SOCIAL DIFFERENTIATION & STRATIFICATION

S. N. Eisenstadt
The Hebrew University of Jerusalem

SCOTT, FORESMAN INTRODUCTION TO MODERN SOCIETY SERIES

Albert J. Reiss, Jr.

Harold L. Wilensky

Editors

Scott, Foresman and Company

Glenview, Illinois   London

Library of Congress Catalog Card Number: *73-147373*

Copyright © 1971 by Scott, Foresman and Company, Glenview,
Illinois 60025.
Philippines Copyright 1971 by Scott, Foresman and Company.
All Rights Reserved.
Printed in the United States of America.

Regional Offices of Scott, Foresman are located in Dallas,
Oakland, N.J., Palo Alto, and Tucker, Ga.

Foreword

Modern societies are complex territorial organizations whose populations are more-or-less integrated by economic, legal, military, and political institutions and by the media of mass communication and entertainment. Sociology reflects this complexity. It is often packaged in separate sociologies such as those of work, religion, minorities, politics, and the community.

By looking at modernization as a process, and urban-industrial ("modern" "affluent") society as a distinctive social system, this series hopes to avoid fragmentation into separate sociologies and at the same time provide intensive treatment of major institutional areas (economy, polity, kinship), units of social organization (society, community, complex organization, family), and of processes that cut across all institutional areas (social differentiation and stratification, social control, demographic and technological change). The series is "relevant" in that all authors address themselves to a single question: "What is modern about modern society?" It is comparative in that all authors know that we cannot answer that question unless we compare the different shapes of modern and premodern societies and of contemporary nations, totalitarian and pluralist, "capitalist" and "socialist." Our abiding concern is the macroscopic, comparative analysis of social structure and change.

Each book in this series can stand alone for specialized courses; each can also be used in combination with others as a flexible substitute for conventional textbooks.

In this introduction to *Social Differentiation and Stratification* by S. N. Eisenstadt, social stratification is analyzed in a general sociological framework. Professor Eisenstadt accomplishes this by examining social stratification on the one hand and functional analysis on the other. Moreover, the book compares social differentiation and stratification in various societies, both traditional and modern.

Eisenstadt indicates that social differentiation and stratification constitute a basic yet distinct aspect of social structure. It is thus closely connected with some of the basic problems of sociological analyses in general—such as the nature of social order, the bases of social consensus, the place of force or persuasion in the maintenance of social order and in institution building. While the author argues that social differentiation and stratification are prevalent in any society, he takes pains to specify the conditions under which social stratification and strata formation tend to develop as a distinct, autonomous organization and a symbolic dimension of social order. After general analysis of the nature of social stratification as related to social order, Eisenstadt presents a detailed analysis of some of the major types of stratification as they develop in different societies.

The analysis starts with "partial" stratification, i.e. with stratification based on age and with stratification in primitive societies. It then proceeds to the analysis of stratification and strata formation in one type of traditional society, Imperial societies.

The third part of the book concentrates on stratification in modern societies—analyzing the general characteristics of strata formation in modern as distinct from traditional societies, as well as the differences between different modern societies, e.g. societies with strong orientations to power, wealth or prestige. If a modern society displays unusual commitment to power, its stratification system will show some similarity to that of any traditional society with a similar orientation. This book should give the reader some sense of how an immensely informed student of comparative sociology traces continuities and discontinuities between modern and premodern structures.

Albert J. Reiss, Jr.
Harold L. Wilensky, editors

Preface

This book is an outgrowth of a larger exploration of stratification problems that I began several years ago in a series of lectures, seminars, and research studies at the Hebrew University of Jerusalem. Although all of these activities are still proceeding, I had often thought that a preliminary stocktaking might be useful and therefore was glad to accept the invitation extended to me by my friend Professor A. Reiss, editor of this series, to undertake the preparation of this work. As usual, this book has taken longer than expected, though it is, in a sense, only a preliminary statement of many of the problems it explores.

During my work on stratification, as in the preparation of this book, I have incurred the debt of many people. In its first phase, I collaborated with Dr. E. Schild of the Hebrew University, and parts of this book owe much to our collaboration.

Throughout the seminars and research work I have concluded, my students and associates have been of great help in discussions, criticism, and investigative assistance. However, I must single out Miss Miriam Curelaru, who has assisted me in many seminars and rendered invaluable aid in reading the manuscript, in commenting critically on it, and in preparing the notes. Mrs. Rotenberg helped with the notes to Chapter 9, and Mr. J. Yatziv helped with the notes to Chapter 10.

Throughout the years, many pertinent discussions with Professor Edward Shils of the University of Chicago have been most helpful and stimulating. Professors A. Reiss and E. Encel of the University of New South Wales also were helpful in making many comments on the manuscript.

In preparing and editing the manuscript, I have been greatly helped by Mr. Michael Edwards, whose assistance far exceeded even that of a meticulous copy editor. He has greatly changed and improved the style of my presentation.

I also thank Mr. David Halfen of Scott, Foresman for his help throughout the preparation of the manuscript.

S. N. Eisenstadt

The Eliezer Kaplan School of Economics and Social Sciences
The Hebrew University of Jerusalem

CONTENTS

Social Differentiation & Stratification

Social Differentiation & Stratification

Social Roles and Social Structure

Imagine that you and a few friends have decided to form a recreational club—a chess club, for example. What sort of people would you want to join it?

If it is to be a real chess club and not just a social club that incidentally provides facilities for chess, you will of course want to recruit real chess players. Thus a prospective member who inquires what sort of club it is might get the reply: "Only serious chess players belong in this club." And you might think, at first, that such an approach is certain to make the club successful. But not all of the members will be free to play a game every time they visit the club.

At least some of them will have to deal with the needs of the club as a whole—general needs that exist independently of the members' private needs. Like most other voluntary associations, a chess club needs a place—a room, apartment, or house—in which to pursue its activities. It also needs a number of chess boards and sets of chess pieces, and a corresponding number of tables and chairs. Some members may want to have refreshments available; others may want to read newspapers, journals, or magazines between games.

Providing these and/or other facilities will require a certain amount of expense and administrative work. Most clubs meet their expenses from two sources: subscriptions and donations; thus even a very small club will find that it needs a treasurer. And even a small club will benefit from having a fund-raising committee. Similarly, if a club holds business meetings or keeps records of its activities—indeed, if it wishes to pursue its activities in an orderly manner—it will need both a secretary and a chairman.

At first, many of these administrative duties may be undertaken intermittently and at random by different members of the club. For instance, some of the tasks, such as removing out-of-date notices from the bulletin board, may be performed by any member who takes it upon himself to do so. But the longer a club is in existence and the larger its membership becomes, the greater the tendency for these duties to be sorted out according to a relatively stable system or pattern. Thus it may be agreed, formally or informally, that only the club secretary has the right and the duty to remove old notices from the bulletin board and to post new ones and that the elected club chairman shall automatically become chairman of the fund-raising committee.

These collections of duties and functions are known to sociologists as *roles,* and the process by which they are sorted into these collections is known as *role differentiation.*[1]

As roles become differentiated, questions naturally arise about the relative importance of the different fixed positions, or *statuses,* associated with the various roles.[2] Is the club chairman, an efficient administrator but a mediocre chess player, to receive as much respect and deference as the club champion, a surely eccentric who demands complete silence when he is playing? What happens if the chairman tries to introduce regulations that would set aside "quiet hours," for a period during which less expert players would be free to invite comment or instruction, but the club champion will not accept the proposed schedule, and the matter is put to a general vote? With whom should the conscientious member consider that his loyalty lies? This is not just a problem for individual members; even on a small scale, it is a social problem—a problem of *social evaluation.*

Evaluation of any kind involves criteria. Thus as long as the overriding intent of the chess club is to play chess, it is unlikely that differences over administrative matters will alter the general

[1]M. J. Levy, Jr., *The Structure of Society* (Princeton, N.J.: Princeton University Press, 1952), pp. 157–166 and ch. 7.

[2]For the distinction between *role* and *status* see R. Linton, *The Study of Man* (New York: Appleton-Century-Crofts, 1936), pp. 113–114. See also T. Parsons, *The Social System* (Glencoe, Ill.: The Free Press, 1951), pp. 25–26.

opinion that more respect is due to good chess players than to good administrators, at least within the context of the club. Of course it is possible that the best administrators will also be the best chess players and that the same individuals will fill both roles, but this is not likely. In any case, there would still be the problem of working out the criteria for evaluating each role in relation to the other, although the criteria need not be elaborate. In our example, there could be a simple understanding that whatever recognition is expressed for administrative services is secondary or inferior to recognition for excellence in playing chess. However, the specific application of such a general criterion may be very complex. Even the most highly respected chess players, if they partake of administrative duties, may expect a separate or extra form of recognition; but this may be something that inferior chess players, who are good at administration, may be unwilling to grant.

Nor is the development of criteria for evaluating different kinds of roles the only problem; seemingly impossible problems are inherent in grading the members' relative ability as chess players. Of course the best player should receive the highest honors and rewards the club can bestow, but what about the less outstanding and the merely competent players? And how (if at all) is their recognition to be differentiated from those whose game is mediocre or even bad? In other words, if chess performance is to be rewarded or recognized, how are the different grades of performance to be differentiated, and how many grades should there be?

The answers to these questions cannot be obtained simply by applying the master criterion of excellence at chess; many other criteria may have to be weighed against it. In any case, the longer the club stays in operation, the less likelihood that its members will be consistent in applying their master criterion, although its dominant role may never be seriously challenged. But even the "pure" chess players (members who are interested only or mainly in chess) may begin to sense the encroachment of another criterion, seniority, on the basis of the length of time the various members have belonged to the club.

No doubt the club champion will always be more highly respected than the senior member, and will receive a greater share of the rewards, but the criterion of seniority may well prevail when it comes to ranking the senior member vis-à-vis a junior member who is a better chess player (as long as the latter is not one of the club's outstanding players).

Seniority may also be felt in a more indirect way, in influencing the distribution of rewards within the club. As in the United States Congress, it may play a large part in controlling access to the positions from which rewards are dispensed. Indeed, it may control access to membership in the club, and it may even control to some degree the possibility of displaying one's prowess at chess after membership has been gained.

Similar considerations apply to criteria that depend on purely administrative goals. Although those who have performed administrative services for the club are not likely to claim that administrative excellence should be esteemed more highly than excellence at chess, they will probably claim that it should be esteemed more highly than mediocre or poor performance at chess. And it would be surprising if they do not take advantage of their positions as administrators to regulate access to club membership or, by scheduling various kinds of tournaments and exhibition matches and deciding who is to play in them, to weight the probability that a particular member will make a name for himself as a chess player.

What a complicated social entity our little chess club has become! It began with a few friends who simply wanted to play chess but now it is involved in all sorts of other activities. To understand how this happens we must examine the concepts of *social differentiation* and *social stratification.*

SOCIAL DIFFERENTIATION

Social differentiation is so significant an aspect of organized social life that it has often been treated as virtually equivalent to it, and especially to the social division of labor. Indeed, Durkheim's famous treatise, *The Division of Labor in Society,*[3] conceives the origins and development of organized life, of social life, in terms of social differentiation. So, too, do many other classic works of sociology and social philosophy, including Plato's *Republic;* and this concept has been studied and refined by sociological analysis.

Social differentiation usually refers to (1) the situation that exists in every social unit, large or small, by virtue of the fact that people with different characteristics perform different tasks and

---

[3]E. Durkheim, *The Division of Labor in Society,* G. Simpson, trans. (New York: The Free Press, 1964) (paperback ed.).

occupy different roles, and (2) the fact that these tasks and roles are closely interrelated in several ways.

One advantage of this loose definition is its broad range of applicability. Small groups, corporate units such as factories, and the larger, relatively self-sufficient units we call "total" societies can be said to be (regardless of historical or ethnological type) socially differentiated in the sense given above. Another advantage is that the definition reflects most of the various schools' sociological thought as it pertains to social differentiation.

Although it might seem that very little is implied about the behavior of a group when its structure is described in terms of social differentiation, our definition draws attention to an important question: What is the relationship between the social structure of a collectivity and the behavior of its members? If we concentrate on the phenomenon of social differentiation as structure rather than process—that is, on part (1) of our definition—we can hardly avoid concluding that the behavior of individuals who fulfill different roles is very much influenced by the ways in which their roles are connected with each other.

At least some degree of role interdependence can almost always be inferred. For instance, the worker in the shop will eventually feel the effects if the company's public relations director botches his job, even if these two employees (or types of employee) never so much as set eyes on each other. Conversely, roles may be clearly complementary, as when certain tasks cannot be performed without the direct, face-to-face cooperation of technical and semiskilled personnel.

Thus role interconnections that affect behavior are a substantial part of what is meant by a *social system*.

Characterization of social systems

Social systems have often been defined as consisting of different roles that involve different kinds of tasks. Thus the family, considered as a social system, has the roles of father, mother, children, and various types of kin, who are expected to perform the different types of activities that are, in some sense, prescribed for them. It may be, for example, that consanguineous relatives (those linked by blood relationship) are supposed to behave somewhat differently toward each other than toward affinal relatives (those with whom there is no biological relationship but only one created by marriage).

In a small social system, such as the modern American family, it is not very hard to single out the principal roles and role relationships, even if their distribution may sometimes call for sociological research. But in dealing with whole societies this analytic task becomes much more complex and difficult. Sociologically speaking, the most intractable aspect of the social division of labor is the mutual interdependence of roles among incumbents who may never meet or directly interact. Indeed, they may be totally unaware of each other's existence, and yet they depend on each other in ways that can be clearly specified in the abstract although they may be hard to detect by observation. Nevertheless, this dependence is much more tenuous than in the case of the factory worker and the public relations manager. In a factory, everyone's job is more or less clearly defined in that he is expected to work for a defined goal, such as making money for the firm.

In other words, a factory has a highly visible division of labor with at least one ready-made master criterion for role evaluation: Does each job contribute to the firm's earnings or doesn't it? Societies, on the other hand, often lack clear goals, except that all presumably seek survival. For this reason, and because they consist of many different kinds of social systems and subsystems, the ramifications of a society's overall division of labor (when economic and noneconomic roles are considered) seem impossible to establish with finality.

Thus it seems that at least two aspects of the division of labor, or social differentiation, have to be distinguished: *direct* division (of the kind that, theoretically at any rate, could involve direct interaction between role incumbents) and *indirect* division (in which role interdependence is mediated by one or more intervening roles). We shall meet this problem again but, for the time being it is enough to have noted that socially differentiated roles, or *social roles* for short, never exist in isolation.

Perpetuation of social systems

Social roles, of course, are performed by people, but in most social systems—even in such ephemeral groups as street-corner gangs and other informal cliques—membership tends to change more often than their roles, statuses, or various activities. Moreover, the very continuity of every group or society depends on its ability to prolong itself independently of the individuals who perform its roles and occupy its leadership positions at any given moment. Indeed, this social fact is recognized by most societies, as can be seen from the nature of the terminology and nonverbal symbols with which they express their identity as collectivities. And this fact, if not its recognition, is characteristic of all social systems to some extent.

Communities, families, business firms, voluntary associations—all are perceived by their members as spanning more than one generation. Although a collectivity may be the creation of one group, or even of one man (a "genius"), and the latter may attempt to mold the collective identity in his own image (Louis XIV's *L'état c'est moi!* is the example that comes most readily to mind, though he has been outdone by several modern dictators), and even to destroy the collectivity if it seems to be slipping from his control (*Après moi le déluge!*), he hardly ever succeeds in either enterprise where whole societies are concerned.

However, the permanence of social systems can be exaggerated. The notion one sometimes receives from sociological and anthropological treatises, that groups are almost "eternal," inevitable entities, constituted of fixed roles or statuses, is extremely exaggerated.

Such work groups or institutions as the family are not eternal inasmuch as their role composition is subject to change, and this is even more true of societies. The division of labor, as well as the entire role system of every group or society is almost constantly changing. Sometimes the change is so slow that it is imperceptible; sometimes it happens so quickly that a generation or two is required for people's thinking to catch up. In any case, new kinds of activities and new roles to go with them develop almost continuously in most social systems. Even the ordinary changes in personnel necessarily affect role structure because of the variations they introduce in the efficiency of role performance. Moreover, the purely individual element in personality, the element that makes up the core of a person's self-perception and identity, may be a powerful force for social change, and it is doubtful whether this element can be described wholly in terms of the roles a person is called upon to perform.

Therefore every social system must perform two basic tasks if it is to remain socially differentiated—if, in other words, it is to remain a viable social system.

It must make or allow for (1) a differential allocation of people to positions and roles, and (2) the socialization—that is, education in the broadest sense—of people for the performance of these roles.[4]

It is very hard, over a period of time, to assign people to different positions and roles without using more or less stable criteria to determine what kinds of individuals should fill these roles and how they should perform the tasks expected of them. Furthermore, the criteria, if they are to mean anything, must be enforced. Although the rigor with which they are enforced may vary greatly, at least theoretical sanctions should be available to ensure compliance; but sanctions that are invoked too often are often self-defeating. Hence the most general or common task of socialization is inculcating the readiness to be assigned a role and the willingness to perform at least some roles, once the assignment has been made. Unless the need for this task is recognized and this attitude is successfully inculcated, the more specific task of developing the necessary skills and abilities for role performances will be undertaken in vain. And, indeed, the overwhelming majority of social systems of which we have detailed knowledge seem to have recognized these two forms of socialization.[5]

Differential evaluation of roles

Another aspect or characteristic of social differentiation, and one that constitutes the bridge between social differentiation in general and social stratification in particular, is what the sociological literature calls the differential evaluation of roles and the concomitant differential allocation of rewards.

The fact that some roles are valued more highly than others is probably a universal fact of social life. Indeed, no two roles are likely to carry identical social price tags, either in one or in different social systems. What, then, are the indicators of differential social evaluation—or, in nonsociological language, how can we read the social price tag?

[4]For the socialization process see K. Davis, *Human Society* (New York: The Macmillan Company, 1949), ch. 8; H. M. Johnson, *Sociology: A Systematic Introduction* (New York: Harcourt Brace Jovanovich, Inc., 1961), ch. 5; and I. L. Child, "Socialization," in G. Lindsey, ed., *Handbook of Social Psychology* (Reading, Mass.: Addison-Wesley Publishing Company, 1954), pp. 655–692.

[5]M. J. Levy, Jr., and L. A. Fallers, "The Family: Some Comparative Considerations," *American Anthropologist*, 61 (1959): 647–651; H. M. Johnson, *Sociology: A Systematic Introduction*, op. cit., ch. 5.

Thus far, the best answer that sociologists can give to this question is provisional. Most people, they have found, habitually make precise and finely graduated judgments about role evaluation, but they can seldom give a precise description of their criteria. Most sociologists agree that, in studying this phenomenon, it is best not to begin with such intangibles as criteria but, instead, with the tangible rewards and benefits from which the existence of criteria is inferred. However, as soon as an attempt is made to specify the various kinds of rewards, it becomes obvious that some of them are as intangible as the values that govern their distribution.

Consider the following classification of such rewards, which can be found, in one way or another, in most sociological works:[6]
1. Rewards that are based on differential allocations of esteem and deference
2. Rewards that are based on differential amounts of obedience that can be exacted from others
3. Rewards that are based on differential allocations of services and commodities
It is clear that only type 3 rewards are tangible in the sense that they can be assigned a relatively precise monetary value. But rewards of types 1 and 2 are no less real than rewards of type 3.

If the reader suspects that "differential evaluation of roles" is just a long-winded way of referring to old-fashioned social inequality, he will be partly right (why only "partly" will be seen in later chapters). Ever since 1755 and the publication of Rousseau's *Discourse on Inequality,* most of the controversies about social differentiation have centered on this topic.[7] But we should distinguish as far as possible sociological from political and

---

[6]See, for example, H. H. Gerth and C. W. Mills, trans. and ed., *From Max Weber: Essays in Sociology* (New York: Oxford University Press, Inc., 1959), ch. 7; K. Davis and W. E. Moore, "Some Principles of Stratification," *American Sociological Review,* 10, no. 2 (1945): 242–249; T. Parsons, "An Analytical Approach to the Theory of Social Stratification," *Essays in Sociological Theory* (New York: The Free Press, 1954), pp. 69–88; E. A. Shils, "Charisma, Order and Status," *American Sociological Review,* 30, no. 2 (1965): 199–213; W. G. Runciman, *Relative Deprivation and Social Justice* (London: Routledge & Kegan Paul Ltd., 1966): and G. C. Homans, *Social Behavior: Its Elementary Forms* (New York: Harcourt Brace Jovanovich, Inc., 1961), esp. chs. 5, 8, 14.

[7]Jean Jacques Rousseau, "A Discourse on the Origin of Inequality," *The Social Contract and Discourses* (London: J. M. Dent & Sons Ltd., 1913–1955), pp. 143–229. For a brief review of the controversies on the nature of inequality see G. Lenski, *Power and Privilege* (New York: McGraw-Hill Book Company, 1966), pp. 10–20 and M. M. Tumin, *Social Stratification: The Form and Function of Inequality* (Englewood Cliffs, N.J.: Prentice-Hall, Inc., 1967). A more detailed exposition, which goes back to ancient times, is S. Ossowski's *Class Structure in the Social Consciousness* (London: Routledge & Kegan Paul Ltd., 1963).

ideological controversies, although all of them may frequently be closely interconnected.

Sociologists have recognized that some kind of social inequality exists in almost every society, and—however deplorable this inequality may be—they try to analyze the phenomena by answering the following questions. Are some roles or positions more highly rated than others in *all* societies? Do similar evaluations of roles always bring similar kinds of rewards? And what are the underlying causes for differential evaluation of roles and differential allocation of rewards?

To explore these and related questions, it is necessary to enlarge the study of social differentiation to include social stratification.[8]

SOCIAL STRATIFICATION

Social stratification is not usually conceived, in sociological literature, as being fully explained by differential evaluation of social roles and differential allocation of rewards. In most sociological studies, it is characterized by several additional aspects.

Whatever the social system, roles are not merely interconnected; they tend to be interconnected along certain lines. It is not always easy to detect this tendency in the smallest kinds of social systems, but in relatively larger ones (as in our chess club example) a skilled observer can see it at work. And this—to simplify a very complicated phenomenon—is what happens. Roles become sorted into categories and these categories (in a way we will explore later) become sorted into levels or layers, each of which is in some way above or below another. Such an arrangement of individuals or groups is usually referred to as *hierarchical,* and much of what most sociologists mean by social stratification is contained in the notion of roles and groups of roles that are conceived both to exist and to be arranged in a hierarchical order.

A more specific definition of social stratification (although the reader is cautioned against thinking he can learn very much from definitions until he sees how they are applied) is the social

---

[8]For some different points of view on the relationship between inequality and stratification see K. Davis and W. E. Moore, "Some Principles of Stratification," op. cit.; M. M. Tumin, "Some Principles of Stratification: A Critical Analysis," *American Sociological Review*, 18, no. 4 (1953): 387–393; M. M. Tumin, "Rewards and Task Orientations," *American Sociological Review*, 20, no. 4 (1955): 419–423; and D. H. Wrong, "The Functional Theory of Stratification: Some Neglected Considerations," *American Sociological Review*, 24, no. 6 (1959): 772–782.

order that is most closely related to (1) a differential evaluation of roles, (2) the existence—especially in large social systems—of categories, or social divisions, of roles, and (3) the existence of a hierarchy or hierarchies of role categories.

The general nature of (1) has already been discussed, and the main thing to note about (2) is that a role category consists, *by definition,* of all the roles that occupy the same position in a hierarchy. Such hierarchically arranged role categories, or social strata (as they are often called in popular speech), have various names in the literature of social science. Marxists call them *social classes.* Max Weber, finding the Marxist approach oversimplified, divided them into *classes, estates,* and *parties.* In certain American community studies, the main distinction is made between *class* and *caste.*[9] As for (3), there is some controversy whether a society has one or several such hierarchies, and, if several, about the nature of their interrelationship.

What kinds of questions does the study of social stratification involve? We have noted most of them already, but only as questions that cannot be satisfactorily dealt with if one limits himself to the study of social differentiation. In slightly restated form, they are:

1. What positions or roles receive (or are given) higher rewards than other positions or roles?
2. What is the nature of these rewards?
3. What criteria are used in distributing these rewards?
4. How have these criteria been established and by whom are they maintained?
5. What criteria are used in regulating individuals' access to the various role categories?
6. How do role categories become arranged in hierarchies and

[9]See Karl Marx and Friedrich Engels, *The Manifesto of the Communist Party* (New York: International Publishers Co., 1932), and H. H. Gerth and C. W. Mills, trans. and eds., *From Max Weber: Essays in Sociology,* op. cit.

For illustrations of some American community studies see W. L. Warner and P. S. Lunt, *The Social Life of a Modern Community* (New Haven, Conn.: Yale University Press, 1941), and *The Status System of a Modern Community* (New Haven, Conn.: Yale University Press, 1942); W. L. Warner and L. Srole, *The Social Systems of American Ethnic Groups* (New Haven, Conn.: Yale University Press, 1946); Allison Davis, B. B. Gardner, and M. R. Gardner, *Deep South* (Chicago: University of Chicago Press, 1941); W. L. Warner and W. C. Bailey, *Democracy in Jonesville* (New York: Harper & Row, Publishers, 1949); and R. Lynd and H. Lynd, *Middletown and Middletown in Transition* (New York: Harcourt Brace Jovanovich, Inc., 1925 and 1937). For critiques of most of these community studies see S. M. Lipset and R. Bendix, "Social Status and Social Structure: A Reexamination of Data and Interpretations," *British Journal of Sociology,* 2 (1951): 150–168, 230–254, and R. Rosner Kornhauser, "The Warner Approach to Social Stratification," in R. Bendix and S. M. Lipset, eds., *Class, Status and Power* (New York: The Free Press, 1966), pp. 224–255.

according to what criteria? And how are these hierarchies maintained?

7. What are the relationships between differential evaluation of roles, the development and maintenance of role categories, and the arrangement of role categories into hierarchies?

8. What relationship do all of the above phenomena bear to a social system's division of labor and to what are often called its "needs"?

SOCIAL DIVISION OF LABOR

Thus far the main emphasis of this study has been—quite deliberately—on social stratification as a part of the social division of labor. Our analysis has implied that all societies have a division of labor and that only within the context of social life can people either attain or meaningfully strive toward the goals that give their lives purpose and value. No isolated individual—or family, for that matter—can be totally self-sufficient in this respect.

Instead, individuals and groups are interdependent because they have to engage in a mutual process of exchange in order to pursue and attain their goals. The crux of this process is the use of resources as social rewards on the one hand and as media of exchange on the other. People find that, to get what they want, they have to exchange some of their own resources for some of other people's, and organizations and institutions are built as mediators of the interaction this process involves. Institutions devise collective goals, and make it possible for their members to pursue these goals in a systematic manner. They also make it possible for people to pursue their personal goals and still contribute to attaining the goals of the collectivities.

The use of resources is the basis for an orderly social life, for the social division of labor. Two other facts about the division of labor are especially important in the present context.

1. *There is a division of labor in all known human societies,* even in the most primitive band of wandering hunters. We do not know how this phenomenon originally came about (although we can make some plausible guesses about why it occurred); we merely accept it as a basic datum of human evolution—as we accept the fact that, at some stage of his evolution, man learned to speak.

2. *The division of labor in all human societies has certain*

basic characteristics in common, which can be detected in both primitive and complex modern societies. Together, these characteristics are a kind of core around which the division of labor grows and develops. Such characteristics as age, sex, and kinship form a basis for the allocation of various roles in all societies, and define the various types of political, economical or ritual activities, which we shall discuss very soon in greater detail.

These two facts enable us to say, in the context of the present discussion, that the division of labor is an *evolutionary universal* of the human species.[10] To repeat: we know of no human society, not even the most primitive band, that does not have a division of labor—even though we do not know how this originated, whether in the history of the human species or in the transition from the subhuman to the human. We must accept it as a basic evolution, like erect posture or the evolution of human speech.[11]

Autonomy of subsystems

All but the very smallest social systems are almost always divided (to some extent) into subsystems. Indeed, some authors maintain that this is true of any group that numbers more than two persons. Subsystems, at any rate, can develop greater or lesser degrees of autonomy; that is, they can develop goals more or less independently of the main system and other subsystems, and then can pursue them more or less effectively. The autonomy developed by a social system's subsystems is a vitally important variable in determining the amount of social differentiation in the system and the system's overall tendency to become socially stratified.

But perhaps this is a misleading way of putting it. What is meant is that social differentiation pertains not only to individual roles, or categories of roles, but to even broader categories of activities—categories that, no less than the division of labor, can be regarded as similar evolutionary universals. In every society, every socially meaningful activity is always categorized—to some extent—as economic, political, cultural, religious, or familial, even if in many (or perhaps most) cases these categories are not wholly distinct from each other.

[10]T. Parsons, "Evolutionary Universals in Society," *American Sociological Review,* 29, no. 3 (1964): 339–357.

[11]Ibid.

Because these different kinds of activities are socially meaningful (as contrasted with wholly private activities, such as—in most societies—scratching one's head), and because they convey their meaning through symbolism, they can be said to belong to different institutional and symbolic spheres. For example, a man wears a suit to work but casual clothing around the house, which is one of the ways he signifies that his activities are economic in the first instance and familial in the latter.[12]

Social institutions and societal needs

The universal existence of basic institutions in any society has often been attributed to universal societal needs or to the goals of a society. The fact that different social systems or "social institutions," (so called if they pursue acknowledged goals in an organized fashion) have different goals should be emphasized because it is closely related to one of the major problems in sociological analysis: the needs of social systems and the extent to which different systems have the same needs.

The sociological literature has described these societal needs in many ways, but the most systematic and probably best-known analysis is that of Talcott Parsons and Edward Shils, who have identified four "functional" needs in every social system: adaptation, goal attainment, integration, and pattern maintenance (which includes tension management). Accordingly, every social system must first adapt itself to its external social and nonsocial environment. Second, it has one or more goals that must be attained through cooperation. Third, it has to maintain interdependence among its various subunits and ensure their loyalty to the system. And fourth, it must maintain the patterns of a social system in the sense that the occupants of the various societal roles learn these patterns and respect them.[13]

Although there is much disagreement about the nature and identity of a social system's most important needs, as well as their universality (we shall touch on some of these controversies later), there can be little doubt that *some* conditions have to be met if a

[12]For symbolism and its relationship to social structure see T. Parsons, *The Social System*, ch. 9, and E. Goffman, *The Presentation of Self in Everyday Life* (Edinburgh: University of Edinburgh Social Sciences Research Center [monograph no. 2], 1958), esp. chs. 1 and 3.

[13]T. Parsons and N. J. Smelser, *Economy and Society* (New York: The Free Press, 1965) (paperback ed.), esp. pp. 46–85; T. Parson, R. F. Bales, and E. A. Shils, *Working Papers in the Theory of Action* (Glencoe, Ill.: The Free Press, 1953), ch. 5.

social system is to be operative. But some conditions, of course, are specific to different systems. Perhaps, therefore, the major problem in general sociological analysis is the extent to which the specific needs of a social system can be derived from its general needs.

Whatever one's view, it seems clear that socially differentiated roles tend to develop in response to a social system's needs, both general and specific. It seems equally clear that a social system's specific roles—that is, the specialized roles that distinguish it from other kinds of social systems—tend to develop in response to its specific needs, which in turn are derived from its specific goals. Only a chess club, for instance, *has* to have a chess champion.

Every specific organizational need varies in its details from one type of group or society to another. A chess club, as we have seen, has certain material facilities and resources, as well as internal arrangements among its members for upholding the club's goals, observing the rules of chess, raising funds, and representing the club to the outside world. In the case of a society that plans to industrialize itself, its specific organizational needs include the development of a labor force that is capable of performing industrial tasks, discovering and training persons with managerial capabilities, establishing various kinds of new organizations (marketing boards, commercial banks, labor relations, councils, etc.), and securing political protection for all of these organizations and activities.[14]

All this requires the cooperation of a great many people. Running a chess club is not always easy, but industrializing a whole society involves complication upon complication. The difference is analogous to many individuals pursuing the same goal independently and a collectivity pursuing its object en masse. It is a well-known fact that no two individuals ever think exactly alike, and it is also a fact that some collectivities achieve their specific goals (even the most complicated ones), but how can a mass of individual goals add up to a collective goal? Or have we been misled by the analogy of societies and voluntary associations? It may well be, as many sociologists believe, that the

[14]These, in fact, are the major problems facing underdeveloped societies that are in the processes of economic modernization; see W. E. Moore and A. S. Feldman, eds., *Labor Commitment and Social Change* (New York: Social Science Research Council, 1960), and J. J. Spengler, "Social Structure, the State, and Economic Growth," in S. Kuznets, W. E. Moore, and J. J. Spengler, eds., *Economic Growth: Brazil, India, Japan* (Durham, N.C.: Duke University Press, 1955), pp. 363–387. See also T. Parsons, *Structure and Process in Modern Societies* (Glencoe, Ill.: The Free Press, 1960), ch. 4.

question should be rephrased: How is it possible for a collectivity to impose a goal on its individual members?

This problem suggests that we analyze some of the basic questions about social order, inasmuch as collective goals are conceived as a basic component of such order or, alternatively, the very maintenance of this order is conceived as a collective goal. Why, then, do people accept such order and/or goals—why are they willing to invest some of their own resources to maintain or attain order or goals?

Autonomy of social stratification

Before, however, addressing ourselves to this question, it might be worthwhile to turn back briefly to the problems of social stratification.

Social stratification is not a component of social order in the same way that a role is a component of a social system. Rather, stratification is a *dimension,* as a single-line arrangement is a dimension of a freight train. And just as the linear arrangement of boxcars defines or limits the shape and operation of a freight train, the fact that all societies (except the most primitive) are socially stratified influences the ways in which social life is organized. This is what is meant by saying—as we shall frequently do—that social stratification is an *autonomous dimension* of social order. In other words, certain characteristics of every stratified society—characteristics that at first sight may seem to have nothing to do with social stratification—may have been produced directly by the workings of the stratification system.

This system is a pervasive social fact that no person or institution can ignore. It is, as it were, the differentiating mold into which everyone is poured and in which everyone must find his own social physique. But it is not a rigid mold. Indeed, in most societies its flexibility makes it more like a net with compartments that selectively admit fish of all different sizes—but the screening process is at best inexact, never working entirely as it is supposed to. Other similes, all equally suggestive and inexact, help to dispel the erroneous, inert image of geological strata that *social stratification* tends to evoke, while demonstrating social stratification as a universal, dynamic dimension of social division of labor. Some aspects of social stratification are as universal as division of labor but this does not mean that *every* division of labor is an evolutionary universal. All the evidence, both historical and contemporary, shows that societies' systems of roles and positions continually change and that the new forms may depend on an infinite variety of circumstances. This is true at both the macrosociological and the microsociological level.

This point about the concrete contours of social division of labor may seem too obvious to require special clarification, but much of the sociological and anthropological literature too often creates the opposite impression. Particularly in monographs that describe the division of labor in primitive tribes, the differential evaluation of roles may receive much more attention than the fact that the roles exist. And often there are good reasons for this, perhaps the best reason being that the rationale for the existence of a particular role or position poses an unanswerable question. But in some contexts such questions are legitimate especially in analyzing the fundamentals of social differentiation.

Therefore, if genuine sociological knowledge is our object, it is not enough to limit our analysis to the ways in which different roles and positions are evaluated or to the ways in which people are allocated to them. We must in addition, analyze the stages by which a particular division of labor, constituted by its various roles and positions, has reached its present state. We must analyze both its origins and its development; we must trace not only its main divisions but its subdivisions as well. Above all, we must look for the stage at which the subdivisions began to develop goals of their own. Since the development of any specific division of labor is, as we have indicated, closely related to different collective goals, we must indeed return to the problem of placement of these goals in the social order and life of the individual—a problem evoking many sociological controversies in general and stratification controversies in particular.

The Davis-Moore controversy

Recent sociological literature has voiced two major and closely related, but not identical, controversies about some of the basic problems of social stratification that touch on central problems of social order. One of these is the Davis-Moore versus Tumin (and others) controversy;[15] the other controversy centers

[15]The main controversy and the major issues are found in R. Bendix and S. M. Lipset, eds., *Class, Status and Power* (New York: The Free Press, 1966), pp. 47–63. See also E. Rosenfeld, "Social Stratification in a 'Classless' Society," *American Sociological Review*, 16, no. 6 (1951): 776–784; R. D. Schwartz, "Functional Alternatives to Inequality," *American Sociological*

on the criticism of the structural functionalist approach (especially Parsons' approach) by Dahrendorf, Rex, and others.[16] The topics and issues in these controversies tend to overlap, and in many ways they touch upon the central problems of the nature of social order.

The excited tone of these exchanges is undoubtedly due to the fact that they have been dominated by the issue of social inequality. Two of the articles are worth quoting at length, not only because of their sociological interest but also because they demonstrate how closely the problem of defining social order is linked to basic issues of political philosophy.

The position of Davis and Moore is based on the assertion—apparently more an article of faith than a generalization from known facts—that social roles are evaluated according to their contribution to a society's essential needs: the greater their contribution, the higher their evaluation. They attempt to explain the obvious exceptions to this rule by a second assertion; namely, that roles requiring skills that are both difficult to acquire and in short supply also are highly evaluated.

> Granting the general function that inequality subserves, one can specify the two factors that determine the relative rank of different positions. In general those positions convey the best

---

Review, 20, no. 4 (1955): 424–430; W. Buckley, "Social Stratification and the Functional Theory of Social Differentiation," *American Sociological Review*, 23, no. 4 (1958): 369–375; D. H. Wrong, "The Functional Theory of Stratification: Some Neglected Considerations," *American Sociological Review*, 24, no. 6 (1959): 772–782; W. E. Moore, "But Some Are More Equal than Others," *American Sociological Review*, 28, no. 1 (1963): 13–18; M. M. Tumin, "On Inequality," *American Sociological Review*, 28, no. 1 (1963): 19–26; and W. Buckley, "On Equitable Inequality," *American Sociological Review*, 28, no. 6 (1963): 799–801.

[16]The Parsonian approach has been presented by its eponymous formulator in numerous books and articles, such as T. Parsons and N. J. Smelser, *Economy and Society* (New York: The Free Press, 1956); T. Parsons and E. A. Shils, "Values, Motives, and Systems of Action," in T. Parsons and E. A. Shils, eds., *Toward a General Theory of Action* (Cambridge, Mass.: Harvard University Press, 1951), pp. 47–243; T. Parsons, *The Social System* (Glencoe, Ill.: The Free Press, 1951); and T. Parsons, "A Revised Analytical Approach to the Theory of Social Stratification," *Essays in Sociological Theory* (Glencoe, Ill.: The Free Press, 1954), pp. 386–439.

For the Parsonian critics see J. Rex, *Key Problems of Sociological Theory* (London: Routledge & Kegan Paul Ltd., 1961); R. Dahrendorf, "Toward a Theory of Social Conflict," *Journal of Conflict Resolution*, 2, no. 2 (1958): 170–183; and also R. Dahrendorf, *Class and Class Conflict in Industrial Society* (Stanford, Calif.: Stanford University Press, 1959), ch. 5; and D. Wrong, "The Oversocialized Conception of Man," *American Sociological Review*, 26, no. 2 (1961): 183–193.

For an attempt to synthesize these two opposing theoretical viewpoints see P. Van den Berghe, "Dialectic and Functionalism: Toward a Theoretical Synthesis," *American Sociological Review*, 28, no. 5 (1963): 695–705.

reward, and hence have the highest rank, which (*a*) have the greatest importance for the society and (*b*) require the greatest training or talent. The first factor concerns function and is a matter of relative significance; the second concerns means and is a matter of scarcity.

Differential Functional Importance. Actually a society does not need to reward positions in proportion to their functional importance. It merely needs to give sufficient reward to them to insure that they will be filled competently. In other words, it must see that less essential positions do not compete successfully with more essential ones. If a position is easily filled, it need not be heavily rewarded, even though important. On the other hand, if it is important but hard to fill, the reward must be high enough to get it filled anyway. Functional importance is therefore a necessary but not a sufficient cause of high rank being assigned to a position.

Differential Scarcity of Personnel. Practically all positions, no matter how acquired, require some form of skill or capacity for performance. This is implicit in the very notion of position, which implies that the incumbent must, by virtue of this incumbency, accomplish certain things.

There are, ultimately, only two ways in which a person's qualifications come about: through inherent capacity or through training. Obviously, in concrete activities both are always necessary, but from a practical standpoint the scarcity may lie primarily in one or the other, as well as in both. Some positions require innate talents of such high degree that the persons who fill them are bound to be rare. In many cases, however, talent is fairly abundant in the population but the training process is so long, costly, and elaborate that relatively few can qualify. Modern medicine, for example, is within the mental capacity of most individuals, but a medical education is so burdensome and expensive that virtually none would undertake it if the position of the M.D. did not carry a reward commensurate with the sacrifice.

If the talents required for a position are abundant and the training easy, the method of acquiring the position may have little to do with its duties. There may be, in fact, a virtually accidental relationship. But if the skills required are scarce by reason of the rarity of talent or the costliness of training, the position, if functionally important, must have an attractive power that will draw the necessary skills in competition with other positions. This means, in effect, that the position must be high in the social scale—must command great prestige, high salary, ample leisure, and the like.[17]

However, Davis and Moore do not make it clear whether their two criteria of functional importance and scarcity of skills are supposed to be associated in the differential evaluation of roles. Are they always considered together? If they are, do people give them equal weight? And what about the prestige that is acquired in many societies solely from the possession of a rare skill, no matter how useless it is from a social point of view? These and many similar questions are not answered by Davis and Moore.

But rather than examine the details of their analysis, let us turn to their critics' principal objections, which are that neither highly evaluated positions nor the criteria by which these positions are evaluated and the rewards by which such evaluation is effected are necessarily explained by the causes cited by Davis and Moore. These causes may sometimes explain the genesis of the importance of some roles (e.g., the feudal warlord in medieval society), but they cannot explain the perpetuation of such roles and their limitation of access. Furthermore, Tumin and others claim that political and economic positions are not always the most highly evaluated and that such evaluation need not always be expressed in the same types of rewards, especially when it pertains to economic and power positions.

This is not to say that functionalist explanations are worthless. Indeed, the social position of the medieval warlord can be traced to the need for a local, highly centralized military authority whose function was to provide at least minimal security for an agricultural society that operated under very insecure conditions. This, however, merely explains the role's origin; its development and later form can hardly be accounted for in functional terms. But Tumin should be allowed to speak for himself.

An effort has been made to raise questions regarding the inevitability and positive functionality of stratification, or institutionalized social inequality in rewards, allocated in accordance with some notion of the greater and lesser functional importance of various positions. The possible alternative meanings of the concept "functional importance" has been shown to be one difficulty. The question of the scarcity or abundance of available talent has been indicated as a

---

[17]"Some Principles of Stratification," by K. Davis and W. E. Moore, from *The American Sociological Review*, vol. 10, no. 2, 1945, pp. 243–244.

principal source of possible variation. The extent to which the period of training for skilled positions may reasonably be viewed as sacrificial has been called into question. The possibility has been suggested that very different types of motivational schemes might conceivably be made to function. The separability of differentials in power and property considered as resources appropriate to a task from such differentials considered as rewards for the performance of a task has also been suggested. It has also been maintained that differentials in prestige and esteem do not necessarily follow upon differentials in power and property when the latter are considered as appropriate resources rather than rewards. Finally, some negative functions, or dysfunctions, of institutionalized social inequality have been tentatively identified, revealing the mixed character of the outcome of social stratification, and casting doubt on the contention that "social inequality is thus an unconsciously evolved device by which societies insure that the most important positions are conscientiously filled by the most qualified persons. . . ."[18]

Functionalism and its critics

A somewhat similar range of arguments can be found in the controversy about the Parsonian approach,[19] which centers on the allegation that the structural-functionalist approach assumes that the common values or goals of a society on one hand and its basic functional needs on the other determine the working of a social system, regulate the behavior of the individuals who participate in it, and assure their compliance in pursuing the major societal needs.

The structural-functional approach, according to its critics, assumes that most participants in every group and society have more or less accepted a central value system that determines the criteria and differential evaluation of roles and assures the acceptance of these criteria by the system's participants. It also supposedly assumes that such evaluation and the concomitant division of labor reflect the specific organizational needs or exigencies of a society.

[18]From "Some Principles of Stratification: A Critical Analysis," by M. M. Tumin, from *The American Sociological Review*, vol. 18, August 1953, pp. 393–394.

[19]For the Parsonian approach see the references cited in no. 16.

For obvious reasons, this general approach is often labeled *structural-functionalism,* or simply *functionalism.* It is related to the functionalism of Radcliffe-Brown,[20] Malinowski,[21] and other members of the British school of social anthropology, but it should be regarded as distinct from the latter. (At any rate, we will not review the anthropological uses of functionalism.)

Essentially, the approach of the critics of these two schools (Dahrendorf, M. G. Smith, J. Rex and others, about which more will be said later) is that a society's dominant values are imposed on it by those individuals or groups that manage to seize and monopolize its strategic positions of power. It is therefore the distribution of power within a society, not its alleged needs—and still less the values shared in common by its members—that determines how its roles are allocated and who has access to them. This, of course, is a version of what is usually called the *conflict model of society,* which implies the existence in all societies, and at all times, of individuals who accept neither the dominant values nor the current institutional arrangements. Most conflict theorists recognize the importance of this implication. Indeed, they see it as a guarantee that even the most rigid system must eventually submit to social change, and as proof that most systems are constantly and noticeably changing—a fact they claim the functionalists do not like to admit.[22]

We will not analyze these various concepts and controversies nor attempt to evaluate or resolve their divergent points of view and explanations of the nature and origin of social differentiation and stratification—but not because we think they are not important or crucial for understanding social differentiation and stratification. Indeed, they are so important that—it seems to us—it would be rather fruitless to pursue them in the abstract. (Unfortunately, the fact that so much of the controversy over these problems has been conducted in very general terms may explain

[20]See, for example, A. R. Radcliffe-Brown, *Structure and Function in Primitive Society* (London: Cohen and West Ltd., 1952).

[21]See for example, B. Malinowski, *Magic, Science and Religion, and Other Essays* (New York: Doubleday and Company, Inc., Anchor Books, 1954), and *A Scientific Theory of Culture and Other Essays* (New York: Oxford University Press, 1960).

[22]See R. Dahrendorf, "Toward a Theory of Social Conflict" and *Class and Class Conflict in Industrial Society;* J. Rex, *Key Problems of Sociological Theory;* M. G. Smith, "Pre-Industrial Stratification Systems," in N. J. Smelser and S. M. Lipset, eds., *Social Structure and Mobility in Economic Development* (Chicago: Aldine Publishing Company, 1966), pp. 141–176; C. Morse, "The Functional Imperatives," in M. Black, ed., *The Social Theories of T. Parsons* (Englewood Cliffs, N.J.: Prentice-Hall, Inc., 1961), pp. 100–152; and A. Hacker, "Sociology and Ideology," in *The Social Theories of T. Parsons,* op. cit., pp. 289–310.

why little progress has recently been made in this field, despite the growing abundance of research and data.) Instead, we shall attempt to discover how some of the problems raised by these controversies are related to our preceding analysis of institution building and what light (even if partial and preliminary) this analysis can throw on these problems.

SUMMARY

This chapter has presented some of the basic concepts we shall use throughout this book, concepts that are part of the basic repertoire of sociological analysis, namely *role, status, social differentiation, social division of labor,* and *social stratification.* We have derived these concepts from our illustration of the chess club, and we have seen how they denote the basic elements of every social system.

At the same time, we have emphasized the fact that, although social differentiation and stratification, the social division of labor, and the autonomy of different institutional spheres exist in all human societies and can be considered *evolutionary universals,* they do not explain the way in which a *specific* division of labor or constellation of roles develops in a given group or society. To understand how a division of labor develops, one must first analyze the social activities prior to labor division.

Here we encounter the problematic relationship between individual goals and behavior, on the one hand, and social order, on the other. We have briefly analyzed some of the important controversies evolving from these problematic relationships, which we shall analyze in greater detail in the following chapter.

2

Social Order and the Individual

REWARDS

The fact that social differentiation necessarily involves a system for the allocation and distribution of rewards to role incumbents—in short, the whole phenomenon of differential role evaluation—implies a great deal about the organization of social life and individuals' participation in the social division of labor. Although we have to assume that taking part in the institutional arrangements created by social differentiation is generally considered to be a rewarding activity, there are good reasons to suppose that if there were no rewards for doing so, people would *not* take part, and society as we conceive it would not exist.

The preliminary classification of the three types of social rewards (in Chapter 1) indicated that they form an important aspect of social life in that they may also serve as individuals' goals and as "resources" for their other activities. Each "commodity" can serve in any of these three capacities, depending on the way it is socially organized. Thus it is time to explore the basic differences between the ways in which different kinds of rewards are institutionally organized.

Rewards and goals

A particular commodity, service, or type of symbolic interaction is not necessarily or inevitably a social reward; this quality or ability is not inherent in the nature of things social. Instead, it proceeds from the actual use of rewards that is always in process in every social system. But rewards cannot be entirely random objects or honors, and therefore they have been classified in various ways. The classification adopted by most social scientists who have investigated the matter is the same, or much the same, as the one already familiar from Chapter 1 (p. 9). Since these three categories clearly correspond to wealth (3), power (2), and prestige (1), the reader may be pardoned for asking: What else is there?

Despite their apparent simplicity, these categories raise many questions, one of which is the extent to which the rewards distributed within a particular group can be used outside it. For example, does the prestige enjoyed by the leader of a street-corner gang when he is with his followers improve his position in the society at large? Or, to state the problem in more general terms, can we know anything about the nature of rewards unless we know the group settings in which they are meant to be used?

Use of rewards

In order to approach this problem, it is necessary to analyze the different uses of such rewards, or what use people who receive these rewards can make of them. The answer to this question has significant implications for the analysis of the stratification process, and therefore it is worthwhile to attend to it.

From an analytical viewpoint, rewards appear to have three different kinds of uses:
1. They can be consumed directly.
2. They can be used for symbolic consumption (discussed below).
3. They can be used for getting something else, that is, as resources or as media of exchange.

The first kind of use, direct consumption, needs little discussion. People may, as the expression goes, "blow" their income, make a purely personal or selfish use of the services they receive from others, order their subordinates around just for the sense of power this gives them, and bask in the deference of their social inferiors without ever wondering if they perhaps expect something in return.

Thus the direct consumption of social rewards can merge almost imperceptibly into symbolic consumption insofar as individuals or groups consume certain commodities in certain ways—in order to prove that they are able to do so and, by implication, that other individuals or groups are unable to do so—and thereby indicate that they are better than the latter. The best-known type of symbolic consumption is *conspicuous consumption,* a term invented by the American institutional economist Thorstein Veblen, whose *Theory of the Leisure Class* (1899) dissected the upper-class extravagances of America's "gilded age."[1] Another type is the *potlatch,* an institution of certain North American Indian tribes whose leading members maintained their status by displays of ritual extravagance.[2] Similar patterns of behavior, by no means restricted to the wealthy classes, are found in most advanced civilizations, and sociologists are accustomed to studying them under the general rubric of *life style.* All of the various aspects of social stratification, especially the process of strata formation, have some connection with the symbolic consumption of social rewards.[3]

The third way in which social rewards can be used is instrumental, that is, as resources for social-institutional interaction and exchange. The use of various forms of wealth provide the most obvious examples, but we will limit ourselves to examining the use of these resources in gaining access to what sociologists call *differential life chances.* In almost all social systems, possession of certain resources brings the possibility of regulating access to the most highly valued positions and roles. Thus friends and relatives, who in a sense are extensions of the self, may be promoted to the highest positions, from which certain classes of individuals are systematically excluded.

Again, we are concerned not so much with the phenomenon's existence (a sufficiently familiar fact) as with its social organization, which is still largely unexplored. But extensive research is not needed to distinguish at least two methods of using resources to secure differential life chances. These may be called the *direct* method, by which resources are actually exchanged (usually by

[1]Thorstein Veblen, *The Theory of the Leisure Class* (New York: New American Library, Inc., 1953).

[2]M. Mauss, *The Gift,* trans. I. Cunnison, with an introduction by E. E. Evans-Pritchard (Glencoe, Ill.: The Free Press, 1954), chs. 1 and 2.

[3]H. H. Gerth and C. W. Mills, eds. and trans., *From Max Weber: Essays in Sociology* (New York: Oxford University Press, 1959), ch. 7, and the American community studies cited in ch. 1 above.

purchase) for the roles or positions in question, and the *indirect* method, by which such resources as the power that comes with wealth or prestige are used for regulating the conditions of access to these roles or positions.

(Two other methods of using resources, both of which involve *restriction,* also should be mentioned: restricting the range of commodities that may be exchanged for other commodities [e.g., not rewarding prowess in battle unless it is conjoined with a high social position or noble birth] and restricting the rates of exchange between different commodities [as when a plain but wealthy girl is regarded as more marriageable than one who is beautiful but poor].)

It should also be pointed out that those who are qualified to accede to high positions usually have some influence in regulating the conditions for accession. And their influence increases greatly once they have gained access and exercise all the privileges of the positions.[4]

Continuous conversion of rewards, resources

Thus we see that, where individual and/or social values or goals are pursued, a particular object may serve equally well as (1) a social reward; (2) a goal; that is, as something individuals pursue for its own sake, whether acting singly or as a group; (3) a general medium of exchange; that is, a resource that, like money, is readily exchangeable for a wide variety of other resources; and as (4) a resource; that is, as something that can be used to reach a goal.

Once this classification has been made, it is easy to see that a commodity can serve any of the four functions. Thus power can be a resource that is used for obtaining other commodities, or a goal in itself, or a reward for services rendered, or—at least in a highly developed political system—a general medium of exchange. The same is true of economic commodities and, as we shall see, prestige.

All this does not mean, however, that people *think* in terms of this classification. For instance, someone who is asked whether he

---

[4]D. H. Wrong, "The Functional Theory of Stratification: Some Neglected Considerations," *American Sociological Review,* 24, no. 6 (1959): 772–782, and *From Max Weber: Essays in Sociology,* esp. pp. 190–191. For a more systematic exposition of this idea see also S. N. Eisenstadt, "Prestige, Participation, and Strata-formation," in J. A. Jackson, ed., *Social Stratification* (London: Cambridge University Press, 1968), pp. 62–103.

wants prestige as a resource or as an end in itself may have a hard time answering. Nor does it mean that the rewards necessarily fulfill individuals' goals (indeed, some goals may be inherently unachievable, but this fact alone does not prevent them from playing an important part in human affairs). Such inferences, in addition to being incorrect, would also be beside the point. In other words, the fact that a commodity can serve all of these functions implies that various institutional patterns are indispensable to social life.

How do goals come to be defined as desirable? How is it that rewards can often be used as resources? How does a commodity, such as gold or silver, become the basis for the general medium of exchange called money? All of these arrangements originate within a social context and are sustained by social organization, without which they would have no motivating force whatever. The process by which resources and rewards are continually converted into general media of exchange, and vice versa, constitutes the very fabric of social life.

The role this process plays in both creating and maintaining the social division of labor should now be at least partly apparent. We have seen how the convertibility or nonconvertibility of a social reward—that is, its value or worth outside the group that conferred it—can pose a problem for its recipient (as in the example of the gang leader). If we are to understand the forces that bind most people to their positions in society and keep them doing "their thing," one of the questions we would do well to ask is: How many of the rewards of each institutionalized subsystem of a society are convertible into media that have currency beyond that subsystem? But we shall have to return to this question later.

PRESTIGE

The traditional classification of social rewards—wealth, power, prestige—at least suggests that there are different kinds of rewards and that having one of them does not necessarily imply or preclude having either of the others. But it does not say why something so intangible as prestige should be put on the same level as wealth and power. The reader may well ask if it deserves special treatment in a section of its own. Is prestige anything more than the icing on the cake of privilege?

The question is worth raising at this stage because, of all the major social rewards, prestige has been least analyzed. It has, of course, been studied, but almost always as a mere symbol or indicator of differential status. Thus much of the research that purports to examine prestige examines, instead, its structural base; that is, the social arrangements it symbolizes. And thus the study of prestige has been subsumed under the study of life styles, and prestige itself has been treated as just another item of consumption. However, it is a very complicated phenomenon, and one that must be discussed in the present context, particularly since it pertains to the whole question of how and why social roles are differentially evaluated.

Bases of prestige

Prestige has often been defined as society's principal symbol of an individual's or a group's social standing, and its symbolic character is what has made the concept so elusive. Prestige does not seem to exhibit the organizational features associated with more concrete social rewards, such as power and money. Esteem and deference, awards, titles, decorations, invitations to the "right" parties, mention in the society pages—these do not, in themselves, look like very substantial rewards, and indeed their insubstantial nature has long been a common motif among poets and moralists.[5] Of the three major uses we have distinguished for rewards, only direct consumption seems to fit prestige. And yet much of the historical and sociological literature on social stratification makes prestige a principal element, and sometimes the *principle,* of strata formation.[6] Each view, if pushed to its logical conclusion, tends to exclude the other; however, there is clearly some truth in both of them. How, therefore, can they best be reconciled?

For an answer, let us return to our chess club and our reasonable assumption that the best player would enjoy the

---

[5]A similar opinion can also be found among some sociologists; see, for example, G. Lenski, *Power and Privilege* (New York: McGraw-Hill, Inc., 1966), esp. pp. 430–431. For an opposite view see E. A. Shils, "Deference," in J. A. Jackson, ed., *Social Stratification,* op. cit., pp. 104–132.

[6]The importance of prestige as the basis of strata formation has been overemphasized by Warner; see his studies (cited in ch. 1 above, no. 9) and the criticism they have received. The notion that prestige is only one of several possible bases for strata formation was introduced by Weber; see *From Max Weber: Essays in Sociology,* op. cit., pp. 190–191. A recent argument in favor of Weber's approach is made by W. G. Runciman, "Class, Status and Power," in J. A. Jackson, ed., *Social Stratification,* op. cit., pp. 25–61, and by S. N. Eisenstadt in "Prestige, Participation, and Strata-formation," in *Social Stratification,* op. cit., pp. 62–103.

highest prestige, inasmuch as chess is the sole rationale for the club's existence. Moreover, we would make the same assumption vis-à-vis other voluntary associations, whether religious, economic, or political: those individuals who best attain, or are most closely associated with, the organizations' main goals are rewarded with the highest prestige they can bestow. We also found that members of the chess club who do not excel at chess but who, by virtue of their administrative positions, are able to regulate the club's activities by interpreting its goals and formulating its rules are also likely to claim high prestige, and even to obtain it. Finally (although this was not part of the original discussion), it seems probable that mere membership in the club would confer a kind of prestige, for we all know of clubs whose principal attraction resides in their exclusiveness.

Having said all this, let us make a systematic attempt to apply these microsociological insights to the construction of a macrosociological plan of human institutions. These insights indicate that most societies have at least three bases for prestige: (1) being a member of a collectivity; (2) occupying a central, and therefore controlling, position in a collectivity (*centrality*); and (3) symbolizing the main goals or values of a collectivity, either by achievement or by participation in the broad sociocultural order (religious, political, scientific, etc.) from which such goals are drawn.

Because of the present state of sociological knowledge, the evidence for these assumptions varies in quality and quantity. Few sociologists would disagree with (1) inasmuch as numerous studies have documented the ways in which groups and societies attempt to reinforce the distinction between members and nonmembers. The universality of this distinction was emphasized by the American sociologist William Graham Sumner in his *Folkways* (1906), when he coined the terms *in-group* and *out-group*.[7]

There is much less agreement on (2), and therefore centrality will be discussed at length in Chapter 4. However, it should be noted that *centrality,* although closely related to *power,* is not identical with it. The analytic utility of this distinction will be demonstrated when we consider some "case histories" of real societies.

As for (3), the factual basis for this assumption is quite clear, but the facts can be variously interpreted. The author's interpretation is that, in every social context, some of the major types of

---

[7] W. G. Sumner, *Folkways* (Boston: Ginn and Company, 1906), esp. pp. 12–15.

symbols and goals are more relevant than others because of the way in which a collectivity defines itself. A business enterprise, for instance, is more likely to be interested in profits than in aesthetics.

In other words, members of a collectivity who best exemplify the values implicit in its goals—who are, in a way, *closer* to those values than the typical members—are also, for the most part, those who have the highest prestige and hold, or are admitted to, the most prestigious roles. This is especially noticeable in societies or communities that are dominated by religious values, where the "keepers of the mystery" or the priestly class are deferred to almost regardless of their personal qualities. The same is clearly true (*mutatis mutandis*) of societies dominated by tradition, as is seen in the attachment of the British to their royal family and to everything connected with royalty.

In short, we maintain that this kind of collective symbolism is a basis for prestige in all social systems, whatever their collective goals may be.[8]

Prestige and social structure

These three bases of prestige, apparently so diverse, have a common denominator: all involve individual participation in a supraindividual structure. However, the nature and the quality of this participation may differ greatly in each case. For instance, participation in a broad, cultural order that transcends the group is not the same as participation in the group's central role-structure. And each type of participation may connote variations in commitment and reward; rarely, if ever, do all members of a group participate to the same degree. Participation also involves leaders, on the one hand, and followers on the other. Thus participation is the institutional aspect of what might be called the *charismatic dimension* of human existence.

Prestige, then, is not simply a trapping of power or the natural response that accrues to a charismatic personality. Rather, because differences in prestige correspond to different levels of participation, it is a recognition of the right to participate in something. Thus it is a genuine social reward in itself and not just

---

[8]Similar points of view can be found in T. Parsons, "A Revised Analytical Approach to the Theory of Social Stratification," *Essays in Sociological Theory* (Glencoe, Ill.: The Free Press, 1954), pp. 386–439, and in E. A. Shils, "Charisma, Order and Status," *American Sociological Review*, 30, no. 2 (1965): 199–213.

the derivative honor that accompanies a reward, more structural than symbolic, and similar to the resources that regulate access to highly valued positions. Therefore prestige, which embodies the right to control access to this kind of participation, is a very important structural aspect of social life.

Like every other social reward, prestige can be a goal of individuals; however, its structural implications may be much more generalized, especially when it tends to become the focus of personal and collective identity. Although it is beyond the scope of this book to analyze all aspects of individual and social identity, our analysis has proceeded too far to ignore the link between prestige and personal and social identity.

From a structural point of view, this link resides in the regulation of access to the pursuit of specific desiderata and goals. Needless to say, many of these goals can be pursued by individuals regardless of the group to which they belong, and yet every society seems to have desiderata or goals, or usually a combination of goals, whose pursuit is restricted to individuals who share certain types of identities. These identities, denoted by particular kinds of personal attributes, are also associated with a particular level of participation in various collectivities, a central position in those collectivities, or a capacity to symbolize the collectivities' principal goals through participation in a broader cultural order. All this may easily result in the cultivation of a particular life style, not only for its own sake but also for the sake of privilege. Aristocracies, for example, justify or defend the tangible advantages of their prestige on the ground that their way of life represents the right social or cultural order.

Inasmuch as prestige, according to the view outlined above, can be a resource, it can also be a medium of exchange, not unlike money or power, although differing from them in its dispersion. The man who has prestige may obtain services and commodities (including obedience) that are unavailable to those who do not have it, or he may receive them at a better price. True, prestige will not buy very much by itself, but it offers an excellent position from which to negotiate.

When a nonmember seeks a favor from a group, he will do well to have an "in" with that group (usually in the form of acquaintance or friendship with a member). A person who enjoys high prestige with all or most of a collectivity's members, such as champion athletes and film stars, has an "in" with every group and subgroup in that collectivity; he is "welcome in every home." No group in our society is more aware of this elementary social fact than the advertising profession, which knows that endorsement of a product by a prestigious individual automatically confers prestige on the product.

Prestige can also be considered a medium of exchange because of its ability to assure and/or prohibit access to various institutional positions. This practice is too common to require illustration, but we shall refer to it later when we analyze the mechanism of ascription.

INDIVIDUAL AND COLLECTIVE GOALS

We have seen that various commodities—wealth, power, prestige—can serve as social goals, rewards, and resources and that their conversion from one such use to another is a crucial mechanism of the social division of labor. But it may seem that, in the meantime, we forgot about the more structural aspects of the social division of labor—the different types of roles in different social groups and societies and, especially, how these patterns of roles may be related to the goals and needs of these groups. Therefore the next step in our inquiry is to discover the nature of goals and needs, the relationship between them, and the social division of labor that develops in every collectivity.

The first thing to note about goals is that they should never be taken for granted. The very decision to form a chess club, build an automobile factory, or industrialize a society should not be taken for granted—something given in the nature of things—but rather as an outcome of a group decision, that group acting in the name of the collective. Thus we return to the above question, closely related to the Davis-Moore-Tumin controversy, namely: how is it possible for a collectivity to impose a collective goal on all, or most, of its individual members?

Sociological knowledge is not yet adequate to settle this issue with finality, but it is possible that individuals accept collective order and goals simply because they want the advantages that can be derived therefrom. This assertion assumes that two of the many motives of individuals are (1) the desire for a broader social or cultural order than that of the family group and (2) the desire to achieve certain collective goals. These desires can exist under any kind of political or economic system, whether democratic or collectivist, industrial or agricultural. They are most likely to be directed at the macrosociological level, but—needless to say—they can also pertain to small groups.

Even as a partial approach to a sociological explanation of social order, this may seem simplistic or naive, but let us consider some of the alternative explanations. Some theorists assume, with rather less justification, that the goal of social order is imposed on individuals by an irresistible external force. Others see social order as the collective outcome of many individual calculations of rational self-interest, or of the social and economic division of labor supposedly engendered by these calculations. In short, individuals are portrayed as wholly egoistical, but this is no more plausible than portraying them as wholly altruistic.

In contrast, our conception allows for the fact that, among all sorts and conditions of men, the quest for a meaningful sociocultural order is, and has always been, a major concern. Even a superficial examination of history will show that the desire to participate in such an order is at least as strong a human motive as anything that can be labeled calculated and individualistic self-interest. Every revolution, every reform movement and religious revival, has had its symbols of the "good society"—symbols that, for the faithful, are identifiable with social order and collective goals.[9] In his immortal *Candide,* even Voltaire, the most disillusioned idealist, recognized that the impulse to construct Utopia dies hard in the human heart.

Admittedly, our view of social order poses some very difficult questions for the sociologist, the foremost being:

1. What, precisely, is the place of collective goals in the total universe of an individual's goals and wishes?
2. Who formulates collective goals, and how do these goals originally arise?
3. Under what conditions are collective goals institutionalized; that is, how do those who originally formulate them succeed in getting the members of the in groups to accept them?
4. How do groups succeed in creating the social mechanisms that are necessary for implementing the attainment of public goods and collective goals.

In answer to the first question, all that can be said is that the desire for social order, even if it often takes the form of a passive or merely potential commitment, is a basic element in the wide panorama of individual hopes and fears, goals, and attitudes. In most societies, this quest for social order tends to be articulated

---

[9]For special reference to the processes of modernization see S. N. Eisenstadt, *Modernization: Protest and Change* (Englewood Cliffs, N.J.: Prentice-Hall, Inc., 1966). For a more general view of the nature of revolutions see C. Brinton, *The Anatomy of Revolution* (New York: Prentice-Hall, Inc., 1952). .

into formal schemes or arrangements for attaining public goods or collective goals, such as the maintenance of internal order, defense arrangements against external enemies, provisions for a basic standard of living for all members of the groups, or promotion of society's special traditions.

Of course, not all individuals want the same kind of social order or public good, nor do all who want a particular kind of order want it to the same extent, and some members of every society may be completely apathetic. All of the many variations among individuals and societies have yet to be fully and systematically explored by sociological analysis. Meanwhile, however, let us be clear about what is *not* being argued. The fact that every individual desires a meaningful social order does not mean that social order in general, or specific types of public good or goals in particular, are the only or even the main goals of individuals. On the contrary, all the evidence seems to show that individuals regularly weigh the importance of social order against "lesser" goals.

Why, then, the preference in some situations for one type of social order? It may be helpful in this connection to mention the views of a contemporary American sociologist, J. C. Coleman, who suggests that at least part of an individual's interest in a particular social order or set of collective goals depends on his perception of the future.[10] The individual, Coleman maintains, is likely to make a calculation of the benefits that will accrue to him, as well as to other members of the same system (including its future members), if the institutions in which his and other members' resources have been invested are allowed to continue. Other things being equal, his support of the system will depend upon his estimate of these benefits.

But this is only one explanation, and although it contains important elements of truth, it is not a complete explanation because the future, as it is envisaged by individuals, is greatly influenced by their conception of a good social order. This is another problem that sociological analysis has only recently begun to investigate, and that space limitations preclude discussing.

Whatever their differences may be, and whatever the real explanation of the preference for one social order over another, a concept of social order in general, and collective social goals in

[10]J. C. Coleman, "Individual Interests and Collective Action," Papers on *Non-Market Decision Making*, Summer 1966.

particular, depends not on the need for it, nor on people's concept of social order, but on the possibility of institutionalizing this conception.

No matter what specific needs may confront a society from time to time, they must be seen in the same symbolic light if they are to be institutionalized. And needs are not likely to be met unless they *are* institutionalized, unless they are both conceived and implemented within an organized pattern of social life.

SUMMARY

This chapter has analyzed some of the ways in which individuals goals and activities are related to the maintenance of social order. We have seen that the crux of this relationship is the fact that the same commodities—wealth, power, prestige—that serve as goals or desiderata of individuals also serve as resources and media of exchange for social interaction and the implementation of collective goals. Thus the conversion of rewards and resources is the fabric of the social division of labor.

Among these commodities and resources, we have singled out prestige as especially important for understanding the relationships between individuals' behavior and social order in general and social stratification in particular. We have also shown that prestige is based on the right of participation in a social or cultural collectivity, order, or center.

It is through the conversion processes of rewards and resources that the various patterns of roles that develop in every social group are crystallized. These patterns tend to vary among collectivities according to the latter's specific needs and goals.

This necessarily raises the question of how the public good and collective goals can be imposed on individuals and how the former become interwoven in the fabric of social life. Our provisional answer is that this is possible because, to some degree, such goals are conceived by individuals as part of their own goals, albeit as goals of a special kind. But this answer has indicated that, to understand how these goals are achieved in social life, we must analyze them in relation to the processes of institutionalization.

3

Social Order and Institution Building

INSTITUTION BUILDING AND RESOURCES

To understand how conceptions of social order, public goods, and collective goals are institutionalized, we must first examine the process of *institutionalization,* or *institution building.* An institution can best be defined as an entity whose regulative principle organizes most of the activities of its members in a society or a collectivity and in a definite organizational pattern that is closely related either to the basic problems or needs of this society, group, or collectivity or to some of its goals. This organization is effected in terms of norms and obligations that are upheld because of their voluntary acceptance by the members of the society and/or by the force of sanctions.[1]

Thus institutionalization is the process by which social patterns are organized in a stable way. This process may occur on all levels of social organization—in microsocietal settings, collectivities, and (most typically) the macrosocietal order.

Resources and their conversion are a vital part of the process of institutionalization. As we have defined them, they are not commodities or services that are sought simply for their own sake;

[1] T. Parsons, *The Social System* (New York: The Free Press, 1964), (paperback ed.), ch. 2.

they are also sought because they can be used as a means for getting something else. Indeed, our analysis of the various ways in which rewards can be used has stressed the point that the conversion and exchange of resources is the crux of social life in general, and the same thing is true of institution building in particular. People will not do things for other people unless they are rewarded or, as we often say, compensated; and thus anything that serves as a means for obtaining a desired goal is also, by that very fact, a resource.

What does it mean, then, to say that resources have been invested in an institution? Is an institution like a business, from which each individual receives benefits proportional to his investment? Or is it a different kind of arrangement altogether?

Because comprehensive answers to these questions would take us too far from the subject of this book, we will limit ourselves to a brief discussion of institutional resources and their relationship to the process of institution building. This discussion, by throwing more light on the way in which collective goals become institutionalized, will enable us to proceed to our next major topic: how institutions provide incentives for individuals to pursue various types of public good or collective goals.

Resources are needed for institution building because of the basic fact of individuals' interdependence (no one can attain his goals by himself) and because, stated purely in terms of exchanging resources, institution building is analogous to a goal-seeking process. Through the direct or indirect exchange of institutional resources, individuals take part in (among other things) the pursuit of collective goals they did not formulate and for which they may have little or no sympathy. Nevertheless, they may support these goals, in keeping with the norms and regulations necessary for pursuing them in an organized fashion, in at least the minimal sense that (on the whole) they do nothing to thwart them. In exchange for their support, which consists of a generalized sentiment and whatever services or commodities they make available in an institutional setting, they receive resources that enable them to pursue their own private goals.[2]

Thus, again, the conversion of resources and rewards into

[2]For a further discussion of these aspects of the process of institution building see S. N. Eisenstadt, "Societal Goals, Systemic Needs, Social Interaction and Individual Behavior: Some Tentative Explorations," in R. L. Simpson and H. Turk, eds., *Institutions and Social Exchange: The Sociologies of T. Parsons and G. C. Homans* (Indianapolis, Ind.: The Bobbs-Merrill Co., Inc., 1971) (forthcoming). For a critical review of some of the sociological literature that deals with the same problem see S. N. Eisenstadt, *Essays on Comparative Institutions* (New York: John Wiley & Sons, Inc., 1965), pp. 16–40.

general media of exchange can be seen as a necessary process for the creation and maintenance of even the most elementary division of labor. The very fabric of the social division of labor depends on the ever increasing convertibility of social rewards that comes with a macrosocietal order. And, again, social exchange is vital for the existence of organizations and institutions.

THE LIMITATIONS OF PURE EXCHANGE

By using the language of exchange in such a way, we may have given the false impression that the exchange model of social interaction, whether that of free economic market exchange or that of purely interpersonal interaction, is adequate to explain the process of institution building. Because, unfortunately, there will be little opportunity to analyze exchange processes in subsequent chapters (indeed, beginning with Chapter 4, the vital role of these processes in social organization will have to be taken more or less for granted), this is the time to state the various limitations of the concept of exchange in the study of institution building, social stratification, and social differentiation.

Large parts of social-institutional interaction cannot be a purely market-type or interpersonal exchange. Exchange, in other words, is only one *type* of interaction, and institutions are formed to promote interaction. However, because this argument could be dismissed as a mere quibble over terminology, and in order to place the limitations of the exchange model in the clearest light, we have to go beyond terminology and analyze the inadequacy of the pure exchange model.

Individual behavior and social structure

The first inadequacy results from the fact that the groups and individuals who take part in the exchange of resources participate from structurally differentiated positions. In other words, groups and individuals are not randomly distributed throughout society; they occupy various cultural, political, familial, and economic positions—positions that, in turn, result from the exchange of resources. Personal aspirations and goals are to a great extent determined by this differential placement in the social structure; so, too, are the resources (manpower, money, political or religious values) that people find at their disposal.

Moreover—at least in complex societies—the most noticeable feature of the social landscape is the tendency for different kinds of resources to become organized in different ways, each in a manner appropriate to the institutional sphere to which it belongs. For instance, in most societies the exchange of economic resources is organized in different ways than the exchange of political or religious resources. This difference in organization is one aspect of what has been called the *autonomy of institutional spheres,* which in turn is an aspect of social differentiation.[3]

But beyond the initial position of individuals in the institutional structure and the fact that most of their resources are organized in an institutionalized way is the process of the institutional exchange, whose continuous conversion of resources sets many different kinds of limitations on the model of pure exchange. These limitations are most clearly seen if we examine the assumptions on which the model is based, but because it would be too time consuming to examine all of them, let us confine ourselves to the two principal assumptions: conditionality and profitability.[4]

Conditionality refers to the assumption that an individual's behavior is always conditioned upon the behavior of others, which is said to happen in two ways.

1. An individual acts in a particular way only in *response* to a particular behavioral pattern of another individual or group of individuals. In this case, behavior can be said to be conditioned upon specified inputs from an external source.

2. An individual acts in a particular way only when he *expects* to experience certain consequences, including the behavioral responses of others. In this case, the controlling factor is not the evoking stimulus, as in (1), but what systems engineers call the feedback of the original behavior.

Profitability refers to the assumption that an individual will always behave in such a way as to maximize his own advantage or profit. It is similar to the classic economic concept of self-interest.

---

[3] See ch. 1 above (pp. 13–14) and also A. W. Gouldner, "Reciprocity and Autonomy in Functional Theory," in L. Gross, ed., *Symposium on Sociological Theory* (Evanston, Ill.: Row, Peterson & Co., 1959), pp. 241–270.

[4] See, for instance, G. C. Homans, *Social Behavior: Its Elementary Forms* (New York: Harcourt Brace Jovanovich, Inc., 1961), chs. 2–4.

Exchange and social identity

Thus the limitations of the exchange model are to be found in areas where the assumptions of conditionality and profitability do *not* hold. One of these areas, and a very important one, is found in the symbols, or at the symbolic level, of social order and norms. For its most primordial aspects, every society develops certain symbols of social order that both connote the fundamental goals of human existence and society (or some part of it) and denote the proper place for cultivating them. In this way they define what may be called—to use Durkheim's nomenclature—the basic pre-contractual norms of society, including its norms of reciprocity and exchange. The important point is that, at the primordial level, certain goals, positions, and commodities are formally exempted from social exchange.

Chief among these nonexchangeable commodities are the constituents—however they may be defined in a particular society—of cultural, societal, and personal identity. Thus the ancient Greeks, though they often fought among themselves, were united in their hostility to "barbarians" (as they called all non-Greeks). Or, in other words, they had a strong sense of cultural identity and were not prepared to bargain away any part of it.

In the modern world, with its conflict and rivalry between nationalities, societal identity usually has a stronger claim on the individual than cultural identity, and the former is regarded as nonnegotiable. Personal values or identity, as expressed in such notions as honor, integrity, and manly or womanly virtue, are even less exchangeable. The medieval Christian notion of selling one's soul to the devil is only one of the many injunctions in myth and folklore against such exchanges.

Indoctrination in the meaning of such basic symbolism is a vital part of socialization in every society. Learning what it means to belong to a collectivity—first the family, then larger social units—is the indispensable first step toward acquiring a notion of social order as such. Indeed, personal relationships would be impossible without it. Thus the basic symbols of collective and individual identity tend to stress similarities between group members rather than differences. They also tend to be perceived as existing prior to any instance of social exchange; that is, as in some way prior to society itself.

But, of course, neither the symbols nor the things they connote are "given"—any more than collective goals are preestablished or eternal. Like other social products, they result from processes of institutionalized interaction between different persons and groups. However, this interaction is of a rather special kind. At least five features set institutional interaction and exchange apart from the narrowly economic conception of exchange relationships and the equally narrow conception of purely interpersonal relations.[5]

1. Institutional exchange includes the definition of the basic goals of human existence and endeavor, and is oriented toward all the varied human activities in society.

2. Institutional exchange cannot occur unless social units exist that are capable of entering into exchange relationships. Accordingly, institution building is partly a matter of establishing initial bargaining positions for different individuals and groups within a society.

3. Institutional exchange cannot take place without media of exchange. And because the nature of these media necessarily varies among the different institutional spheres, each type of institutional commodity is governed by different norms of exchange and is part of a different exchange order. Thus money is one kind of medium, and political support is another, and they are not supposed to be exchanged for the same sorts of things. (This is why the giving or taking of bribes is not considered a legitimate part of political life, just as awarding contracts for political reasons is not considered a legitimate part of economic life.)

4. Institutions need various kinds of organizations and administrative devices as channels of exchange, and in this way the relatively smooth functioning of exchange processes is assured.

The history of stock exchanges is an excellent example of this principle. It is not necessary to create a formal organization, called a stock exchange, in order to buy and sell stocks, but a stock exchange both facilitates and promotes this type of business, not only by providing opportunities for the greatest possible number of transactions but by upholding the norms that make it both possible and desirable to participate in such transactions. Thus the New York Stock Exchange has never hesitated to cooperate

---

[5]For interpersonal exchange see G. C. Homans, *Social Behavior,* and P. Blau, *Exchange and Power in Social Life* (New York: John Wiley & Sons, Inc., 1964). *Sociological Inquiry,* 34, no. 2 (Spring 1964) contains an extensive and many-sided critical review of Homan's approach. For the limitations of this approach in explaining macrosocietal exchange and the processes of institutionalization see also S. N. Eisenstadt, "Societal Goals," op. cit.

with federal authorities in policing the behavior of its members whenever the adverse publicity attending this behavior has seemed likely to diminish the volume of its business.

5. The need for legitimation, the fifth facet of an institutional setting, is fulfilled by conferring on someone or on some thing that which we say he or it "is entitled to" or "has a right to." There need not be a sanctioning law or regulation; a general agreement (however achieved) is sufficient to legitimize possession or behavior.

Since people cooperate reluctantly or not at all with arrangements they regard as illegitimate, it is crucial for social exchange that it both achieve and maintain legitimation. It must do this on no fewer than three levels: norms, media, and channels.

Institutionalizing collective goals and public goods

Various individual goals can be attained either through the direct interaction of people or the more complicated fabric of institutional interaction (analyzed above). However, most direct interaction necessarily takes place within the broader contours of institutional frameworks, and therefore the maintenance of these frameworks is a necessary condition for obtaining most individual and all public goods and collective goals. How then are such goals institutionalized?[6]

Institution building in general, and the institutionalization of collective goals in particular, depend to a great extent on the type of social interaction that is designated *leadership* or *entrepreneurship.* Institution building in every instance depends largely on leaders or entrepreneurs who (1) articulate specific goals in such a manner as to create or consolidate favorable and general symbolic orientations vis-à-vis these goals, (2) establish organizational frameworks for the pursuit of these goals, and (3) obtain and deploy the resources necessary to achieve these goals, including the kind of motivation that effectuates their organizational arrangements.

These are not ordinary abilities. Indeed, all the available data indicate that an active elite, endowed with these abilities, is crucial for an institution's development.

[6]See S. N. Eisenstadt, "Societal Goals," and S. N. Eisenstadt, "Institutionalization and Change," *American Sociological Review,* 29, no. 2 (1964): 235–247.

Charismatic leadership, institutional entrepreneurs and group interaction

It may well be that different types of leadership are appropriate for different aspects of institution building in general and for the conception, implementation, and achievement of public goods and collective goals in particular. It takes a rather unusual individual to turn the latent desire for social order into a personal quest, and a rather special response from other individuals if that quest is to become more than a private dream. Sociologists call the capacity to evoke this kind of response *charisma*. Originally theological in application (*charisma*, a Greek word, means "that which is bestowed by *charis*," or divine grace), the term was first given sociological currency by Max Weber, who was interested in the truly exceptional leader's capacity to, as we say, "cast a spell" over his followers.[7]

All charismatic leaders, insofar as they are concerned with propagating values, are concerned with the problems of social order. So, too, are their followers—a fact that tends to be forgotten, perhaps because *charismatic* is so often used to denote no more than a strong or pleasing personality.

If charisma were no more than a set of personality traits, it would be impossible to explain another important phenomenon noted by Weber: the routinization or, as it will be called in this book, the *institutionalization of charisma*. What Weber meant by this phrase is that, although the charismatic leader dies, his goals and his conceptions of social order, envisaged for the collectivity—and something of his personal authority—live on in the institutions he founded or that have been founded in his name.[8]

Pursuing a concept of social order and collective goals via membership in a duly constituted organization, with all the routine duties and petty compromises this implies, is inevitably more mundane than pursuing a great vision under the immediate direction of a great leader. This is why Weber spoke of charisma becoming routinized, and stressed its disillusioning aspects. But from another point of view, we might marvel at the way in which,

---

[7]For charisma, as discussed by Weber in various contexts, see E. A. Shils, "Charisma, Order and Status," *American Sociological Review*, 30, no. 2 (1965): 199–213, and *Max Weber on Charisma and Institution Building*, edited and with introduction by S. N. Eisenstadt (Chicago: University of Chicago Press, 1968), esp. pp. 48–65 and the introduction.

[8]For the meaning of "routinization of charisma" see S. N. Eisenstadt, *Max Weber on Charisma and Institution Building*, esp. pp. 54–65 and the introduction.

through routinization, new values and ideals—originally the dream of one person—not only take root but flourish in the social order.

Again, however, this process will be called institutionalization, instead of routinization, to emphasize the fact that the goals of the charismatic leader are in some way adopted by the society in question, whatever that society may eventually make of them because of its ongoing organizational needs. Thus the task of social elites is not simply to invent solutions to new problems but to pose these solutions in *institutional* terms, and therefore a type of leadership somewhat different from the charismatic type may be needed.

Accordingly, members of this elite should perhaps be called *entrepreneurs* rather than *charismatic leaders,* although they could not get far without at least borrowing the aura of charisma. This is not to disagree in any essentials with Max Weber, who of all modern sociologists came closest to recognizing that the creation of new institutional structures often depends on the "push" supplied by charismatic individuals and groups. On the contrary, it stresses the fact that Weber's routinization of charisma is crucial for the establishment and continuation of institutional structures.

In spite of several descriptive studies, we know very little about the phenomena that produce charismatic people. Similarly, we have very little systematic knowledge of such people and the conditions they need for success. Perhaps they represent the closest sociological analogy to biological mutation. Whatever the explanation, the unpredictability of mutation may well reflect the curiously indeterminate character of social differentiation; that is, the fact that, at any given time, an institution seems to contain not one but several, often competing, development potentialities.[9]

It would be a mistake, however, to conclude that all collective goals and institutional frameworks are formed through the activities of a central person or group. In most societies, a wide range of entrepreneurial and other groups is always at work, producing a correspondingly diversified range of goals.

Indeed, various public goods and collective goals frequently become institutionalized through the relatively dispersed interaction of many individuals and groups. The institutionalization of marriage and kinships norms is perhaps the best (but least understood) illustration of this possibility.

[9]S. N. Eisenstadt, "Social Change, Differentiation and Evolution," *American Sociological Review,* 29, no. 3 (1964): 375–386.

Once more, we must admit that we know very little about these processes; they have yet to be studied in depth. But whatever their precise explanation, and no matter whether the goals in question are oriented toward the fulfillment of specific needs or the universal human need for a meaningful social order, it is clear that the role of entrepreneurial individuals and groups is crucial in at least some of the processes, and especially in those that form the symbols of collective identity.

It is here, moreover, that leadership—that asymmetrical form of interaction which is inherent in institutionalization—is of utmost importance, because a society's basic symbolism is, in fact, formulated by entrepreneurs and charismatic leaders who present it to the less articulate social strata from within which their followers are recruited. At this point we return to some of the special problems in this type of institutional interaction.

If leadership involves a process of social exchange, how does it happen that the symbols of a society's identity, although formulated by leaders in the course of interaction with their followers, are regarded as nonexchangeable? The present state of scientific knowledge allows us only to guess at the answer, but it probably has something to do with the emphasis on solidarity that is so prominent a feature of primitive societies and small informal primary groups. Solidarity, after all, is nothing if not unconditional; tribesmen help each other in battle because they are members of the same tribe, not as the result of an exchange transaction. And the same principle applies to members of a small, informal in-group.

The norms that govern solidarity are quite unlike those that govern exchange. Because there is some degree of solidarity in almost all societies, it can be inferred that participation in most social orders usually involves some degree of participation in unconditional relationships.

Exchange and titles

Interaction that involves the basic forms of social identity is not the only kind that is considered exempt from (and even prior to) the norms that govern social exchange. The fact is that social exchange tends to develop its own limitations in keeping with its own norms.

The most important mechanism by which such limitations

are effected, which thus far lacks a standard designation, will be referred to in this book by the made-up term *titles*,[10] and the title mechanism differs from the pure exchange mechanism roughly as follows.

When a simple case of exchange is effected by an exchange medium, the person who, as we say, "purchases" a commodity usually ends up with more of the commodity and less of the medium of exchange than he possessed before the transaction. The "cost" of the commodity is measured in terms of the number of exchange medium units that have to be given in return for a particular number of commodity units.

But let us also consider the many cases of social exchange in which this kind of transaction does *not* occur. When an officer orders the soldiers under his command to do various things, and obtains their compliance, he does not thereby diminish his stock of power. When a religious elite exacts certain observances from its followers, it does not surrender a portion of its influence in a quid pro quo exchange. When an aristocracy habitually obtains deference from commoners, it gains in prestige, even though prestige is the expended medium of exchange.

In short, the very possession of a medium of exchange, such as prestige or power, is tantamount to a title to certain rewards. This anomaly, of course, greatly impairs the "purity" of a social exchange system. Although other resources, such as money, can be exchanged for power and prestige, the use of power and prestige, once they have been gained, does not involve entering into the pure type of exchange relationships. Rather, their use entails different types of unconditional and asymmetrical relationships and exchanges between the holders of the titles and the nonholders.

One of the many other ways in which social exchange tends to develop its own limitations should at least be mentioned before we conclude our discussion of social exchange, and this is a mechanism we encountered earlier: *the creation of scarcities.* As we saw on page 44, institution building involves the setting up of bargaining positions. Therefore the groups and individuals who secure monopolies (or virtual monopolies) of the skills and resources needed within the various institutional markets may be able to preempt the most favorable bargaining positions. More-

[10] A fuller discussion of titles as characteristics of media of exchange and their role in exchange processes that involve norm setting in stratification is available in S. N. Eisenstadt and E. Schild, "Stratification and Exchange" (ms).

over, they may also be able to acquire various titles in this way, and the sole right to them. But this feature of social organization can best be discussed under social stratification, the topic of Chapter 4.

SUMMARY

This chapter has concentrated on analyzing institution building in general and the processes of the institutionalization of the public good and collective goals in particular.

We have given special emphasis to the importance of these processes as they pertain to charismatic leaders and institutional or organizational entrepreneurs, and we have shown that their interactions—their exchanges with other individuals and groups in a society—are crucial for institutionalization.

Such interaction, however, is not molded along the same lines as the models of pure market exchange, and it imposes several important limitations on these models in every institutionalization process. The most important limitations are closely related to the implementation or achievement of collective goals and the processes of stratification, that is, to the establishment of collective and individual identities and "titles."

Finally, these considerations lead to the new problem of the relationship between the processes of institutionalization and those of social stratification.

4

Social Stratification and Institution Building

We shall now attempt to connect the preceding analysis of the processes of institution building with the central problem of our analysis, stratification, by analyzing the ways in which the criteria of differential evaluation of positions are established and how they are related to the various aspects of institution building that were analyzed above. In doing so, we necessarily touch again, and in greater detail, on some basic controversies about the nature and beginnings of social organization and order, issues that have been examined by both classical and contemporary sociological theorists.

SOCIAL ORGANIZATION

First, we must ask if social organization and order can be derived from individuals' drives, goals, and aspirations, or is it rooted in the systemic nature of social organization, that is, in purely societal needs, role requirements, and developmental laws?

Secondly, are social organization and order rooted in the normative order of society, that is, in the values a society's members share in common, or can they be traced to the distribution within society of power and other resources that are exchangeable for power?

These issues are very closely related to the central problems of the Davis-Moore-Tumin controversy, and we are now in a somewhat better position to approach them.

Power and persuasion

Functionalists and antifunctionalists seem to differ primarily on the question of power—what it is and the part it plays in social organization. Most dictionaries, and probably most people as well, associate power with coercion, especially physical coercion. In this book, however, power will be considered as a quality or asset of entrepreneurship. Because the role of entrepreneurial groups and individuals is of crucial importance in institution building, no less than in the formulation of collective goals by charismatic personalities, and although it may indeed be a fact that this relationship always or almost always involves some form of coercion, power—at least in an institutional setting (and very few noninstitutional settings are of much interest to the student of social organization)—must involve much more than coercion. As a motivating device, coercion is self-defeating in the long run; the purely negative benefit of not being physically abused or deprived of a valued possession is an obverse, minimal social reward. The prospect of being hanged, as Dr. Johnson said, may concentrate a man's mind wonderfully, but it is not likely to make him the hangman's faithful servant in the interim.

Institutional leadership, as explained above, contains a strong element of exchange, albeit of a special type. The majority—that is, the followers—contribute to collective goals to derive an exchange from the elite that formulated those goals. It has been suggested that what they receive in return is principally assurance, however minimal, that they belong to a meaningful social order—an assurance no human being can long bear to be without. It has also been suggested that most people may be more or less conscious that in their relations with the elite they are getting the short end of the exchange and that they are unable to do anything about it. In other words, they realize their relative lack of power. Nevertheless, a collectivity cannot pursue its goals without these people, who in a very real sense *are* the collectivity. In Chapter 2 we asked the question: How is it possible for a collectivity to impose a goal on all (or most of) its members? Now we must ask: How are the charismatic and entrepreneurial elite able to institute and perpetuate a state of social differentiation that is so favorable to themselves?

For an answer, we shall have to resume the discussion of needs and goals begun in Chapter 3, redirecting it in order to explain, or begin to explain, the phenomenon that Davis and Moore have called the *differential scarcity of personnel.*

Goals, needs, and entrepreneurs

There seem to be two ways in which an individual or a group can impose role criteria on an entire social system: (1) through interpreting the system's goals and needs and/or (2) by creating a scarcity of the skills the system requires in order to pursue its goals and satisfy its needs.

It was emphasized in Chapter 3 that goals can never be taken for granted. For instance, a club's goal of playing chess is not a "given," like a biological or physical fact, but something upon which certain individuals reached a decision at a particular moment in time. The close relationship between goals and needs has also been mentioned, and two classes of the latter have been distinguished: general needs, which are present in all social systems, and specific needs, such as a chess club's need for certain equipment and facilities. What has not been stressed thus far is the extreme flexibility with which needs, even specific ones, may be interpreted.

Of course the goals and needs of social systems must always be affected to a greater or lesser extent by what we call natural causes—by a group's genetic composition, for example. It is equally clear that, once a goal has been selected, specific needs are bound to arise. But the crucial point in the study of social differentiation is that these needs do not announce themselves in some easily understood form, like so many unpaid bills. On the contrary; before they can be met they have to be defined. True, the basic needs of some social systems, particularly small ones, are sufficiently obvious. This is the case with our chess club, but even here it is hard to make an objective estimate of its *minimal* requirements. And deciding what is needed to make the club operate at the optimal level is clearly an area in which much disagreement is possible.

A system that fulfills only its minimal needs is not functioning very satisfactorily from an objective point of view, even though its members may be satisfied with its operation. What, then, is the task of a group that wishes to gain power over the social differentiation of such a system? Inasmuch as persuasion (as we have seen) is the better part of leadership in general and institution-building entrepreneurship in particular, this task would appear to be to persuade the majority of the members that the system has certain higher needs and that these needs are being neglected. The charismatic or entrepreneurial elite, engaged in such persuasion, will of course choose to emphasize needs that it, either alone or preponderantly, has the resources and skills to fulfill. If it is successful, its resources and skills will be at a premium.

We are not dealing here with the creation of scarcities so much as with the creation of goals and the recognition of their associated needs. From the entrepreneurial elite's point of view, the aim of the latter process is to convince the other members of the collectivity that they should accept certain collective goals and broad conceptions of social or cultural order. In other words, the elite may succeed in so changing the image of the collectivity in the eyes of its members that various new collective goals and needs are recognized as both legitimate and important. And there are at least four levels at which such conviction may be attempted.

1. The charismatic or entrepreneurial elite may attempt to convert the members to a broad conception of social and cultural order: "The kingdom of heaven is within you"; "Liberty, equality, and fraternity"; "From each according to his ability, to each according to his need." Such, in brief, are some of the revolutionary conceptions of society formulated by charismatic leaders and their disciples. Persuasion at this level, because it questions the nature of all established social institutions, must have strong charismatic elements to be effective.

2. The elite may attempt to persuade the members that providing for certain needs beyond the minimal level is an appropriate goal for the collectivity. This is often done not by supplanting established goals but by showing how the new goals are subsidiary to them. In this way the collectivity may develop a set of secondary goals and needs, and the people who minister to them, like the administrators of the chess club (administrators anywhere, for that matter), may consider themselves entitled to specific rewards.

3. The entrepreneurial elite may attempt to persuade the members that ministering to certain collective goals and needs will personally benefit each member; that is, help them attain their individual goals.

4. The entrepreneurial elite may attempt to persuade some or most of the members not to pursue certain goals. At the same time, it may take steps to ensure that these goals are pursued only by individuals who will not endanger the elite's pursuit or enjoyment of them.

Of course an elite that has sufficient resources at its disposal may decide to substitute coercion for conviction; but coercion, as such, will probably never ensure acceptance of either its goals or its needs. Moreover, an elite must employ coercion already regarded as legitimate (in which case its use probably is not strictly necessary). Force cannot produce acceptance, which may be regarded as a continuum whose extremes may never characterize every member of a population at the same time. At an intermediate point on this continuum, the claims of the entrepreneurial elite to receive special rewards on the grounds that it provides for certain necessities may be accepted by most people as simply a regrettable fact. This will happen when most people—though they do not attach as much importance to various collective goals as do the members of the entrepreneurial elite—recognize, to some extent, that these goals must be provided for and that only the elite (because of its monopoly or virtual monopoly of certain resources) can provide for them.

Creation of scarcities

Up to this point we have dealt mainly with the power gained by the entrepreneurial elite in its self-appointed role as interpreter of collective goals and needs. We now have to deal with the possibility that the elite may obtain special rewards for its members by creating a *scarcity* of the skills and resources that are needed to pursue certain collective goals. Such an artificial scarcity should be carefully distinguished from the natural scarcities that affect the behavior of most groups, often without their knowledge. Nevertheless, the creation of scarcities is not unlike the creation of goals and needs. Just as collective goals and needs would not exist beyond the minimal level without entrepreneurs, elites, or leaders to define them, the higher rewards that are allocated to leaders would not exist unless the latter had chosen collective goals toward which they could make, or appear to make, a major contribution. This situation is a major factor in the related social process of *institutional exchange* (discussed below), but there are important differences between these two entrepreneurial activities.

For example, the creation of scarcities probably offers more scope for the exercise of coercion than does the creation of goals and needs, but even here coercion will be self-defeating unless it is to some extent legitimized. Political opportunists and adventurers—the successful ones, at least—have always realized that after a position is seized by force it must be maintained by social exchange, or by some combination of force and social exchange that is much less obtrusive than the means by which they originally gained their power. Then the sheer length of role incumbency brings legitimation in due course.

It does not seem that entrepreneurial elites can count on coercion to the same extent in formulating their concepts of social order and collective goals. Apart from the need for legitimation, there is the problem of maintaining a high level of commitment to the collective goals. And this problem, to judge by the evidence of history, is insoluble. Most people do not seem capable of wholehearted involvement in the pursuit of a highly generalized collective goal over a considerable period of time, unless this goal is the survival, in a minimal sense, of the collectivity itself. It is therefore necessary, if a stable pursuit of collective goals is to be possible, to appeal to private ambitions and needs and to create a system in which the pursuit of individual goals will enhance or supplement the collective goals. For this reason alone, such involvement in collective enterprises as can be stimulated by coercion is not likely to be worth much, in the long run, to those whom these enterprises chiefly benefit.

SOCIAL ORDER AS UNSTABLE BALANCE AND EQUILIBRIUM

What point have we reached after this long discussion of social order and the mechanisms that sustain it? The model that emerges is a system based on some kind of *balance*—usually a temporary balance, and rarely a stable balance—between (a) the resources at the disposal of individuals and groups, (b) their private goals, (c) the collective goals sustained by the system's role structure, that is, by the division of labor that has developed through the processes of social differentiation, and (d) the resources needed for implementing these collective goals.

If there is to be social order, such balance must be achieved at two levels: the levels of (1) nonexchangeable commodities and (2) institutional exchange.

The balance that must be achieved at level 1 is between the processes by which a society develops its basic symbolism and those by which individuals and groups acquire titles (in the sense discussed above). This sounds complicated, but it is something we have already encountered: the institutionalization of social order, collective goals and public goods. Clearly, entrepreneurial elites are motivated by the desire to appropriate titles, but if, at the same time, they do not provide a society with at least a sense of collective identity that will enable it to function as a society, their success will probably be short lived. The crucial mechanisms at this level are socialization and communication (pp. 8, 53–55).

The balance that must be achieved at level 2 is between the various institutional "markets" and their continuous interchange of resources and rewards. The crucial mechanism at this level is therefore the conversion of resources into general media of exchange, so that each institution will have something to offer the others. Through the use of general media of exchange, individuals and groups are also able to create the artificial scarcities that enable them to pursue their goals without interference.

Neither type of balance, however, is automatically present as an attribute of society. In other words, they are not "givens." They are, instead, the results of social interaction, in both the microsocietal and the macrosocietal setting. But because the nature of this interaction varies greatly at each level, it is necessary to turn from the study of social differentiation (with its model of a society differentiated into separate roles and institutions) to the study of social stratification to see how two social processes of such importance can be so different and yet so intimately connected.

First, however, we must analyze the nature of the macrosocietal order in greater detail, for it is within this order that social stratification is most visible.

SIZE, COMPLEXITY, AND MACROSOCIETAL ORDER

Till now we have talked about social differentiation and social divisions of labor without making explicit distinctions between small groups (microsocietal settings) and total societies (macrosocietal groups).[1] Thus a great many generalizations have

[1]For some of these distinctions see: E. A. Shils, "Society and Societies: The Macro-Sociological View," in T. Parsons, ed., *American Sociology: Perspective, Problems, Methods* (New York: Basic Books, Inc., Publishers, 1968), pp. 287–303.

been put forward without an attempt to assign them to either a microsocietal or macrosocietal level of analysis, but it should be clear from the context of each case that most of them were primarily macrosocietal. Indeed, the issue of macrosociology versus microsociology has been deliberately avoided because it would have unduly complicated matters. Nevertheless, it was pointed out that social stratification is a complex phenomenon and is seen in its most complex guise only in large societies. It therefore seems best to list, without further introduction, the differences between the microsocietal and macrosocietal orders that are most relevant to the subject of this book.

The first difference is that of complexity, which can be analyzed as follows.

1. Because the organizations, groups, positions, and roles that make up a macrosocietal order are more numerous both in type and quantity, the relationships between them, particularly those involving interdependence, are much more complex than in a microsocietal order.

2. Because the relationships between these various components of social order are more complex in a macrosocietal setting, the importance of institutionalized media of exchange is greatly enhanced.

3. Because of the high level of development of institutionalized media of exchange and the social mechanisms that control them in a macrosocietal setting, a much greater variety of individual goals is available to those who participate in a macrosocietal order.

The flow of resources in a macrosocietal order—that is, the process by which resources are converted into social rewards and general media of exchange—takes on what may be called *totality*. This totality, which is the systemic element in social differentiation, is characterized by two features.

1. In almost every macrosocietal order certain basic institutions, resources, and goals are sufficiently stable, at least from a structural viewpoint, to be taken for granted. Thus in a particular society the relationship between its political, economic, and religious spheres may be comparatively stable, even though there is considerable variability of goals and activities within each sphere. Accordingly, the flow of resources among these institutional spheres must be regulated in keeping with the goals and needs of each sphere.

2. The extent of this kind of regulation is determined by the generality attained by the exchange processes within the systems,

and especially by the degree to which the internal resources and exchange media of a particular subsystem can be exchanged for those of other subsystems. Accordingly, this exchangeability of resources (if we may call it that) is a major aspect of totality.

Centrality, by which we mean a central and therefore controlling position in a collectivity (and which has already been described as one of the three principal bases for prestige [p. 31]), is much more likely to be a major factor in a macrosocietal order (with its complex division of labor and semiautonomous institutional spheres) than in a microsocietal order, where everyone, so to speak, is already at the center. Centrality usually takes the form of political organization, but it can also be seen in cultural, religious, scientific, and other broad social spheres.

The position of the individual in a macrosocietal order is very different from his position in a microsocietal setting. Both the complex relationships between institutional spheres and the importance of centrality affect him in very specific ways. Every macrosocietal order tends to organize the lives of its members. At the structural level, life is organized in four respects.

1. It is through the family and other agencies of socialization that are very much part of the macrosocietal order, that the individual is taught most of the goals toward which his activities will eventually be oriented. Indeed, as sociologists are increasingly becoming aware, there are socialization agencies for adults no less than for young people.

2. Most of the goals the individual is taught to pursue can be attained only within the macrosocietal order. This is true even for reformers and revolutionaries, who, after all, do not usually wish to abolish social order as such. And some of these goals, such as participation in various institutions, are essentially social.

3. The range of qualities and attributes that may become foci of personal identity is much greater in a macrosocietal order. In addition to participating in the primordial qualities and institutions of the family and kinship, it is possible to take part in the great variety of collectivities associated with the other major institutional spheres.

4. In a macrosocietal setting, an individual may not only occupy several positions but may develop a relationship between them that involves and enhances his whole personality. In a microsocietal setting, by contrast, relationships between the few positions a person can occupy simultaneously are likely to be much more functional. That is, they are likely to be determined by the nature of the duties performed for his particular group.

Moreover, the rewards an individual receives from one position usually are not easily exchangeable for the rewards allocated to other kinds of positions, nor do they serve as easy means of access to other positions.

Because of the greater variety and flexibility of role relationships and the availability of generalized media of exchange (money, for instance) in a macrosocietal order, each position a person holds will tend to affect most of his other positions.

1. Participation in a major institutional sphere, such as politics, will affect the amount and level of participation in other spheres, and vice versa.

2. The rewards received from each position become relevant to the chances of access to virtually all other positions an individual may reasonably desire to occupy.

3. The positions an individual occupies in the various collectivities and subsystems encompassed by a macrosocietal order may reflect (as already pointed out) not only his collective but his personal identity.

SUMMARY

Thus a macrosocietal order provides opportunities for the development of personality that do not arise at the microsocietal level. And thus it is primarily within the macrosocietal order that the roles performed by an individual in various institutional spheres can be connected in a way that will be crucial in terms of his identity. This does not mean, of course, that all individuals are equally sensitive to the symbolic possibilities of a macrosocietal existence, but it means that macrosocietal man is more of an individual than his microsocietal brother.

5

Social Stratification and Social Organization

Chapter 4 concluded with an account of two important social processes that involve exchange and balance and the conversion of resources. At the level of nonexchangeable commodities, the entrepreneurial elite that succeeds in formulating a society's basic symbolism, including its major institutional goals, uses its resources of power and prestige in such a way that it can be said to hold titles to various kinds of social rewards. At the level of institutional exchange, each institution seeks to convert its resources into a general medium that can be exchanged for the commodities available in other institutional markets.

The two types of resource conversion that were analyzed at the end of Chapter 4, though analytically distinct, are closely interwoven in every social system in a way especially pertinent to our central concern: the analysis of social stratification.

The basic components of social stratification have been identified as the differential evaluation of roles and positions, the resultant allocation of social rewards, and the use that is made of these rewards. Also, three kinds of use have been distinguished: direct consumption, symbolic consumption, and exchange. In regard to exchange, we have emphasized the use of social rewards in procuring differential life chances, particularly through the control of access to highly valued roles and positions (pp. 27–28). By what mechanisms, then, are the three component processes— evaluation, allocation, and use—linked together in the complex phenomenon of social stratification?

CRYSTALLIZATION OF SOCIAL STRATIFICATION

The most important mechanisms—in descending order—are the setting up of various personal and collective identities, with their structural and symbolic implications; the acquisition of titles; and ascriptive limitations on access to the most important positions.

All of these mechanisms necessarily constitute important limitations on free, market-like institutional exchange, and all of them are, to a large extent, connected with or focused upon the various structural derivatives of prestige. These derivatives, in turn, are the most important foci around which the different aspects of stratification become interconnected, although they are variously important in different societies.

Although most of the structural derivatives of prestige can be found in all relatively continuous social groupings, they are especially manifest and visible in the macrosocietal order, where, as we have seen, the crystallization of the basic personal and collective identities assumes several special dimensions.

First, these identities become closely related to participation in primordial family, kinship, and territorial groups, which are the starting point from which other possibilities of participation in other types of social or cultural units tend to branch out.

Second, a person's desiderata and goals, on the macrosocietal level, include not only a great variety of discrete goals but a propensity to participation (usually differential) in the major types of subgroups in the total collectivity and in the broad symbolic orders and their centers.

Ascription

One of the mechanisms of social stratification (mentioned above but not yet analyzed) is ascription. This concept seems to have been developed by anthropologist Ralph Linton in the

1930s[1] and systematically formulated by Talcott Parsons and Edward A. Shils in the early 1950s as part of their "general theory of action,"[2] and both the noun and the adjective *(ascriptive)* are now standard sociological terminology.

According to Parsons' and Shils' theory of interaction, an individual who is confronted by a social object (that is, one or more individuals) must react in one of two ways: he can react to the object in terms of what it does *(achievement)* or in terms of what it is *(ascription)*. (In a later version of the theory, achievement is called *performance* and ascription *quality,* but the older terminology is more widely used.) Most elites or upper classes, once they are well entrenched, tend to emphasize the ascribed qualities of their members and to take their achievements for granted. Some qualities (a reputation for wisdom is a time-honored example) can be acquired either through achievement (the hard way) or ascription, but just as there are some things that a person has to achieve on his own in order to be credited with them, there are others (noble birth, for instance) that must be ascribed. No man can change the circumstances of his birth and early upbringing; nor can he usually determine the general qualities (the symbols of his class, bestowed on him through socialization) that will be ascribed to him as a result of that birth and upbringing. The same applies to his occupation: various qualities, including association with persons of a certain type, will be ascribed to him regardless of his occupational performance.

Clearly, the mechanism of ascription offers an elite or special group a powerful means of legitimizing its differential life chances. If only persons of good birth (that is, members of the elite) are to be considered fit for certain positions in society, access to those positions is restricted much more effectively (from the elite's point of view) than if they were open, say, only to persons of outstanding intelligence. Of course a member of the elite who occupies such a position may not be entirely bereft of intelligence (he may even perform with distinction), but once intelligence becomes secondary to birth or another ascribed quality, the typical occupant is under no social obligation to demonstrate that his intelligence is anything out of the ordinary.

---

[1] R. Linton, *The Study of Man* (New York: Appleton-Century-Crofts, 1936), ch. 8.

[2] T. Parsons and E. A. Shils, "Values, Motives, and Systems of Action," in T. Parsons and E. A. Shils, eds., *Toward a General Theory of Action* (Cambridge, Mass.: Harvard University Press, 1951), esp. pp. 57, 65–66, 76–84.

Instead, he must demonstrate his cultivation of a certain life style—or, in terminology that should be familiar by now, his differential participation in a broad cultural order.

Such participation, to be socially visible, must be symbolic. Indeed, an important aspect of every system of stratification—as we saw in our discussion of the uses of resources in general and prestige in particular—is the attempt of individuals and groups that have attained a position through achievement to substitute ascription as the basis for their position. The first steps in such attempts are usually various forms of conspicuous consumption and the development of life styles exclusive to some categories or groups of people.

Thus, in a society mainly concerned with the individual's pursuit of wealth, a rich, self-made man who makes a great display of disposing his wealth as he pleases can be said to participate symbolically in the sociocultural order to a greater degree than the ordinary workingman.

Varieties of stratification systems

It is through the various mechanisms outlined above that the basic components of social stratification become linked together. But the scope and strength of this linkage vary greatly among different societies and different sectors of the same society. Often the links are very weak, which enables each component of the overall stratification to develop separately. Thus roles and positions may be differentially evaluated even though people who occupy them do not cultivate a distinctive life style. People may receive differentially allocated social rewards but not automatically use, or be able to use them, for controlling access to highly valued positions. They may not even use the mechanism of ascription for this purpose, and thus a hierarchical arrangement of role categories need not arise, or not to a marked degree.

Relatively weak linkages among the components of stratification are especially characteristic of groups whose members interact only or mainly at one level—as the members of the so-called ecological systems interact at the level of their physical environment. Full-fledged systems of stratification—systems that are characterized by strong linkages—rarely arise in such groups, and they are unstable when they do.

These linkages also tend to be weak among such basic demographic attributes as age and sex and various physical characteristics, such as height. In all societies, individuals are classified to some extent in terms of these attributes; but only rarely does one of these attributes function as the sole principle of stratification, decisively linking a differential evaluation with the allocation and use of social rewards. For instance, one seldom encounters a society in which most of the significant rewards are allocated according to age, or in which sexual differentiation gives rise to a distinct, wholly exclusive style of life and the power of controlling access to *all* highly valued positions. In most societies, such a system of stratification is precluded by the nature of the family unit, which is usually the focus or model of a style of life that is shared by individuals of all ages and both sexes.

Unfortunately, the relationships between the basic component mechanisms of stratification have not yet been systematically explored and analyzed by social scientists. True, there are many studies that deal with differential allocations of rewards on the one hand and differential access to positions and roles on the other, but each of these two lines of research has gone its own way, seldom troubling itself about the other. And attempts to combine the two have been rare indeed.

Although most researchers point out the well-known fact that those who occupy high positions in certain institutional spheres, or whose parents do, usually have a good chance of gaining access to high positions in similar or related spheres, this observation does not take us very far.[3] In fact, the realization that the various forms of access are closely related aspects of the same phenomenon is very recent. Thus the anthropologist Lloyd Fallers has designated the differential evaluation of positions as the primary aspect of social stratification and the regulation of access to positions as its secondary aspect.[4] But even Fallers' exposition— to our mind—does not adequately emphasize the need to study the relationship between these two aspects over a long period of time.

What is needed is a systematic analysis of the social mechanisms by which differential evaluation and differential access become linked in various kinds of societies. For instance, we do not yet know the extent to which the different types and degrees of social rewards that are allocated to different positions in a society

[3]For a summary of such research see S. M. Miller, "Comparative Social Mobility," *Current Sociology*, 9, no. 1 (1960).

[4]L. Fallers, "Equality, Modernity and Democracy in the New States," in C. Geertz, ed., *Old Societies and New States* (New York: The Free Press, 1963), pp. 161–168.

affect the life chances of their occupants, as well as the occupants' children, in the long run as compared with the short run. Similarly, although it has long been recognized that the symbolic consumption of rewards is a crucial part of social stratification, reflecting one of the major uses people make of their social rewards, the connection between such use and the other basic components of stratification has never been properly investigated.

Strong and weak linkages

Accordingly, the next task before us, now that we have succeeded in isolating the basic components of social stratification, is to decide what conditions are likely to make the linkages between them either strong or weak.

By their very nature, these linkages are most prominent in the macrosocietal order—although, as we shall see, there may be macrosocietal orders in which such linkages are weak. And although, as we have seen, the linkages that develop between the different components within partial groups and around primordial categories are usually weak, they are not random, and they tend to vary systematically among different groups and societies.

PARTIAL STRATIFICATION: AGE AS A CRITERION

Partial stratification can be defined as a condition of the social structure in which the linkages between the basic components of social stratification remain weak. Despite variations among societies in this respect, some types of linkage are inherently weak, especially those formed by basic demographic and physical attributes, in the so-called primordial categories (p. 65). One of these is age, of which we remarked that although all societies evaluate people to some extent in terms of this category, very few of them use it as a master criterion of evaluation. But to illustrate how even a relatively weak linkage may vary from society to society, we will briefly investigate age as a principle of stratification. (Unfortunately, for reasons of space, this investigation must be confined to the macrosocietal level). This will also help explain the notion of social stratification as a dynamic relationship between variables, in contrast to a static arrangement of strata.[5]

Age is a basic aspect of life and a major determinant of human destiny, and every human being passes through various ages. At each stage he acquires and uses different physical and mental capacities, and performs different tasks and fulfills different roles vis-à-vis other members of his society. The child becomes a father, the pupil a teacher, the stripling an adult; a man in "the prime of life" is later considered to be "aging," and finally "old." This gradual unfolding of power and capacity is not merely a biologically conditioned and therefore inescapable fact. Although the biological processes of maturation (within the limits set by such factors as relative longevity) are more or less similar in all human societies, their cultural definition is not. To what end, then, is this process of definition directed and of what does it consist?

The principal end would appear to be the differential allocation of social roles, but this is not just a matter of matching roles to numerical ages. Whereas the numerical definition of age is objective and universally applicable, every cultural definition of age and age differences has different yet complementary elements, all of which are variables. Possibly the most important of these is the relationship between age and a society's division of labor. Clearly, the way in which members of a society perceive differences in age will be related to the kinds of jobs their society requires them to do. And this in turn will be related to the ways in which people perceive themselves.

An individual's view of his place in society—indeed, his whole conception of his life—is intimately bound up with the cultural definition of whatever age he happens to have attained. This definition, in turn, is made up of evaluations of this age according to its supposed relationship to such basic human traits as physical and sexual prowess, ability to cope with the environment (whether material, social, or supernatural), and that higher kind of ability that is usually labeled "wisdom" or "inspiration." The age brackets that are held to embody these and similar qualities vary from society to society, but in no society does one such bracket embody all of them. Rather, these various qualities are seen as unfolding from one age to the next, each age emphasiz-

---

[5]For analyses of the role of age in society see S. N. Eisenstadt, *From Generation to Generation* (Glencoe, Ill.: The Free Press, 1956), and *Essays on Comparative Institutions* (New York: John Wiley & Sons, Inc., 1965), pp. 109–130.

ing various features of the entire range of possibilities. Thus the cultural definition of an age span is always broad, stating the potentialities, limitations, and obligations at a particular stage of human life. It is in terms of these definitions that people map out the broad contours of their lives, with their own expectations and opportunities, and place themselves and their fellowmen in social and cultural positions by ascribing a distinct position to each individual.

Age and social structure

The various qualities associated with different ages are usually interconnected in many ways. Indeed, the attributes of a particular age span can be fully appreciated only in relation to those of the others. Whether seen as a gradually unfolding continuum or as a series of sharply contrasting attributes, they are fully explicable and intelligible only in terms of each other. This appears to be true in all societies; but societies differ greatly in the roles they allot to age as a structural principle.

Specifically, there are at least three major areas in which these differences can be detected.

1. The extent to which similarities and differences in age are basic criteria for the allocation of roles and the rewards that go with them.

2. The extent to which social rewards can be used by role incumbents to control their own or their descendants' access to major institutional positions.

3. The extent to which age is a criterion for the development of groups with exclusive, symbolic life styles.

In (1), several major aspects of social and cultural organization play a determining role. At the level of social organization the most important of these, as we have seen, is the relative complexity of a society's division of labor. The evidence seems to show that, in general, the simpler a society's social organization—that is, the less social differentiation it exhibits—the greater the influence of age as a criterion in allocating roles.

At the level of cultural organization, where we deal with a society's major value orientations, it seems clear that insofar as a society's values emphasize participation in a transmitted, traditional sociocultural order, the importance of age as a criterion is enhanced. Emphasis on a particular age is largely related to constellations of specific values. For instance, primitive societies that emphasize military values and orientations also emphasize young adulthood as the most important age, whereas those whose activities are sedentary emphasize older ages. Similarly, within some traditional societies a particular period, such as old age, may be emphasized if it is seen as the most appropriate one for expressing major cultural values and symbols (scholarly wisdom, for example).

It follows that the societies in which age is most important as a criterion for allocating roles and social rewards are those that lack social differentiation and emphasize tradition. Conversely, the more highly differentiated a society, an institution or a group, and the less emphasis it gives to tradition, the smaller the importance of age as a criterion. Therefore it is in primitive and traditional societies, or in the more primitive and traditional sectors of developed societies, that we expect to find age as a basic criterion for allocating social, economic, and political roles.[6]

In regard to (2), we encounter the paradox that the greater the importance of age as a criterion for role allocation the smaller the chances that incumbents of highly valued roles can convert them into hereditary titles. The reason for this is that such conversion would have to involve appropriating the social rewards that accrue to these roles for the purpose of regulating access to them over several generations, or at least until their hereditary transmission is established as legitimate. But the greater the importance of age as a criterion for role allocation the greater the stress on the differences *between* different ages. And these differences are ascriptive. It follows, then, from the very nature of ascription (see pp. 63–64), that social rewards that are allocated mainly by age cannot be used by someone who is not yet or no longer the correct age, and such a person cannot use them to control access to his position either on his own or his children's behalf.[7]

Age groups

In (3), a more complicated situation exists where the development of specific age groups with distinct styles of life does not depend on the extent to which age is a criterion for role allocation. The two phenomena may sometimes be closely related, but age

[6]See S. N. Eisenstadt, *From Generation to Generation,* op. cit., esp. ch. 4.

[7]M. G. Smith, "Pre-Industrial Stratification System" in N. J. Smelser and S. M. Lipset, eds., *Social Structure and Mobility in Economic Development* (Chicago: Aldine Publishing Company, 1966), pp. 150–151. For a preliminary analysis see S. N. Eisenstadt, *From Generation to Generation,* ch. 2.

groups in general and youth groups in particular tend to arise in societies in which the family or kinship unit cannot ensure, indeed may even hinder, its members' attainment of full social status. Such conditions are characteristic of (though not confined to) societies in which family or kinship groups are not the basic unit for the social division of labor. Membership in these societies is not defined in terms of membership in a family or kinship group, nor is it mediated by such groups. The major political, economic, social, and religious functions are performed not by family or kinship units but by specialized groups (political parties, occupational associations, etc.) that individuals may join irrespective of their family, kinship, or caste. Furthermore, the orientation of the major roles adults are expected to perform in these societies is different from that of the roles performed in family or kinship groups. Nor do the children's identification and close interaction with older family members ensure that they will attain full self-identity and social maturity.

Under these circumstances, there is a tendency for peer groups to form, and especially youth groups, which can serve as a bridge between the world of childhood and the adult world.[8]

The societies that are most likely to employ age as a master criterion of role allocation are, as we saw, primitive societies that have little social differentiation, although age groups may be found to varying degrees in every society, whether primitive, historical, or modern. However, the level of social differentiation in each case affects the nature of the age groups. In modern societies, for instance, the development of various youth organizations is connected—paradoxically—with a decline in the importance of age as a criterion of role allocation. In fact, very few roles are explicitly allocated by age in modern societies. Instead, most socially valued roles are allocated in terms of "achieved characteristics" (see pp. 63–64), such as wealth or acquired skills. Family background may be of great importance for the acquisition of these attributes, but very few positions are allocated solely because of family standing.

A decline in the importance of age is usually connected with the rise of autonomous youth groups and movements, a fact that has several interesting effects on the organization and structure of such groups. In primitive and traditional societies, youth groups are usually part of a wider organization of age groups that cover a

[8] S. N. Eisenstadt, *From Generation to Generation*, chs. 3 and 4. For a brief analysis of youth cultures in the United States see T. Parsons, *Essays in Sociological Theory* (Glencoe, Ill.: The Free Press, 1954), pp. 342–345.

very long period of life—from childhood to late adulthood, and even old age. To be sure, it is during youth that most of the dramatic elements of the transition from one age group to another are manifested, but this stage is only part of a longer series of continuous, well-defined stages. In modern societies, however, the situation is entirely different: a youth group, whatever its composition or organization, usually stands alone. It is not part of a fully institutionalized and organized series of age groups.

It is true that in many traditional sectors of modern societies the more primitive or traditional archetypes of youth still prevail. Moreover, elements of these primitive archetypes still exist even in the modernized sector of many modern societies. Nevertheless, full development of these elements is lacking under such circumstances, and the social organization and self-expression of youth are not accorded full legitimation or meaning by the society. Thus we again seem to encounter the paradox of an inverse relationship between the development of life styles based on age and the degree to which age serves as a criterion of role allocation.

In less differentiated societies, or sectors thereof, the rewards received by every age group can be used for the development of its own style of life. But from the individual's point of view, these rewards are necessarily transitory and therefore cannot serve as foci of family life or be transmitted, like other property, to members of one's family. Conversely, insofar as a society has a nonfamilial division of labor with a high degree of specialization, age is not a criterion for role allocation. At the same time, a common style of life tends to develop within specific age groups, especially youth groups. The intensive and segregated nature that these styles of life sometimes attain is a remarkable phenomenon, but they rarely attain the degree of exclusion that characterizes strata formation.

CONDITIONS FOR PARTIAL STRATIFICATION

The preceding analysis illustrates the great difficulty with which age becomes the focal point for combining all the components of stratification. At the same time, it shows that the extent to which these components become combined is not the result of an entirely random process but varies systematically according to various criteria (which we shall also encounter in analyzing stratification on a macrosocietal level).

This analysis also specified two general conditions under

which weak linkages between the basic components of stratification may develop: (1) when access to major institutional positions is distributed either more or less equally among all members of a group or society or according to criteria that are applied more or less equally to all members of that group or society and (2) when the relationship between one or more of the basic components of stratification and the rates that determine the convertibility of resources (see p. 28) is fixed by ascription, so that the only possibility for variation resides in the personalities of the occupants of the society's major positions and roles. Either condition may exist in conjunction with the other, and either may be responsible for partial stratification (that is, weak linkages).

The following passage from the anthropologist M. G. Smith may help to clarify the nature of partial stratification and at the same time disclose some of the complexities in the apparently simple concepts of social equality and inequality.

> In studying institutionalized inequality, two questions are essential, and a third perhaps even more important. Descriptively, we must ask "In what does inequality consist? What is its form, degree and scale?" Analytically, we must ask "On what is this distribution based, and how does it relate to other features of the social order?"
>
> ... These principles differentiate systems in which inequalities are temporary, random or contingent from others in which access to advantageous positions is differentially distributed, so that, whatever the grounds, some persons are privileged and others disqualified. Systems of the latter sort may be stratified if the differential distribution of opportunities characterizes ranked strata having some internal homogeneity and external distinctness. Excluding biologically given differences ... inequality in the distribution of access to favored positions is decisive for societal classification as stratified; only some societies having differentially distributed opportunities may in fact be stratified, and stratification never consists in the mere existence or occupancy of these differential positions, but in the principles by which the distribution of access and opportunities is regulated.
>
> Even when all members of a society enjoy equivalent opportunities to obtain positions of social precedence and advantage ... these must be distributed "unequally," in the sense that some persons hold them while others do not. "Photographic" accounts of current distributions fail to provide an adequate basis for social classification or analysis,

simply because they assimilate sharply different types of society on the basis of superficial similarities.[9]

Because this quotation stresses only the importance of condition 1 above, condition 2 requires comment. In some so-called primitive societies (certain chiefdoms, for example), a full-fledged system of stratification does not tend to develop because the linkages between the major components of stratification have become fixed by ascription. Thus the principal social rewards may be allocated to certain families that are not able to convert them into media of exchange for use in any kind of a "free" institutional market. As a result, there is no variation in rates of exchange, and therefore no bargaining for the sake of individual goals; the society is "set" to function in the same way forever, without any increase in complexity. Under such circumstances, social stratification does not develop into an autonomous dimension of social order, one that is distinct from social differentiation. Instead, its major components remain embedded in other, more primitive aspects of social structure.

Structural characteristics of primitive societies

Partial stratification is the norm for the microsocietal order (see p. 66), especially in groups that interact at only one level and in spheres of social life that are dominated by basic demographic attributes. However, it may also occur at the macrosocietal level, especially in the so-called primitive societies. What, then, is the meaning of *primitive*?

It is hard to be precise about a word that is habitually used with vagueness, but perhaps the most significant characteristic that all such societies appear to share is a low level of social differentiation and a correspondingly limited capacity for accumulating a surplus of any kind. Nor is there far-reaching occupational or economic specialization in such societies. Signs of a tendency toward specialization—craft guilds, for example— can be found in the more "developed" ones, but specialization never goes beyond certain limits; the low level of technology, together with the lack of surpluses, does not permit this. Also, the absence of writing, and hence the failure to accumulate and transmit experience more efficiently than can be done by word of mouth, should probably be attributed to this same lack of a

[9]M. G. Smith, "Pre-Industrial Stratification Systems," in N. J. Smelser and S. M. Lipset, eds., *Social Structure and Mobility in Economic Development*, op. cit., pp. 148–149.

surplus. But all of these characteristics are merely symptoms of a basic structural characteristic: a low degree of social differentiation, a relatively small accumulation of surpluses of any kind.[10]

At this point it may be useful to borrow two classic terms from the French sociologist Emile Durkheim (1858–1917), who summed up many of the differences between various levels of social differentiation when he distinguished *mechanical* from *organic* solidarity.[11] By mechanical solidarity he designated the cohesive relationships among groups of relatively small social differentiations. These groups, which are very similar in their functions and activities and therefore not greatly dependent on one another for most services and resources, share some common identity, which is often symbolized in common rituals. Organic solidarity, on the other hand, is based on complementary differences between roles and persons. The various parts, although they differ in their needs and functions, do not conflict or compete but rather complement one another and make each part more directly dependent on the other parts.

We are now in a position to list four major structural characteristics of primitive societies—and it will be noted that all four of them are related to the low level of social differentiation discussed above.

1. Primitive societies have a high degree of structural equivalence between their various units.

2. Primitive societies are characterized by a high degree of mechanical solidarity.

3. In primitive societies the sociopolitical sphere is scarcely (if at all) differentiated from the cultural sphere.

4. Because of their strong emphasis on primordial relationships and symbols, primitive societies tend to be almost centerless; that is, they do not have a fully differentiated central political organization.

The alleged centerlessness of primitive societies

Items 1, 2, and 3 have already been adequately covered, but item 4 requires more comment, especially since it will be the main topic of discussion in Chapter 6. According to the traditional

[10]See G. Lenski, *Power and Privilege* (New York: McGraw-Hill, Inc., 1966), esp. chs. 5 and 6, and M. Gluckman, *Politics, Law and Ritual in Tribal Society* (Chicago: Aldine Publishing Company, 1965), esp. ch. 2.

[11]For elaboration of the concepts of solidarity see Emile Durkheim, *The Division of Labor in Society*, G. Simpson, trans. (New York: The Free Press, 1964) (paperback ed.).

anthropological terminology (which stems from the work of Robert H. Lowie [1883–1957]), societies that lack specifically political roles or role structures are designated *stateless*.[12] But this is probably a misleading term: *center* denotes only part of what is usually meant by *state,* and the "centerlessness" of primitive societies is only relative.[13]

In some of these societies, as in the kingdom of the Zulus, the so-called Bemba federation, and the "divine kingship" of the Shilluk (all of which have been labeled *federative* by anthropologists), and in the various so-called associational states, such as that of the Yako, some centralized political organization, including specialized political and administrative roles, can be seen, together with various symbolic foci of power and authority. It can easily be demonstrated that, in addition to these developments (and in many ways independently of them), several major attributes of centers, especially the symbolic and structural expression of relationship between the social and the cosmic order, are very prominent in such societies.

Does it make sense, then, to talk of *centerlessness* or *statelessness*? If every society has some kind of center, or can be called a state in some sense, perhaps these attributes are only part of what we mean by a *society*? The answers to these questions lie in the fact that the phenomenon suggested by this viewpoint is neither the presence nor the absence of certain features but the degree of structural differentiation with which they present themselves. Thus it is true that primitive and nonprimitive societies make some provision for symbolizing the relationship between the social and the cosmic order; the tribal war dance and the war bond rally fulfill much the same function.

But in primitive societies this symbolic function is institutionalized in a different and characteristic way. It is not embodied in a structurally distinct center but in a ceremony or other special occasion that seems to involve all the society's structural units simultaneously. Moreover, there is no hard-and-fast rule that one of these units can fulfill this function by itself and the other units cannot.[14] The function can be conceived as being dispersed

[12]See R. H. Lowie, *The Origin of the State* (New York: Harcourt Brace Jovanovich, Inc., 1927). See also L. Krader, *Formation of the State* (Englewood Cliffs, N.J.: Prentice-Hall, Inc., 1968), and M. N. Fried, *The Evolution of Political Society: An Essay in Political Anthropology* (New York: Random House, Inc., 1967).

[13]See S. N. Eisenstadt, "Primitive Political Systems" (in the introduction to the section "Primitive Societies"), in S. N. Eisenstadt, ed., *Political Sociology* (New York: Basic Books Inc., Publishers, 1971).

[14]S. N. Eisenstadt, "Primitive Political Systems."

throughout the society because the symbolism in which it deals, both cosmic and social, is of the primordial, highly generalized sort that can best be embodied in kinship and other basic social units.

Primitive societies can therefore be said to have a decentralized centrality—if this expression is not too paradoxical. However, this does not mean that all units exert an equal amount of power and influence—only that such differences in power as may exist between them are not reflected in corresponding structural differences. Structurally, one basic unit cannot be distinguished from another. This holds true for the various types of kinship groups, as well as for groups that are based on a combination of kinship and territorial units, such as some of the wider forms of tribal organization. Thus the royal household of the Zulu, the aristocratic lineages of the Annuak, or the central association of the Plains Indians do not differ structurally from other basic units of these societies.[15] True, the former are both more powerful and more respected, but they do not differ in their fundamental principles of social organization or in the kind of primordial symbolism that expresses their collective identity from other such units.

All this, of course, is only another way of saying that primitive societies exhibit a high degree of mechanical solidarity. In fact, it does not matter whether we speak of them as centerless or as composed of centers; the important point is that the distance between center and periphery in primitive societies is minimal. That is why social differentiation in such societies does not give rise to social stratification—not, at any rate, as an autonomous dimension of the social order.

Such linkages as may exist among the different components of stratification either remain relatively weak or—what amounts to the same thing (p. 63)—are fixed by ascription. The conversion of resources remains an "automatic" process. Those who have a greater amount of one or another resource are not thereby enabled to change the structure of the society in their favor, nor does it occur to them to try to do so. As we shall see on pages 78–80, 83–84, strata formation cannot begin until the social "rules of the

[15]See M. Gluckman, "The Kingdom of the Zulu of South Africa," in M. Fortes and E. E. Evans-Pritchard, eds., *African Political Systems* (London: Oxford University Press, 1940); E. E. Evans-Pritchard, *The Political System of the Annuak of the Anglo-Egyptian Sudan* (London: London School of Economics, 1940); and Hoebel E. Adamson, "Associations and the State in the Plains," *American Anthropologist*, 38 (1936): 433–438.

game" have been so altered that a society can no longer be called primitive.

STRATA FORMATION AS AN AUTONOMOUS DIMENSION OF SOCIAL SYSTEMS

As an autonomous dimension of the social order, stratification tends to arise insofar as there is an absence of *automatic* or fixed forms for the conversion of resources and/or random distribution of access to positions. Also, it must be possible to convert resources or rewards derived from one set of positions to others in different ways. The process by which stratification becomes crystallized as an autonomous dimension of the social order we shall call *strata formation*. It varies in societies that have developed beyond the primitive stage and that are characterized by:

1. Technological innovations and concomitant "ecological" adaptation, which result in the production of surpluses and the possibility of accumulating further surpluses;

2. Ecological and demographic trends result in the development of various centers, be they economic (urban), ritualistic (temples), or political;

3. A growing differentiation among the prevalent structures of the broad social units of the society—that is, between the periphery and the structures of the centers;

4. A growing internal socioeconomic differentiation within the centers and the periphery and a concomitant development of wider strata or classes;

5. A growing symbolic differentiation between the prevalent units and the symbolic expression of the centers; and

6. A general disembedment of symbolic spheres from their anchorage in primordial symbols, and the development of varied autonomous symbolic (religious, philosophical, etc.) spheres.[16]

In historical terms, these propitious conditions for the formation of social strata were first developed in various archaic societies, such as tribal federations, city-states, patrimonial regimes, and (in a more articulated way) imperial systems. Thus the focal point of the development of social stratification as an autonomous dimension of social order is the process of *strata formation*.

---

[16]For additional structural characteristics of these societies see S. N. Eisenstadt, "Major Types of Breakthroughs from Preliterate Societies: Introduction," in S. N. Eisenstadt, ed., *Political Sociology*, op. cit. See also M. H. Fried, *The Evolution of Political Society*, op. cit.

Basic characteristics of strata formation

It would, however, be premature to inquire into the origins of strata without first defining them. Social strata are categories or groups of people who

1. Are incumbents of institutionalized positions or roles who receive similar social rewards;
2. Have a similar degree of control over basic economic, political, or cultural resources;
3. Are able to control access to their roles and positions to such an extent that they can transmit them more or less exclusively to their children or to other persons whom they see as extensions of their own identities; and
4. Seem to stand in some kind of hierarchical relationship to other categories or groups of people in the same society.[17]

Taken together, these four elements virtually exhaust the various meanings usually given to the term *social strata.* But a "classificatory" approach to strata formation in terms of the relative standing of certain categories or groups of people vis-à-vis a particular resource does not enable us to understand how such standing is related to the standing of these groups vis-à-vis the distribution of other resources.

Every macrosocietal order necessarily presents the problem of relationships and linkages among the different positions in the major institutional spheres. Effecting such linkages is a basic aspect of strata formation, whose most crucial aspects are the attempts to monopolize or regulate (directly or indirectly) the conversion of resources among such institutional positions and the rules of access to them according to ascriptive criteria that stress certain components of personal and collective identity. These tend to be defined, as we have seen, by the combination of various personal attributes and differential participation in the major types of societal and cultural orders, which exist in every macrosocietal setting and tend to be manifested in the way a group upholds its style of life.

The emphasis on upholding a certain style of life connotes the symbolic consummatory aspects of various rewards or resources. A style of life, in turn, denotes the ways in which commodities—owned as resources or received as differential

[17]For a somewhat similar approach see S. Ossowsky, *Class Structure in the Social Consciousness* (London: Routledge & Kegan Paul Ltd., 1963), esp. ch. 9, and H. H. Gerth and C. W. Mills, trans. and eds., *Max Weber: Essays in Sociology* (New York: Oxford University Press, 1958), ch. 7.

rewards—are used to obtain various goals and desiderata and to manifest, by their use in this distinct pattern, the exclusiveness of those who participate in this style of life.

The latter (as every society matron knows) is not *merely* exclusive; the pleasure of exclusiveness lies in *enjoying* something that many other people would like to enjoy but cannot. Accordingly, the style of life upheld by a successful and secure upper group must at least appear to be supremely desirable in terms of the society's dominant values and goals. It is here that the importance of symbolic consumption, as remarked above (pp. 63–64), is greatest. Thus a style of life is a demonstration of (1) the ways in which commodities, already owned as resources or received from time to time as social rewards, are used to attain various goals, and (2) the ways in which commodities symbolize, by their use for these purposes, the attainment of qualities (including qualities of participation) that define a special kind of social identity.

At the same time, of course, there is more or less continuous effort by such groups to deny these goals and this kind of social identity to outsiders, or at least to make it difficult for outsiders to attain them. Thus the development and maintenance of an exclusive style of life necessarily involves a high degree of *in*clusiveness and *ex*clusiveness: the inclusion of clearly designated people and the concomitant exclusion of others. Exclusiveness, no less than ascription, is a mechanism by which social strata are formed and maintained.

Strata formation and kinship

The exclusiveness of a social stratum does not imply a total isolation from other strata; on the contrary, the *emphasis* on exclusiveness connotes interrelationhip, even if it is no more than the one-sided relationship involved in the exercise of titles (pp. 48–50). But because this aspect will be explored in later chapters, let us turn to another major aspect of strata formation: the ability to transmit roles and positions and to control the rates at which resources are converted and the rules for access to various roles and positions are applied vis-à-vis individuals (especially family members) who are seen as extensions of one's own identity.

In most societies—in contrast to less inclusive kinds of groups—the extension of personal identity is effected almost entirely through the primordial social units of family and kin. At the macrosocietal level, these units make a number of important contributions (though not necessarily to the same degree) to the process of strata formation:

1. They serve as the basic agents of socialization; that is, they provide the basic orientations toward collective and individual goals, as well as toward personal and social identity, by inculcating these orientations in immature individuals.

2. They serve as agencies through which access to highly valued roles and positions can be transmitted, either directly through ascription, or indirectly by providing the resources that will enable an individual to qualify himself for such roles and positions.

3. They enforce various limitations on intermarriage, limitations that are often an important part of social stratification.

The relevance of family and kinship units to strata formation is that—from both a structural and a symbolical point of view—the former are social strata in miniature. The solidarity that may characterize the life style of a family is not very different from the solidarity of an exclusive social stratum, which may also be true of a family's symbolic consumption of its resources. It is hardly surprising, then, that the family is a principal (though far from unique) means of transmitting roles and positions and thereby of converting mere occupancy and function into secure privilege.

Unification problems in social hierarchies

The process of strata formation, at least at the macrosocietal level, is based on the ownership and use of resources and control of the rules that govern their use and conversion. However, it would be a serious error to conclude that the end result of this process is normally a unified hierarchy of strata in which everyone not only "knows his place" but is in full accord with the system of values that *makes* that place his. As we saw in the chess club example, different criteria of role evaluation may be applied to different categories of roles within a group, and it may be impossible to reconcile these criteria within the group's overall value system. Thus the quarrel between "pure" chess players and "pure" administrators is likely to remain unresolved.

A chess club, after all, is a voluntary association that occupies only part of its members' time, and therefore it is likely that its value conflicts will be settled by various forms of compromise. But a society is, more or less, an involuntary association, and it is difficult to "opt out" of roles whose criteria of evaluation are incompatible. Indeed, role incumbents may find themselves locked in a life-and-death struggle for the control of scarce resources and/or for establishing a different criteria for evaluation.

Although such contestants may sometimes come to terms with each other, having decided that it is more profitable for all of the "haves" to ally themselves against the "have nots," history seems to show that contestants are more likely to seek the support of the have nots, or even of someone outside the system. Alternatively, and after a long process of alliance and counteralliance, a relatively homogeneous and cohesive leadership structure has sometimes emerged to dominate a whole society without bequeathing it a substantial legacy of dissent, but this is rare, and the result of a special constellation of social forces. Such an outcome cannot be taken for granted or as inherent in the nature of social stratification systems.

Class, status, and party

By the end of this section, we will have reached the point at which it is possible to state how our approach differs from the standard approach to social stratification.

The overwhelming majority of modern sociologists accept some version of Max Weber's distinction between *class, status* (or *estate*), and *party* (or *power*), the three *dimensions*—or, in the terminology adopted in this book, the three sets of *criteria*—by which people can be ranked. A person's *class* denotes his economic and material opportunities, or what Weber called his "market position." (In modern societies this is largely determined for most people by their occupation.)

A person's *status* is more or less what is ordinarily meant by prestige—not personal prestige but the prestige one enjoys by virtue of occupying a certain position in society.

> In contrast to the economically determined "class situation" we wish to designate as "status situation" every typical component of the life fate of men that is determined by a specific, positive or negative, social estimation of honor . . . . In content, status honor is normally expressed by the fact that a specific style of life can be expected from all those who wish to belong to the circle.[18]

[18]*Max Weber: Essays in Sociology*, op. cit., pp. 186–187.

A person's *party* pertains to his affiliation with a group that seeks and wields "social leverage" in order to forward its members' interests, however these may be conceived. Such a group need not, of course, be a political party of the sort encountered in parliamentary democracies. What is essential is that membership in such a group defines one's place in the *political* order.

Most post-Weber writers on social stratification have recognized that class, status, and power rest on different bases in different societies inasmuch as they control the access to different kinds of positions and the control of different kinds of resources.[19] However, few attempts have been made to show exactly how these three dimensions are connected. In practice, those who follow Weber tend to one of two extremes.

One class of scholars, while paying lip service to Weber's three dimensions of stratification, assimilates everything in only one dimension, stressing prestige and honor (for example) at the expense of more narrowly political and economic factors.[20] (Even Weber himself, did not produce a convincing account of just how honor and class are related to power.) The other class of sociologists writes as if each dimension constitutes a wholly separate hierarchy that involves different people.[21] (This viewpoint is supported by an overliteral interpretation of historians' and legal theorists' traditional use of *estate* to denote a segment of the body politic.)

It is only recently, partially in connection with studies in what has come to be known as *status congruence,* that some sociologists have realized there is no need to regard Weber's three dimensions as wholly separate *or* wholly assimilable. Nevertheless, it is too often assumed that "incongruence" between the different dimensions of stratification is necessarily harmful both to societies and individuals—as if the natural order of things

[19]See, for example, R. Dahrendorf, *Class and Class Conflict in Industrial Society* (Stanford: Stanford University Press, 1959), esp. pp. 267–276; W. G. Runciman, *Relative Deprivation and Social Justice* (London: Routledge & Kegan Paul Ltd., 1968); and S. M. Lipset and H. L. Zetterberg, "A Theory of Social Mobility," in R. Bendix and S. M. Lipset, eds., *Class, Status and Power* (London: Routledge & Kegan Paul Ltd., 1966), esp. pp. 561–564.

[20]See the remarks in no. 6, ch. 2 above. This approach is also implicit in many studies of occupational prestige, especially when occupational prestige groupings are employed as the sole basis for measuring social mobility. In this connection see S. M. Miller, "Comparative Social Mobility," *Current Sociology,* op. cit. For a critique of this approach see S. M. Lipset and H. L. Zetterberg, "A Theory of Social Mobility," and S. M. Miller's remarks in "Comparative Social Mobility."

[21]One of the few empirical studies that attempts to overcome this approach is W. G. Runciman's *Relative Deprivation and Social Justice,* op. cit.

somehow demands that every person and group have the same ranking in all three dimensions (or, as is true of some Marxists, that there should be no rankings of any kind).

For these reasons, and because the growing body of comparative studies cannot be properly accommodated in any other way, this author stands squarely in favor of the multidimensional approach, which holds that the extent to which the various dimensions of stratification meet and overlap in different societies is an integral problem of our investigation of comparative stratification, not an insignificant subtopic that can be relegated to a separate, marginal place in the inquiry.

The multidimensional approach to strata formation

Our analysis of strata formation therefore stresses the different elements—institutions, resources, and positions—that must be present in a society before the process can begin. As a preliminary statement of our conclusions (which will be put to the test of historical fact in later chapters), we submit the following three points.

1. Strata formation can occur only in societies where it is possible to use the resources of one institution to bargain for those of others. It cannot occur if the rate at which resources can be converted is unalterably fixed, if the process of conversion has an "automatic" or mechanical quality, or if access to all positions is distributed equally throughout the society. Thus strata formation requires, and occurs through, the conversion of resources.

2. Control of the conversion of resources and the right to evaluate—to establish the criteria by which different positions are evaluated and the rights to legitimize different styles of life—are crucially important for strata formation.

Societal centers, in turn, are crucially important mechanisms for controlling the differential participation of various categories of people in the major collectivities and cultural orders, as well as for converting resources into other resources, into institutional positions, and into access to institutional positions. Needless to say, such centers are not the only mechanism by which such conversions are effected (many other mechanisms, such as market or bargaining processes, also are very important), but societal centers play a crucial role in this process.[22]

[22]For the concept of *center* see E. A. Shils, "Center and Periphery," in *The Logic of Personal Knowledge* (London: Routledge & Kegan Paul Ltd., 1961), pp. 117–131.

The special place of the centers in this process derives from the fact that they combine, or attempt to combine, the formation of the basic symbols of personal, societal, and cultural identity; the control of participation in the various collectivities and sociocultural orders, the establishment of societal goals, and the more "mundane" regulation of economic, legal, etc., relationships within a society.

In other words, these centers are the points at which the two major mechanisms of social control—the control or stimulation of desiderata and the creation and maintenance of artificial scarcities—may come together. All of these components are common to the process of strata formation in all societies.

3. The component processes of strata formation include such things as establishing social identities, regulating access to positions, transmitting positions through familial or semifamilial arrangements, upholding life styles, and inculcating basic attitudes through socialization. But these components are not associated in the same way or to the same extent in all societies. Indeed, this is one of the major ways in which societies *do* differ.

Systems of social stratification are therefore multidimensional, and their dimensions rarely coalesce into a single hierarchy. And now it is time to move from a general to a comparative analysis of strata formation.

SUMMARY

In this chapter we have made a general analysis of the problems of social order, the division of labor, and stratification and are now ready to analyze some aspects of social stratification.

Our major concern in this chapter was the phenomenon of partial stratification—that is, the development of only weak linkages between the various components of stratification, or in other words the partial development of stratification as an autonomous dimension of the social division of labor.

We have seen that partial stratification is characteristic of most microsocietal settings, as well as of those aspects of the social division of labor that are connected with various primordial categories of social stratification, such as age, sex, and kinship. We have also illustrated the conditions for the development of partial stratification by analyzing the allocation of differential statuses on the basis of age.

On the basis of our general considerations and this analysis, we have concluded that partial stratification tends to develop when (1) access to the major institutional positions is distributed more or less equally among all members of a group or society, or according to criteria that are applied more or less equally to all members of that group or society, and when (2) the relationship between one or more of the basic components of stratification and the rates that determine the convertibility of resources are fixed by ascription, so that variations can be achieved only by virtue of the personalities of the occupants of society's major positions and roles.

We have seen that, in macrosocietal settings, these conditions tend to develop—if at all—only in primitive societies, and we have analyzed some of the characteristics of primitive societies that are most pertinent from this point of view.

We have also pointed out the general conditions under which the process of strata formation—as a full, autonomous dimension of social order—tends to develop. And we have stressed, following Weber, the multidimensional aspect or nature of social status.

In the next chapter, we will analyze various types of stratification in macrosocietal settings.

6

Strata Formation in Traditional Imperialistic Societies

Having analyzed some of the general characteristics and problems of social differentiation and stratification, we proceed to a comparative analysis of actual social systems, paying special attention to the process of strata formation. We have indicated that social stratification, as an autonomous dimension of social order, tends to develop in societies that are characterized by (1) a relatively high level of social differentiation, (2) possibilities for the accumulation of surpluses, and (3) the development of societal centers; and we will use two of these variables—social differentiation and center formation—as starting points for our analysis.

In regard to social differentiation, distinctions must be made, not only between traditional and modern societies but between their different subtypes. Within traditional or premodern societies we may distinguish (1) tribal chiefdoms, (2) tribal federations, (3) patrimonial and feudal systems, (4) city-states, and (5) imperial systems;[1] and at least as many subtypes can be distinguished in modern societies. In both cases the classification into subtypes points to variations in the degree of social differentiation and

[1]For these societies see the introductions in S. N. Eisenstadt, ed., *Political Sociology* (New York: Basic Books, Inc., Publishers, 1971), and S. N. Eisenstadt, *The Political Systems of Empires* (New York: The Free Press, 1963).

various other criteria, such as major value orientation, the structure of centers, and so on.[2]

Because of space limitations, we shall not be able to analyze all of these types of society and their strata formation; we must, instead, limit our analysis of traditional societies to one subtype (the most highly developed subtype from a structural point of view): the imperial systems. Within this broad subtype, we will analyze several cases that will be distinguished according to the structure and orientations of their centers. Later, we will analyze stratification and strata formation in different types of modern societies.

TRADITIONAL IMPERIALISTIC SOCIETIES

What, then, did the traditional imperialistic societies—e.g., imperial China, Russia under the czars, precolonial India, and western Europe during the age of absolutism—have in common?[3] Because detailed analyses of these and similar systems have been published elsewhere, the reader should be aware that what follows is a summary of these analyses (which he should consult for their historical data and sociological justification).[4] Bearing this in mind, we can say that all of these societies have similar levels of technology and hence similar ranges of occupational and institutional positions.[5] The basic types of such positions are the following.

1. The peasantry, which comprised the majority of the population and lived either in free or servile village communities. It can sometimes be subdivided, on the basis of ownership and wealth, into various subgroups, such as gentry, middle and/or lower groups of peasants and laborers, and the "agricultural proletariat."

[2]See n. 1 above and E. A. Shils, "Society and Societies," in T. Parsons, ed., *American Sociology* (New York: Basic Books, Inc., Publishers, 1968), pp. 286–303. See also S. N. Eisenstadt, *Modernization: Protest and Change* (Englewood Cliffs, N.J.: Prentice-Hall, Inc., 1966).

[3]More detailed analyses of these societies can be found in S. N. Eisenstadt, *The Political Systems of Empires* and the introductions by S. N. Eisenstadt to the sections "Patrimonial Systems" and "Centralized Empires" in *Political Sociology,* op. cit.

[4]For the data on which this analysis is based see the items cited in no. 3 above.

[5]This conclusion is based on data supplied in the works cited in nos. 1, 2, 3, 6, 7, 8, and 9 of this chapter.

2. Various upper or middle urban, economic, and professional groups, which include merchants, craftsmen (possibly subdivided into prosperous and less prosperous groups), and the traditional professional groups of lawyers, doctors, etc. These groups were usually organized into corporate units.

3. Lower urban groups, composed of laborers, unskilled workers, etc.

4. Cultural or religious groups (especially priests and officials of centrally organized religions or local cults), which include members of religious orders, priestly castes, and men of learning who were concentrated in universities or in centers of learning of either a religious or secular nature. The latter were sometimes closely related to some of the professional groups, providing the schooling for many professionals.

5. Various administrative and political echelons (especially on the central but also on local levels), of which the most important group was the bureaucracy.

6. The aristocracy. In most of these societies (with the notable exception of China and to some extent India) an upper class, composed of aristocratic lineages, had a high degree of control over land and varying degrees of control over the central political and cultural resources.

7. The upper political elite, which centered on the king or emperor. (Membership in this elite sometimes coincided with membership in one or more of the aristocratic and upper religious groups.) By definition, this upper elite had the highest degree of control over the established center or centers of these political systems.

All of these role categories existed, even though in different degrees, in the traditional imperial societies. However, the details of each category's organization, and especially the ways in which each category crystallized into a social stratum, differed greatly from one society to another.

Social and cultural organization of traditionality

Beyond the aforementioned similarities (which we will analyze later), these societies' processes of strata formation were affected by their *traditionality,* a characteristic they had in common with other societies that were not imperial systems.

Perhaps the most significant manifestation of traditionality has been the persistence of a marked differentiation between the center and the periphery at both the symbolic and the structural level. This has been accompanied by severe limitations on the access of nonelite, peripheral groups to the political and religious center or centers. In such societies, tradition not only provided symbols of continuity but set very definite limits on creativity and innovation, and served as the major criterion of their legitimacy. This was true even if the symbols of tradition were developed by a great innovatory movement that, in its day, destroyed much that had been considered traditional.

The implications of traditionality were not confined, however, to the cultural and symbolic spheres; they had important structural consequences. The most important of these was that, in certain parts of the social structures, various groups were (or attempted to become) designated as the legitimate upholders and interpreters of the collective symbolism, and hence became the only ones who were able to legitimize innovation or change. In the more highly differentiated traditional societies, these functions became crystallized into distinct political and cultural centers that occupied special organizational positions. These centers became symbolically and organizationally distinct from the periphery, and tended to monopolize the symbolic representation of the society and authority within it. Thus the structural and symbolic implications of traditionality tended to coalesce.

The traditionality of these societies also had many repercussions on the linkage of their major components of stratification. Of particular importance was the way in which the relatively sharp difference between the center and the periphery affected the conversion of different resources on the macrosocietal level.

This was especially true of the status components that are important from the point of view of strata formation: regulation, through ascriptive and/or legal injunctions, of access to at least some positions; regulation of the symbolical use of resources by different groups (as is evident in the tendency to promulgate sumptuary laws); and even in restrictions on the use of some of the resources and exchange activities (as in the regulation of the output of guilds).

Because the groups at the center were usually able to arrange relatively fixed conditions for entry into different institutional spheres, they were able to prevent numerous categories of people from converting their resources among the institutional spheres and from moving from the periphery into the center. Merchants, for instance, could not usually buy their way directly into the aristocracy.

Another important consequence was the development, albeit in different degrees, of a tendency to make both official and semiofficial ideological evaluations of different groups and roles. This was often accompanied by a legal definition of their status or its various components. Again, this was especially true of those components of status that are important from the point of view of strata formation (see pp. 78–80). And it is here that the power of centers is most clearly seen.

Centers are one of the most important mechanisms for the control of differential participation, as well as the conversion of resources. Needless to say, centers are not the only regulatory mechanisms in these areas; various bargaining processes are also very important, especially in the more peripheral spheres of the society. Nevertheless, the role of the centers is crucial because of the way in which they combine, or attempt to combine, a monopoly of basic societal symbols (see pp. 46–48) with the control of differential participation on the one hand and the definition of societal goals—with all that this implies—on the other. In these societies, in other words, the centers have been focal points at which the two major types of mechanisms for social control (the definition of goals and the creation of artificial scarcities) were to some extent combined.

Despite the fact that the range of basic institutional positions (especially economic and administrative ones), as well as the structure and traditionality of their centers, seem to have been major features that all of these societies shared in common, they developed many differences in the basic characteristics of their respective social strata. Specifically, they differed in

1. The extent of their symbolic and organizational autonomy
2. The components of their identity
3. The strength of their internal solidarity
4. The extent to which they developed distinct styles of life
5. The extent to which these styles of life were normatively prescribed
6. The extent of strata consciousness at the macrosocietal level
7. Access to the different centers
8. The place of family and kinship groups in the process of strata formation
9. The patterns of interstrata relationships in general and social mobility in particular.

Although we cannot deal with all these differences, we will try to decide the extent to which some of them can be explained in terms of (1) the center's predominant orientations and goals,

(2) the multiplicity and the characteristics of the centers in specific societies and the relationships between them, and (3) the degree to which different groups have access to them.

Centers in traditional society

The orientations of centers can be classified according to their major types of goals and rewards (see p. 26) and to various mixtures or combinations thereof. As for the multiplicity of centers, it is clear that all of the traditional imperial societies usually had several centers: political, religious, cultural, and even social. Moreover, these societies had many local subcenters, centers of various "little traditions." From the point of view of our analysis, the most crucial aspect of the relationships among these centers, both central and local, has been their relative predominance. The degree to which membership in one center entails the possibility of access to another is a related factor that we shall also have to study. We shall proceed on the not implausible assumption that the incumbent elites of all centers attempt to maintain their monopoly of access to them and to uphold the orientations and societal goals that they see as representing the essence of their own collective identity. In these attempts they use several mechanisms.

In addition to ascription (see pp. 62–64), the elite had another highly effective regulatory mechanism: it could create an artificial scarcity of the commodity or resource that was most closely related to its own basic orientation (for the major types of basic orientations see pp. 94–95). This, of course, was equivalent to "rigging" the rates of institutional exchange in its own favor, since such monopoly of the "central commodity" (as we may call it) made it extremely difficult for anyone outside the elite to obtain this commodity—no matter what other kinds of resources he may have had at his disposal. It was made especially difficult to buy such a commodity on any terms other than those set up by the elite, which were necessarily rigged in their favor.

If that were all there is to it, an elite's monopoly could never be broken. In practice, however, the limitations on access to the central commodity always tend to be partial. No elite, unless it is established by absolute conquest, can afford to deny outsiders *all* right of access to the center and the central commodity. If it were to do so, its only means of obtaining commodities other than the central commodity would be by the use of coercive measures, which would make excessive demands on the resources of the center and thus limit its ability to implement its collective goals.

For these and similar reasons, most of the traditional imperial elites attempted to develop a balance between encouraging outsiders to seek central commodities and regulating their level of participation in the center. Accordingly, one of these mechanisms was prescribing the distribution of titles, which was done by a variety of methods. Perhaps the commonest method was sumptuary legislation that prescribed the "proper" style of living for various groups and strata. Such legislation tended to emphasize the ways in which different groups could "properly" use the resources at their disposal and the relative distance of these groups from the center.

Another such mechanism was retention of the control of access to the center and the central commodity entirely in the hands of the elite. This was achieved through the subsidiary mechanism of ascription, or by the centers' control of the ascriptive titles to the central positions that bore the highest rewards, whether political, religious, or cultural.

A similar method was to make access to such positions contingent on the new incumbent's unconditional surrender of some of the resources at his disposal. Specifically, he might have been required to relinquish the right to convert these resources into the central commodity or commodities. Another method was to make the price for access to these positions very high indeed, which made it almost impossible for those who attained such positions to use their resources for taking an independent stand vis-à-vis the elite. Finally, elites often attempted to direct or influence outsiders to use their resources for the acquisition of non-central commodities and positions.

Of course, the central elites were not always successful in these endeavors; nor were their various manipulations always accepted by all groups or strata in their respective societies. As is well known, many groups in these societies were marginal to the central institutional core and maintained their own traditions without much reference to the major centers. Also, there were various secondary centers, some of which attempted either to undermine the major centers or to develop wholly independent hierarchies and orientations. Indeed, the very institutionalization of a center or regime tended to give rise to various "countercenters."

Classification of centers

Our main concern in this section is not to analyze the conditions under which elites were successful or unsuccessful in maintaining their positions; instead, we must ask: Insofar as the elites were successful, how did they influence the process of strata formation in their respective societies? We must also ask a subsidiary question: In each case, what role in the strata formation process was played by the orientations and structures of the centers?

Since the best way to answer the first question is via the second, we should first try to classify the different types of centers. One such classification, which is not intended as exhaustive (because we are interested only in types that actually occurred, not in theoretical combinations of characteristics), might be as follows.

Power-oriented centers.

These are found in societies whose centers (in a sense that will emerge below) are based on power and the quest for power. A good example of such a society is Russia from the time of the joint rule of Ivan V and his half-brother Peter—or possibly from the year 1689, when the latter became sole ruler as Peter I—until the death of the empress Catherine the Great (1796) and then through the nineteenth century until the Russian Revolution.[6]

Power- and culture-oriented centers.

Such centers are found in traditionalistic cultures that nevertheless have universalistic orientations. The outstanding example of a society with such a center is imperial China, at least from the Han dynasty (202 B.C.–A.D. 220) to the end of the imperial rule in 1911.[7]

[6]For Russia in this period see especially M. Beloff, *The Age of Absolutism* (New York: Harper Torchbooks, 1962), ch. 6 and "Russia," in A. Goodwin, ed., *The European Nobility in the Eighteenth Century* (London: A. & C. Black Ltd., 1953); J. Blum, *Lord and Peasant in Russia* (New York: Atherton Press, 1964); B. H. Sumner, "Peter the Great," *History*, 32 (1947): 39–50, and *A Short History of Russia* (New York: Harcourt Brace Jovanovich, Inc., 1949); J. Young, "Russia," in J. O. Lindsay, ed., *The New Cambridge Modern History*, vol. 7 (London: Cambridge University Press, 1957), pp. 318–338; and M. Raeff, *Origins of the Russian Intelligentsia: The Eighteenth Century Nobility* (New York: Harcourt Brace Jovanovich, Inc., 1966).

[7]For China see E. Balazs, *Chinese Civilization and Bureaucracy: Variations on a Theme*, H. M.

Religious-ritualistic-oriented centers.

The kind of religion referred to here is intensely ritualistic; and the society will be exemplified by India.[8]

Polycentric centers.

A polycentric society not only has a variety of centers but centers that have different orientations, all of which are, to some degree, continuously maintained. Such societies arose in western and central Europe during the age of absolutism—roughly from the Peace of Westphalia in 1648 to the beginning of the French Revolution in 1789.[9]

Wright, trans., and A. F. Wright, ed. (New Haven, Conn.: Yale University Press, 1964); D. Bodde, "Feudalism in China," in P. Coulborn, ed., *Feudalism in History* (Princeton, N.J.: Princeton University Press, 1956), pp. 49–92; W. Eberhard, *A History of China* (London: Routledge & Kegan Paul Ltd., 1960); W. Eberhard, *Conquerers and Rulers: Social Forces in Medieval China* (Leiden: E. J. Brill, 1952); J. K. Fairbank, ed., *Chinese Thought and Institutions* (Chicago: The University of Chicago Press, 1957); D. S. Nivison and A. F. Wright, eds., *Confucianism in Action* (Stanford: Stanford University Press, 1959); K. A. Wittfogel, *Oriental Despotism: A Comparative Study of Total Power* (New Haven, Conn.: Yale University Press, 1957); and A. F. Wright, ed., *Studies in Chinese Thought* (Chicago: University of Chicago Press, 1953).

[8]For Indian civilization, with special reference to the caste system, see Max Weber, *The Religion of India,* Hans H. Gerth and Don Martindale, trans. (Glencoe, Ill.: The Free Press, 1958); L. Dumont, *Homo Hierarchicus: Essai sur le systeme des castes* (Paris: Gallimard, 1968), and the nine issues of Durmont, ed., *Contributions to Indian Sociology* (The Hague: Mouton, 1957–1966); M. Singer, "The Social Organization of Indian Civilization," *Diogenes,* 45 (Winter 1964): 84–119; and M. Singer, ed., *Traditional India: Structure and Change* (Philadelphia: American Folklore Society, 1959). Some of the earlier expositions of the caste system are J. H. Hutton, *Caste in India* (London: Cambridge University Press, 1946); H. M. C. Stevenson, "Status Evaluation in the Hindu Caste System," *Journal of the Royal Anthropological Institute,* 84 (1954): 45–65; and E. A. H. Blunt, *The Caste System of Northern India* (London: Oxford University Press, 1931).
More recent expositions are F. K. Bailey, "Closed Social Stratification," *European Journal of Sociology,* 4 (1963): 107–124; A. Beteille, "A Note on the Referrents of Castes," *European Journal of Sociology,* 5 (1964): 130–134; and McKim Mariot, "Interactional and Attributional Theories of Caste Ranking," *Man in India,* 39, no. 2 (1959): 92–107.
For the most comprehensive analyses of the changes or differences between the traditional and the modern Indian caste system see M. N. Srinivas, *Caste in Modern India* (New York: Asia Publishing House, 1962), and *Social Change in Modern India* (Berkeley and Los Angeles: University of California Press, 1966).

[9]See M. Beloff, *The Age of Absolutism;* J. O. Lindsay, ed., *New Cambridge Modern History,* vol. 7; G. Clark, *The Seventeenth Century* (London: Oxford University Press, 1950), and *Early Modern Europe (1450–1720)* (London: Oxford University Press, 1957); A. Goodwin, ed., *The European Nobility in the Eighteenth Century;* and B. Barber and E. G. Barber, eds., *European Social Class: Stability and Change* (New York: The Macmillan Company, 1965).

RUSSIA

From about 1689 onward, the rulers of Russia attempted to define the basic orientations and goals of their society in terms of centralized power. In other words, they defined the center very largely in terms of the monopolization of power and the pursuit of goals that were oriented to both the maintenance and the accumulation of power. Hence the major problem of the ruling elite was to limit and control the access of other groups both to power itself and to the positions of central institutional power. The Russian center attempted to do this by creating a general situation in which power could be used to get other resources but in which it was much more difficult to get power through such other resources. Groups that had other resources at their disposal had to give them up and wait on the favor of the holders of power to attain positions of power. Especially (but not only) among the lower orders of society, the rulers encouraged the development of a passive orientation toward the center. They did this by keeping the major collectivities segregated from one another and by making participation in central activities entirely dependent on the center but different for each collectivity.

The center also attempted to control the goals and identities of the various main groups and strata. Establishing and maintaining the components of titles that referred to participation in the center remained perquisites of the center. So did the sanction and regulation of most other components of titles, even those that referred mainly to peripheral spheres of action. But the elite, in general, tended to be relatively permissive toward the use of such resources for various "segregated" desiderata and goals—so long as the latter were not too ostentatious and did not tend to create too great a demand for new skills, which could have created too many new and independent positions that, in turn, could become foci of independent central markets or new collective identities. And so long, of course, as they did not impinge on access to the central power positions.[10]

It did not encourage development by these groups of the rigid styles of life sanctioned by the norms and symbols of the center. On the contrary, it minimized the legitimation of such styles of life and, instead, encouraged a rather indiscriminate dispersal of these groups' resources. If a member of a peripheral group succeeded in getting into the symbolic and power structure, he

[10]See M. Raeff, *Origins of the Russian Intelligentsia*, esp. chs. 4 and 5. For a detailed account of this tendency during the nineteenth century see H. Seton-Watson, *The Decline of Imperial Russia, 1855–1914* (New York: Frederick A. Praeger, Inc., 1964).

had to give up his convertible resources, which left him in a relatively weak bargaining position vis-a-vis the major holders of power (the imperial court and, ultimately, the czar).

Weakness of class consciousness

These various mechanisms, which upheld the predominance of the center until the end of the nineteenth century, had several repercussions on the process of strata formation. Perhaps the most general effect was the relative lack, throughout Russian society of that period, of class consciousness and class organization. This was most evident among the lowest group, the peasants. There was almost no way of extending participation of the peasants' local collectivities into some wider, or nationwide, framework, despite the well-established tradition of informal association for various purposes between peasants of different villages and regions.

Nor were the various urban groups very different in this respect. An important indicator of their weakness was their ineffective organization, even among all the so-called middle-class occupations in the city. Every occupational group and guild was completely dependent, for the development of its organization, on the official sanction of the center. Thus the self-identity of most of these groups had a narrow occupational and geographical basis. They seem to have been concerned with the wider society only to the extent that the legislation of the center compelled them to be.

Strangely enough, this was also true, though to a somewhat lesser degree, of the aristocracy, which had a much higher social standing and greater control of resources than any other group. Moreover, by virtue of its proximity to the center, as well as certain survivals of its semifeudal traditions, it had rather more countrywide links than the urban middle classes and the peasantry. Yet even the aristocracy tended to develop a weak class consciousness or autonomous class organization. Whatever autonomy it managed to save from the pre-absolutist period was shattered by the czars, who succeeded in transforming it into a "service" aristocracy. Such autonomy as it later developed was almost entirely a voluntary concession of the czars. And it was only at the end of the eighteenth and the beginning of the nineteenth century that this situation began to change.[11]

The second major characteristic we have attributed to strata

[11]J. Blum, *Lord and Peasant in Russia,* op. cit., esp. ch. 18, and M. Raeff, *Origins of the Russian Intelligentsia,* op. cit., chs. 2, 3.

formation in Russia—the fact that the major status groups were to a great extent segregated from each other—had important psychological effects. The way in which various groups (or at least their more socially aware members) habitually perceived the social structure can be described as starkly dichotomous: there were those who had power and those who did not. In the last resort, however, because only the czar had power, there was little chance that any group would develop enough class consciousness to insist on a measure of autonomy.

However, the ultimate source of power was distinguished from its bearer and administrator, the service bureaucracy, a remarkable body (immortalized in Russian literature) that ruled over other groups as the representative of the ruler while remaining controlled by and subservient to him. This situation could only emphasize the sharp cleavage between ruler and ruled.[12]

Weakness of rigid life styles

Another peculiar feature of the Russian system was that a closed, normatively prescribed style of life did not develop within most of these status groups, although customary patterns of course developed, especially among the aristocracy and some urban groups. Similarly, the peasantry, living in village communities, tended to follow old and traditionally accepted patterns of life. But these patterns were, on the whole, neither wholly regulated by internal or external normative sanctions nor upheld as models and symbols by those who participated in them. Among the aristocracy, normative prescriptions tended to develop in the capital as a by-product of state service and by virtue of participation in the life of the court, but this was far less true of life on its own domains. Thus there were few, if any, normative restrictions on aristocrats' engagement in business—as there were, for instance, in prerevolutionary France.[13]

The relative lack of a normatively prescribed style of life can be seen in the patterns of intergroup intermarriage, for the available evidence (meager though it is) indicates that the crossing of class boundaries was not at all uncommon. And this brings us

[12]M. Raeff, *Origins of the Russian Intelligentsia*, esp. pp. 45–51, and H. Seton-Watson, *The Russian Empire*, 1801–1917 (London: Oxford University Press, 1967), pp. 10–21.

[13]Cf. J. Blum, *Lord and Peasant in Russia*, chs. 8, 12, 15, 20, and F. L. Ford, *Robe and Sword: The Regrouping of the French Aristocracy after Louis XIV* (New York: Harper Torchbooks, 1965), pp. 22–29.

to another crucial aspect of the Russian status system: the place of family and kinship groups in strata formation. As in all traditional (and probably other) societies, the family or kinship group was the prime agency of socialization. Moreover, family groups that belonged to the same stratum usually formed the frameworks of social intercourse, and thus largely determined who could marry whom within a particular locality or region. But since members of different status groups did not *have* to pursue distinct and rigidly prescribed styles of life, the role of families in fostering class consciousness was correspondingly less. Especially conspicuous was their failure to link family-based identities to a broader, more active orientation toward participation in the center or centers.

Similarly, although there was probably much intergenerational occupational continuity within families, most families had no real control over the access to occupations. Such control as they possessed rested on force of custom, or on making the proper use of the resources needed for the acquisition of various positions. The resources at the disposal of a family, including its prestige, could easily be used to make the most of the available opportunities. But this, in itself, did not assure access by the sons of these families to "better" positions than those their fathers had enjoyed.[14]

Social mobility

The preceding analysis (necessarily somewhat conjectural because of the scarcity of systematic data) seems to be borne out by what little we know of the movements from one social stratum to another (or *interstrata mobility,* as sociologists call it).[15] Given the relatively free use of resources (on which we have already remarked), the main impediment to such mobility was not a lack of ability, or unwillingness to use resources to acquire higher positions, but the legal status of certain groups, especially the serfs. Insofar as there was mobility, it usually gave rise to new patterns of local and occupational group life that were just as segregated as the old ones. Thus the overall pattern remained much the same as before.

Of special importance in this context was the Orthodox

---

[14]M. Raeff, *Origins of the Russian Intelligentsia,* chs. 2, 3.

[15]See J. Blum, *Lord and Peasant in Russia,* ch. 15, and M. Raeff, *Origins of the Russian Intelligentsia,* ch. 3.

church, which was the major channel of mobility from the lower strata. But it seems that the basic pattern of mobility was repeated even here. Entrance into the church's orders entailed, on the one hand, breaking most of one's ties with one's family and renouncing its style of life, but it did not provide compensatory opportunities for forming links with other strata. In theory, the church provided access to the center, and therefore to political power, but in practice it was not permitted to become an independent entity, either politically or socially.[16]

The same thing appears to be true of mobility into the aristocracy and the bureaucracy, although additional characteristics typify the process. The most significant of these was that, since the rulers had almost total control of initial access to the bureaucracy, upward mobility had to be *sponsored* by the ruler or by somebody who acted on his behalf. But even at this level there was an obvious dissociation between the family as a primary agent of socialization on the one hand and as a provider of ascriptive access to high positions on the other. Although, in principle, most scions of the aristocracy were expected to enter some sort of government service (whether civilian or military), the decisions as to who should enter was not theirs but the czar's.

The mere fact of belonging to an aristocratic family did not entitle one to access to such positions, though it certainly made it easier. Once such access was obtained, however, the style of life of the aristocrat in government service differed greatly from what his life would have been like as a landowner on his estates. This was not just a matter of the superficial differences between life in the imperial or a provincial capital and life in the countryside; the main difference was that life as a government official or professional soldier carried its own fairly rigid normative prescriptions while life as a provincial landowner did not. In fact, the courtly style of life tended to emphasize its dissociation from the family life of aristocrats in their localities.[17]

This analysis of strata formation in imperial Russia has attempted to relate the characteristics of this process to the predominance of power orientations in the Russian center. To test the validity of the analysis, it would be worthwhile to see whether other traditional societies, with a similar emphasis on power,

[16]M. Raeff, *Origins of the Russian Intelligentsia*, pp. 51–52; J. Blum, *Lord and Peasant in Russia*, pp. 362–366; H. Seton-Watson, *The Russian Empire, 1801–1917*, pp. 29–35; J. S. Curtiss, *Church and State in Russia: The Last Years of the Empire, 1900–1917* (New York: Columbia University Press, 1940), ch. 1.

[17]M. Raeff, *Origins of the Russian Intelligentsia*, pp. 30–33 and ch. 3.

evinced similar characteristics of strata formation. Space limitations do not permit us to attempt far-reaching comparisons, but several recent studies of another such society, the Ottoman empire, seem to bear out the validity of this analysis.[18]

CHINA

From the beginning of the Han dynasty, the center of Chinese society was defined in terms of a combination of political power and participation in a traditional cultural order—in this case Confucianism.[19] As is true of other cultural orders of this kind, the contents of Confucianism were conceived as fixed in a relatively unchanging pattern of basic precepts and orientations. But in several other aspects, Confucianism was one of the most open systems among traditional societies. First of all, it was only partly a system of revealed religion. Much of Confucianism was oriented toward upholding a tradition whose basic contents came from the activities and precepts of its founder, but this framework allowed for the cultivation and teaching of a purely secular system of ethics in which ritual played no part at all. Also, Confucianism conceived the cultural order as encompassing and enfolding all strata and portions of the society—in principle almost all mankind—and as open to everyone, even if in different degrees.

Confucianism and the political order

The relationship of this cultural order to political power had two major aspects. On the one hand, Confucianism tended to find its natural focus within the confines of the empire; on the other hand, it was the major legitimist of the political order.[20] Hence the Chinese imperial system, unlike the Russians', had an absolutist center that was defined in terms of both political power and cultural tradition, each of which offered an independent basis of access to the center.

[18]H. A. R. Gibb and H. Bowen, *Islamic Society and the West* (London: Oxford University Press, 1950).

[19]See for example, E. Balazs, *Chinese Civilization and Bureaucracy;* K. A. Wittfogel, *Oriental Despotism: A Comparative Study of Total Power;* and H. H. Gerth and C. W. Mills, trans. and eds., *From Max Weber: Essays in Sociology* (New York: Oxford University Press, 1958), ch. 17.

[20]*From Max Weber: Essays in Sociology,* op. cit., ch. 17; G. O. Hucker, "Confucianism and the Chinese Censorial System," in D. S. Nivison and A. F. Wright, eds., *Confucianism in Action,* pp. 182–208.

Whatever the vagaries of emperors and the insecurity of officials, the center was always an arena for interplay between the two major status groups: the holders of political power and the representatives of the cultural order. Each group, of course, attempted to limit the access of the other to the center, but neither was able to deny the right of the other to exist in a state of relative independence. The possession of power, whether by virtue of heredity, military command, individual ability, or proximity to the imperial household, guaranteed access to the center, but it did not guarantee the tenure of positions within it. Power itself had to "buy" access to the center by participating to some degree in the cultural tradition. Similarly, those who enjoyed the prestige conferred by participation in the cultural order had the right of access to the central positions. Once they were in the center, however, they could consolidate their position only by sacrificing some of their independence.

Thus the center of the Chinese system had a more diversified set of values than the Russian one; and, more importantly, the former permitted greater heterogeneity of criteria in its avenues of access. On the whole, however, it was a very closed and monolithic center, and sharply distinguished from the periphery. This is in contrast to the equally important fact that the cultural order the center represented was conceived as *potentially* encompassing all groups and strata of the population. Hence there existed— to a much greater degree than in Russia—an affinity between the identity of the center and the various separate identities of the peripheral groups. Nor, in the official ideology of the center, was there a basic separation between the societal order represented by the center and the order represented by the various types of peripheral collectivities. A not entirely passive orientation to the center, and participation in it, was a basic component of the collective identity of many of the local and occupational groups.

Titles in Chinese society

The distribution of titles in Chinese society exhibited the same duality as the structure of its center, and three features of this distribution are especially worth remarking.

1. A strong emphasis on the general affinity between the central and the peripheral groups as members of the same cultural order gave everyone, even the humblest members of most peripheral groups, a title to at least the possibility of access to the center.

2. This emphasis on participation in the cultural order tended to limit the number of ascriptive titles vis-à-vis central positions.

3. The central elites attempted to regulate not only the collective goals and identities of various strata and groups but also their use of the resources at their disposal. They did this by regulating such use from access to the center and by directing it toward needs whose provision was monopolized by the central elites. For instance, the various peripheral collectivities were officially encouraged to have some of their members participate more actively in the center by taking examinations and graduating as literati.[21]

Thus, because of these and other limitations on its ascriptive capabilities, the elites could not (as they could in Russia) entirely control access to the center. Rather, they had to regulate the price that could be exacted for the right of entrance. In this way they made sure that most resources accumulated by peripheral groups would be invested in the quest for participation in the center instead of in the development of independent power centers. The price of access (again in contrast to Russia) was not renunciation of the right to convert one's resources in exchange for attaining access to high positions. In Chinese society, the retention of this right was not only taken for granted but even encouraged. At the same time, the amount of resources required for gaining access was very high, and varied widely for different groups and strata, according to their standing in the official scheme of things. The highest prices were exacted from groups (especially the merchants and the military) that rated low in terms of the official ideology but had a wealth of resources that they were willing to part with.

Strata formation in Chinese society

At least four consequences of these institutional arrangements for the process of strata formation in Chinese society can be distinguished.

1. A relatively clear ideological evaluation of different occupational positions developed, based on their ideological proximity to the basic tenets of the Confucian order. The literati, and to

---

[21]T'ung-Tsu Ch'u, "Chinese Class Structure and Ideology," in J. K. Fairbank, ed., *Chinese Thought and Institutions*, pp. 235–250; *From Max Weber: Essays in Sociology*, op. cit.; E. Balazs, *Chinese Civilization and Bureaucracy*, chs. 3, 4.

some extent the gentry, had the highest prestige, followed by the peasants. The merchants and the military had less prestige, and vagabonds, beggars, entertainers, etc., had the least.[22]

2. The official picture of society enshrined in the Confucian ideology was complemented by a strong normative definition of the styles of life and collective identities of different social strata. Part of this style of life, in each case, was a strong orientation toward the center and toward participation in it.

3. The various family groups not only served as the chief agents of initial socialization but cultivated distinctive styles of life, according to the social strata or localities to which they belonged (in contrast to the role of family groups in Russia [see pp. 98–100 ff.]). Although there was a strong correlation between family status and the possibility of gaining access to the center, this was never fully legitimized and—as in Russian society—was not automatic. At the same time, because of the importance of kinship in Chinese society, the fact that kinship units were oriented toward the center was a major incentive for attempting to participate in it.[23]

4. The highest groups—that is, the literati and the bureaucracy, developed a high degree of countrywide class consciousness and solidarity. This was rooted in (*a*) the common cultural tradition, (*b*) the sharing of common avenues of access, and (*c*) the fact that these avenues—the schools and the academies—were to some extent independent of the center, although very strongly oriented to it. This common consciousness also resulted in a measure of autonomous organization in the various schools and academies.

For parallel but obverse reasons—that is, because of their distance from the center and their lack of direct access to it—this common consciousness could not develop among the merchants and the other urban groups. In China, as in Russia, these groups never coalesced into a common stratum, although there were, of course, many ties between localities. And the same was true of the Chinese peasantry. This was due not only to the lack of adequate channels of communication; access to the center, although permitted and even officially encouraged, was not given automatical-

---

[22]T'ung-Tsu Ch'u, "Chinese Class Structure and Ideology."

[23]Such attempts are best exemplified by the networks of mutual kinship aid that were created to assist their members through the educational system; see Ho-Ping-ti, *The Ladder of Success in Imperial China: Aspects of Social Mobility, 1368–1911* (New York: Columbia University Press, 1962), esp. pp. 209–212.

ly to the peasant group as a corporate entity but only to individuals, who were nonrepresentative members.[24]

Mobility and stability

So much for the process of strata formation in China. Let us now turn to some of the general structural characteristics of its fully formed stratification system, the most important of which, perhaps, was the absence of a legal distinction between free and unfree strata.

As is well known, China did not have a hereditary aristocracy of the European type; its highest group was the bureaucracy, which anyone could enter by passing examinations in the literary classics. Thus the social mobility of imperial China was probably one of the major mechanisms that accounts for the stability of the Confucian system.

Fortunately, we have more data here than in the case of Russia,[25] and we can say that China's was a "sponsored" type of mobility, directed at the attainment of positions within a very fixed institutional framework. The same was to some extent true of Russia, but the effects of China's sponsored mobility on interstrata relations were quite different. At least from the peasants' point of view, and no doubt that of other groups as well, there was greater continuity between the life styles of the groups from which mobile persons originated and those that they later adopted or attained.

In the whole of human history, only the traditional Jewish society is closely analogous to emphasis on traditional learning and scholarship as in Chinese society. The former was also very much oriented toward a cultural tradition that embraced not just an elite but an entire society. In many ways—especially in the structure of their scholarly class and in the patterns of mobility in and out of that class—there seems to be a very close resemblance

---

[24]Ibid., esp. pp. 1–20, and J. Gernet, *La Vie quotidienne en Chine à la veille de l'invasion mongole, 1250–1276* (Paris: Hachette, 1959), ch. 2.

[25]Chung-li-chang, *The Chinese Gentry: Studies in Their Role in 19th Century Chinese Society* (Seattle, Wash.: University of Washington Press, 1955), pt. 4; R. Marsh, *The Mandarins: Circulation of Elites in China* (Glencoe, Ill.: The Free Press, 1961); Ho-Ping-ti, *The Ladder of Success in Imperial China;* W. Eberhard, "Social Mobility and Stratification in China," in R. Bendix and S. M. Lipset, eds., *Class, Status and Power* (London: Routledge & Kegan Paul Ltd., 1967), pp. 171–182.

between the two societies.[26] Unfortunately, however, we do not have sufficient space to investigate this interesting topic.

INDIA

The Indian caste system is one of the most baffling systems of stratification to come within the purview of our comparative framework. Although we will not enter into a detailed discussion of whether the phenomenon of caste is confined to India or can also be found in other societies (a problem that has occupied scholars for a very long time), it seems clear that some elements of caste, such as the emphasis on endogamy and ritual position, can also be found in many other societies. On the other hand, it is clear that only in India has caste become the ordering principle of a whole macrosocietal system of stratification.[27] It is on this feature, therefore, that we will concentrate our brief analysis, which deals with the system as it existed before Indian independence and makes no attempt to assess the effects of the present Indian government's various efforts of legal regulation.

Caste and social identity

The ideological basis of the caste system in India, as is well known, was the Brahmanic system of values and its emphasis on the supposed parallel between the cosmic and the social orders, especially in the matter of purity and pollution. Thus the caste system reflected the ritual standing of different occupations and tasks, and served both to transmit and perpetuate these differential statuses through the basic primordial family and kinship units. This sociocultural order, unlike the Chinese order, was closed both in terms of its ideological contents and social access. In other words, it was ideologically ascriptive; there was almost no possibility of transcending it by achievement.

Closely related to the nature of this order—from the very beginning—was Indian society's lack of a political center. Such a center came later, under the Mogul and the British rule, but long before this the Brahmanic ideology had become established as the

[26]J. Katz, *Tradition and Crisis* (New York: The Free Press, 1961), esp. chs. 18, 19.

[27]The problem of the uniqueness of the Indian caste system is discussed most fully in Dumont, *Homo Hierarchicus: Essai sur le système des castes*, op. cit.

major ideological center of Indian civilization. The various political centers held a secondary role, which even the greater continuity provided by the Mogul and the British rulers did little to enhance. This situation—the relative weakness of the political centers vis-à-vis the cultural centers—is almost unique in the history of the traditional "great civilizations."[28] Naturally, this had several distinctive effects on the process of strata formation in Indian society, which can be enumerated as follows.

1. Because of the emphasis on the connection between family units and ritualistic-cosmic standing, differences between the styles of lives of the various status groups, or castes, were both normative and very sharply defined. The rules of caste included provisions that covered the proper symbolic consumption of resources and differential rights of access to the major institutional positions.

2. Because of the emphasis (reinforced by ritual) on ascription and heredity, there was a very strong connection between family and kinship groups on the one hand and status identity and organization on the other. The family and kinship group was simultaneously the major socializing agency, the major focus of collective identity, and the major channel for the transmission of ascriptive access to major positions. The possibility of intercaste mobility was almost totally negated by the rules that governed marriage.

3. For the reasons already noted, occupational positions were inseparably linked with ritual status. Every occupational position—that of agricultural laborer, landowner, artisan, and merchant—was clearly assigned to one of the four major status (caste) categories. This practice was closely connected with a strong tendency to put some of the lowest groups (the "Untouchables") beyond the pale of the system, which was sometimes tantamount to legal servitude.[29]

4. In theory (and the gap between theory and practice was broad), the different castes were defined as countrywide. Accordingly, they should have engendered a countrywide caste consciousness and organization, but this did not happen. This was due primarily to the discrepancy between the relatively uniform, homogeneous, countrywide demands of the cultural order and those of the more dispersed and diversified political and economic systems. The Brahmanic ideology and system of worship

---

[28]Ibid., ch. 7.

[29]Ibid., pp. 94, 103.

extended throughout India and was, as we have seen, the basis for the society's cultural identity.

Among the Brahman groups, moreover, as well as other castes (especially the higher ones), there was occasional countrywide contact and intermarriage, but the basis of caste organization and relationships was generally local or regional. Hundreds, if not thousands, of caste organizations were organized locally—in villages, regions, and principalities.

The ideal of the caste division of labor, while ostensibly based on a countrywide ritual order, could not be fully applied on either the regional or the local level.

Caste power and money

With regard to the use of political power and money, a great variety of activities developed that could not be bound by the ritualistic caste prescriptions. First of all, there was not full correspondence between occupational positions and caste category. As occupations became more diversified, they developed into more or less independent hierarchies that could often undermine the status of the local Brahmans, and even change the caste order in significant respects.

The relationships between the Brahmans and the political powers show even more clearly the limits of the Brahmanic ideology, in which the political was subservient to the ritualistic. The ideology, of course, did not change, but the Brahmans' dependence on the rulers for upholding their status became ever more obvious. In many cases, it was up to the rulers to define the ritualistic standing of various caste groups. And yet all this did not necessarily undermine the system in general, as we can see from the pattern of social mobility that developed.

This was not sponsored mobility, as in Russia or China, nor did it apply mainly to occasional individuals or family groups. On the contrary, it seems to have been a form of *contested mobility;* that is, it occurred as a result of open competition, and the social units that were involved were entire kinship groups. This mobility consisted in the formation of new types of political and economic units on the one hand and innumerable subcastes on the other.[30]

What accounts for this curious state of affairs, in which upward movement in the system created new subcastes? It can

[30]For patterns of caste mobility see M. N. Srinivas, *Social Change in Modern India,* op. cit., ch. 1, and *Caste in Modern India,* op. cit., ch. 3.

probably be attributed primarily to the combination of a country-wide religious-social ideology with a decentralized political actuality and, secondly, to the strong connection between family and stratum identity. On the one hand, therefore, this mobility undermined the status of particular local caste hierarchies, as well as the ideal patterns for the conversion of resources. On the other hand, however, many of these mobile groups sought higher ritualistic standing, or "self-Sanskritization," thereby upholding the basic ideological assumptions of the system.[31]

WESTERN AND CENTRAL EUROPE

For reasons of space, we shall treat only those broad structural characteristics that seem to have been common to all the traditional imperial societies of western and central Europe during the late feudal period and the age of absolutism and that distinguish them from other societies of the same type.[32] This society (there is no doubt that these areas had sufficient cultural homogeneity to be treated, for the present purposes, as a single unit) was polycentric in the fullest sense of the term. At its various political centers, of course, was a strong orientation toward power and the extension of power. But additional orientations, especially toward certain types of prestige, were also of great importance. Among the latter was the prestige afforded by participation in the cultural and religious tradition of Christianity and in the communal traditions that were carried on by various local groups from the tribal and early feudal periods.

Contest between centers

This multiplicity of orientations produced a continuous struggle for predominance among the centers and among different sets of values within each center. The outcome differed, of course, in various countries, but on the whole it seems that a combination of power and some form of prestige usually proved victorious.[33]

---

[31]M. N. Srinivas, *Social Change in Modern India,* ch. 1.

[32]M. Beloff, *The Age of Absolutism;* H. Trevor-Roper, *The Rise of Christian Europe* (New York: Harcourt Brace Jovanovich, Inc., 1965); M. Aston, *The Fifteenth Century: The Prospect of Europe* (London: Thames & Hudson Ltd., 1968).

[33]M. Beloff, *The Age of Absolutism;* J. O. Lindsay, "The Social Classes and the Foundations of the States," in J. O. Lindsay, *New Cambridge Modern History.*

But perhaps the most important aspect of most European center structures was not their multiplicity of orientations but the extremely varied possibilities they afforded for relationships among the different major and minor centers and the broader strata of society. Any group that controlled certain kinds of resources enjoyed legitimate and autonomous access to the center, even if the degree of access was not the same for all. Not only the church but many local or status groups were, to some degree, autonomous in converting their resources so as to move from the periphery to the center and from one institutional sphere to another.

One of the most important components of the identity and life styles of these groups and strata was primordial kinship and territorial ties. But these identities, and the concomitant organizational frameworks, were not closed, or entirely ascriptively fixed, in their relationship to other groups and to the centers. They were open toward the various centers, both the national (or "state") political centers and various cultural and supranational centers;[34] and some of them had full access to positions of control over institutional markets. No group ever had total autonomy, and the regulation of access to the center was rarely controlled by a single group with the consent of the center. Within this framework, mobility was considerable. Resources were continually converted from one institutional sphere to another as new types of institutional positions were created.

Polycentrism and strata formation

These general characteristics of western and central European centers had marked effects on the process of strata formation. Given the strong orientation of most peripheral groups toward the center, as well as the strong orientation of the center toward power and prestige, it was only natural that a strong tendency in favor of hierarchically arranged strata and definite ideological and legal distinctions should develop throughout the society.

In addition, many of the contractual and political arrangements that developed among various local and occupational groups after the beginning of the feudal period tended to crystallize into differences between legally free and unfree social strata.

[34]M. Beloff, *The Age of Absolutism*, esp. pp. 47–49; A. Cobban, "The Enlightenment," in J. O. Lindsay, *New Cambridge Modern History*, vol. 7, esp. pp. 105–107; J. O. Lindsay, "The Social Classes and the Foundations of the States"; M. Aston, *The Fifteenth Century: The Prospects of Europe.*

This reinforced the ascriptive, castelike tendencies of many of these groups and emphasized the importance of primordial ties of kinship and territorial affiliation as elements of their collective identity. At the same time, however, powerful forces were working to counteract these tendencies, such as the following.

1. The polycentric nature of European society prevented the development of a castelike occupational system, despite the strong tendencies in that direction. Every major autonomous social unit—the church, the court, and the different social strata and collectivities within those strata—tended to develop a different scale of evaluation, each with a logical claim of general validity. As a result, a multiplicity of status hierarchies tended to develop. Persons who ranked high in one hierarchy might rank low in another, and vice versa—a phenomenon that sociologists have labeled *status incongruency.* Thus another result was a gradual blurring of the distinction between free and servile groups.

2. There was a strong tendency toward a relatively unified class consciousness and class organization. This was especially evident among the higher strata, but it certainly was not unknown among the middle and even the lower free strata. The fullest expression of this tendency is found in the system of representation that culminated in the French estates, whose roots go back to the possibility—available to most groups simply by virtue of their identities as corporate or semicorporate bodies—of political participation in the center. In sharp contrast to the situation in China, countrywide class consciousness and organization were not confined to the higher status groups they could also be found among the middle and even the lowest free groups and strata.

3. Unlike Russia and China, but not entirely unlike India, western and central Europe tended to develop a close relationship between family and kinship identity on the one hand and class identity on the other. Family and kinship groups were very important agencies, not only for orienting their members toward the attainment of high positions but also for transmitting these positions to them by ascription. In Europe, however, there was a good deal of open conflict over the degree to which each stratum should participate in the center. Theoretically, at least, this could not happen in India, where the levels of differential participation were fixed by ritualistic ascription (although as we have seen, the practice was subject to exceptions).[35]

[35]M. Aston, *The Fifteenth Century: The Prospects of Europe;* J. O. Lindsay, "The Social Classes and the Foundation of the States"; M. Bloch, *Feudal Society,* L. A. Manyone, trans., with a

4. Each social stratum, especially the middle ones, tended to encompass a great variety of occupational positions and organizations and to link them in a common way of life with a common avenue of access to the center. Thus Europe again resembled India more than Russia or China.[36]

5. Closely related to the four preceding characteristics was the possibility of differential yet common participation in various cultural orders and centers by different groups and strata. This, in turn, made the life styles of different strata overlap. Thus the availability of several channels of access to the same center—channels that could be used by various social strata—made contact between the strata much easier.[37]

Social mobility

Turning once more to social mobility, we find a high degree of family mobility among strata at all levels of society. This had its roots, as Marc Bloch has indicated, in the feudal period, and it seems to have continued up to the end (or at least the middle) of the absolutist era. Thus the fact that Europe's social strata had a collective consciousness and organization that embraced the whole society facilitated continuous changes in the family and ethnic composition of various groups. This mobility was, on the whole, more of the contested than the sponsored type, although the latter was also present. In sharp contrast to China, but in some ways like India (with its process of subcaste formation), European society developed not only a process of mobility within a relatively fixed system of positions but a process that, in itself, created new positions and status systems. The most obvious illustration of this phenomenon is the development of cities, which occurred,

foreword by M. M. Postan (London: Routledge & Kegan Paul Ltd., 1961), bk. 2, pt. 6, chs. 24–26.

[36]J. Blum, *Lord and Peasant in Russia,* chs. 8, 15; E. Balazs, *Chinese Civilization and Bureaucracy,* chs. 3, 4; H. Seton-Watson, *The Russian Empire, 1801–1917,* pp. 534–540; R. A. Feldmesser, "Social Classes and Political Structure," in C. E. Black, ed., *The Transformation of Russian Society* (Cambridge, Mass.: Harvard University Press, 1960), esp. pp. 235–245; M. Bloch, *Feudal Society;* J. O. Lindsay, "The Social Classes and the Foundations of the States"; H. Pirenne, *Economic and Social History of Medieval Europe,* I. E. Clegg, trans. (London: Kegan Paul, Trench & Trubner & Co., Ltd., 1937), esp. chs. 2, 6, 7.

[37]J. O. Lindsay, "The Social Classes and the Foundations of the States." For more detail see F. L. Ford, *Robe and Sword;* E. Barber, *The Bourgeoisie in Eighteenth Century France;* M. Ashley, *England in the Seventeenth Century* (London: Pelican Books, Ltd., 1963); J. H. Plumb, *England in the Eighteenth Century* (London: Pelican Books, Ltd., 1963).

of course, long before the age of absolutism. Especially in the late medieval city, new points of contact arose between different groups and strata and served as foci for the development of new forms of political and social consciousness.[38]

BASIC COMPONENTS OF STRATA FORMATION

We can now attempt to formulate (in a brief and tentative way) some of the analytical propositions that can be derived from the preceding comparative analysis. In doing this, we will attempt to indicate how the basic components of strata formation become linked. We shall especially emphasize:

1. The extent to which different groups and strata develop distinct styles of life,
2. The extent to which these styles of life are normatively prescribed,
3. The distribution and structure of titles in a society,
4. The patterns of interstrata relations in general and social mobility in particular,
5. The place of family and kinship groups in the strata formation process,
6. The extent to which a unified, as opposed to a multidimensional, status hierarchy tends to develop and
7. The amount and types of countrywide strata consciousness.

Centers and strata formation

The cases we have reviewed suggest that the following propositions are at least worthy of further investigation.

1. A tendency toward a strong normative definition of the life styles of different status groups will most likely be found in a social stratification system whose center is culture oriented.

1a. The extent to which this tendency prevails throughout a society will depend on the different kinds of prestige that are cultivated by the society's center. It will be greater in a society whose center is orientated toward participation in a cultural order *and* in such primordial units as the kinship group than in a society whose center is orientated toward only one of these.

[38] *Max Weber on Charisma and Institution Building,* selected papers, edited and with an introduction by S. N. Eisenstadt (Chicago: University of Chicago Press, 1968), esp. pp. 238–249.

1*b*. Insofar as the center is orientated toward power, the emphasis on normative definitions of life styles will tend to be much smaller.

2. The extent to which different status groups are likely to be segregated from each other depends, to a considerable extent, on the structure of the center and its dominant orientation.

2*a*. The more monolithic a center—that is, the more it stands out from the various subcenters and the periphery and the more it is dominated by a single orientation—the more it will tend to encourage segregation of the different local, occupational, and territorial-kinship groups.

2*b*. Insofar as a *relatively* monolithic center has multiple orientations, the number of its channels of access is increased. This, however, has little effect on the patterns of segregation.

2*c*. On the other hand, the less monolithic the center and the greater the number of subcenters that have direct access to it, the greater the number of potential meeting points for the different status groups and the more their respective styles of life will tend to overlap.

3. As for the entire range of orientations that are available to a center, power and prestige tend to represent polar positions.

3*a*. A power-oriented center will attempt to maximize the segregation of status groups; a prestige-oriented center will encourage them to meet, but the degree of encouragement will depend on the nature of the prestige to which the center is oriented.

3*b*. A center that cultivates prestige by upholding participation in a relatively open cultural tradition (such as the Chinese) will tend to attract the higher status groups, which then converge on the center—but at the same time it will encourage the segregation of lower-level groups of social life, which therefore remain peripheral.

3*c*. A center that upholds participation in a closed cultural tradition (as in India)—especially if one of its orientations is toward more universalistic, open, cultural, or religious traditions—and regulates access to it by means of ascription, will tend to stress the bringing together of various groups (in highly differentiated ways) around common foci of cultural or political identity, while maximizing their segregation in other spheres of life.

3*d*. A center that is oriented toward different kinds of prestige (such as those in western and central Europe during the age of absolutism) will also tend to minimize the segregation of different status groups and to maximize their chances to participate (albeit to different degrees) in the various social and cultural spheres.

4. The orientation and structure of the center greatly influence the extent to which a unified hierarchy of status may develop within a society. As we have seen (pp. 80–81ff.), it is most unlikely that such a hierarchy would develop in a complex society. On the other hand, the centers of traditional societies tend to develop an official ideology of status that may support the notion of a unified status hierarchy. From the interplay between these two tendencies, different kinds of status hierarchies developed in different types of imperial societies.

4.*a.* In general, the more monolithic a center the more it tends to establish a unified hierarchy. The degree of uniformity varies greatly, however, according to the basic orientation of the center. Thus a power-oriented center may attempt to establish a uniform hierarchy vis-à-vis the center, but not elsewhere in society.

4*b.* The "steepness" and the development of a power-oriented center's hierarchy will largely depend on (*a*) the degree to which various groups have access to the center and (*b*) the form of the various peripheral institutional positions and occupations.

4*c.* A prestige- and culture-oriented monolithic center is more likely to encompass—in its official evaluative hierarchy— not only the central position but many other, more peripheral positions. It will probably evaluate them on a general scale, while permitting them to develop their own, secondary scales of evaluation vis-à-vis their various internal subdivisions.

5. What we have called a *unified hierarchy of status* can be defined in terms of the relationships between class, status, and power (see pp. 81–83). The preceding analysis clearly indicates that none of the societies treated above had complete correspondence between (*a*) the hierarchies of evaluation that develop within these three institutional spheres and (*b*) the group membership that forms in each of these spheres in accord with the institutional hierarchy.

5*a.* There is a tendency for greater coalescence among these three dimensions of status to be accompanied by an increase in the convertibility of the resources derivable from the positions in each of the three dimensions.

5*b.* The more power oriented the center, the more it will seek to prevent the coalescence of status hierarchies and minimize the possibility that peripheral resources and positions may be converted into central ones.

5c. Class, status, and power coalescence can be measured by two criteria: (a) the amount of resources held by a group in any of these three institutional spheres and (b) the degree to which position in each institutional hierarchy provides opportunities for the conversion of peripheral resources into central resources.

5d. The most extreme example of normative dissociation between the hierarchies of class, status, and power is found in India, where primordial kinship groups and participation in a closed ritualistic order were emphasized. This was accompanied by an official ideological proscription against the conversion of peripheral resources into central resources. Even in Indian society, however, the multiplicity of centers permitted the development of a strong tendency—at least in middle echelons—toward the convergence of hierarchies and a greater convertibility of resources.

5e. The strongest tendency toward a convergence of hierarchies is exemplified by western and central Europe in the age of absolutism, where nonmonolithic centers developed in combination with large numbers of relatively autonomous kinship and territorial units.

5f. The greater the degree to which peripheral groups have autonomous, nonascriptive access to the center, the greater the coalescence of class, status, and power. If such multiple access is not fully legitimized (as in India), these three hierarchies will never become fully competitive. In Europe, where multiple access was fully legitimized, the different hierarchies competed with each other.

6. The major variables in the development of countrywide strata consciousness and organization are (a) the orientation of the center and (b) the degree to which different strata want, and are able, to participate in the center by the autonomous conversion of their resources.

6a. The more autonomous the access of peripheral groups to the center, the more likely they are to develop countrywide strata consciousness and organization.

6b. The degree and the scope of countrywide strata consciousness and organization tend to be greater insofar as the access of status groups to the center is based on the corporate right of primordial kinship or territorial groups.

6c. Other conditions being equal, the more the center is oriented toward prestige, as opposed to power, the greater the development of countrywide strata consciousness and organization.

7. The role of family and kinship units in the social structure

is also determined, to a great extent, by the major orientation of the center and the modes of access to it.

7*a*. A power-oriented center will tend to minimize the extent to which family and kinship units can serve as basic foci of strata consciousness.

7*b*. A center that is oriented toward participation in a uni-model cultural tradition tends to (*a*) uphold the relationship between family and status identity and (*b*) minimize the functions of the family as an ascriptive regulator of, or access channel to, central positions.

7*c*. A center that is oriented toward participation in a closed cultural tradition—that is, one in which primordial qualities are conceived as part of the basic definition of the sociocultural order—tends to encourage almost every possible connection between family and status.

7*d*. The greater the number and diversity of orientations that coexist in a single center, and the greater the number of units that have relatively autonomous access to it, the stronger the forces that counteract the ascriptive tendencies of primordial kinship groups.

8. In every society, the patterns and the scope of social mobility tend to be strongly influenced by the major orientation of the center and the modes of access to it.

8*a*. A monolithic center tends to encourage the patterns of sponsored mobility. The exact form of such mobility, as well as its effects on the segregation of strata, are largely determined by the major orientation of the center.

8*b*. Centers that have more than one orientation encourage contested mobility. This is especially true insofar as the primordial and kinship units are important and independent bases for access to the center.

8*c*. Insofar as the criteria for access to the center are fixed in terms of a closed cultural order (as they were in India), the units of social mobility will be broad occupational or other extended social groups. Insofar as these criteria are *not* fixed, the units of social mobility will be individual families (as happened in Europe).

Possibilities of change

Our analyses of the various systems of stratification in traditional societies have emphasized the attempts of the various centers to control the processes of strata formation. At the same time, however, we have stressed that these attempts were not always successful. Although it would be nonproductive to analyze every instance in which the will of the imperial elite was met with rebellion, resistance, or subversion, it might be worthwhile to cite some of the possibilities of change that inhered in these highly developed traditional systems of stratification. This will also give us an opportunity to single out the factors that had a bearing on the transition to modernity, the subject of the next chapter.

Let us start, then, with a general analysis of the conditions of equilibrium and change in stratification systems. As we have already pointed out, the stability of such systems depends on an equilibrium between resources, goals, media of exchange, the distribution of positions and roles among the members of groups, and the regulation of access to highly valued institutional positions and styles of life (pp. 17–22, 34–37, 39–45, 52–57 and 61–64). Such equilibrium can never be taken as given or assured in any society. On the contrary, forces within every society continuously operate to disturb it. Hence the maintenance of this equilibrium depends on the success with which mechanisms are developed to countervail the processes that make for disequilibrium.

One such process occurs with increases in the level or amount of the resources available in a society—whether the same types that already exist within it or new types (such as those associated with the development of new economic products or new religious and political orientations). Another process is change, and especially elevation, in a population's level of aspirations. As with resources, this kind of change or elevation may develop in two different directions; toward social and cultural order and toward things an existing system cannot provide. At least three stages can be distinguished in which these two processes combine to disturb the equilibrium of an established system.

1. They may create a demand for new services and media of exchange—a demand that is likely to increase the flow of social exchange and make it more independent of the center. This, in turn, is likely to give rise to new demands and needs, especially of an organizational nature.

2. This, in turn, may create the possibility that the relationships between different sets of positions will be disrupted by changes in their "terms of trade." Clearly, if the elite positions can no longer control resources or take care of the needs and demands of various subordinate groups, these positions cannot be maintained much longer.

3. As a result of the processes in (1) and (2), pressures for change emerge in the entire system of social exchange and in the social distribution of titles and privileges.

At any one of these three stages, changes may occur in the distribution of positions among the population, with corresponding changes in the patterns of access to these positions. Especially at stage 3, there may be pressure for the creation of new positions, new institutional frameworks, and even a new kind of sociopolitical order. Hence the major issue for every system of stratification is the extent to which the needs and goals of its component status groups can be accommodated within the institutional framework.

How centers try to control change

Our analysis of traditional imperial systems has revealed some of the methods by which ruling elites attempted to neutralize or contain possibly disruptive developments. One of the most important methods was the control of the formulation of collective goals, which was effected by monopolizing the mechanisms of communication and socialization. An elite that can make people *want* to pursue certain goals, and *only* those goals, can preserve the existing social order indefinitely. Almost as important was control over the conversion of peripheral into central resources. The major social mechanisms of this method were usually the diversion of surplus resources into secondary positions (positions that could not be used to change the basic structure of society), preventing (or attempting to prevent) the conversion of resources into positions and goals, subsidizing the holders of positions on which the security of the established order depended, and regulating the levels of consumption and investment.

Despite numerous rebellions and the widespread development of dissenting subcultures, these mechanisms were generally successful. Indeed, it was not until the great breakthrough to modernity that they began to lose their effectiveness.

SUMMARY

In this chapter we have analyzed the processes of strata formation in traditional imperial societies. First, we outlined some of the characteristics of traditional societies that were common to all of them and are of special importance from the point of view of strata formation: traditionality, the structure of centers, the symbolical and structural distinctions between center and periphery, and monopolization by the centers of access to themselves.

This stratification was accomplished by (1) the tendencies of the centers to serve as the major evaluators of the major positions, (2) couching these evaluations in metaphysical-religious terms, (3) placing strong emphasis on normative definitions of both the ascriptive linkages among the basic components of stratification and the life styles of different strata, and (4) focusing the stratification struggles of various groups on the centers' acceptance or legitimation of their respective statuses.

We then analyzed several aspects of strata formation in a single type of traditional society—the so-called great civilizations or imperial systems—concentrating on Russia, China, India, and western and central Europe. The major focus of this analysis was on the ways by which the different orientations of these centers may have influenced some of the most important aspects of strata formation, especially the normative definitions of styles of life, the patterns of segregation among different strata, the patterns of social mobility, the development of countrywide strata consciousness, and the place of the family in the system of stratification.

In the following chapters we will analyze the development of specific characteristics of stratification in modern societies and attempt to discover how they are similar to and/or different from those of traditional societies.

7

Social Stratification in Modern Societies

The societies we term *modern* or *modernizing* have developed from a great variety of traditional, premodern societies, which means that the breakthrough to modernity can take place in many kinds of settings. In western Europe, modern societies developed from feudal or absolutist states that had strong urban centers; in eastern Europe, from autocratic states and less urbanized societies; in the United States and Canada, from immigration that was based on both religious and economic motives; in most of Latin America, from the conquest and exploitation of a native population rather than immigration per se (though of course conquest was also a factor north of the Rio Grande). More recently, we have seen the beginnings of modernization in most Asian and African societies from no less varied backgrounds—imperial or patrimonial societies with ancient religious or literary cultures, whether colonized or always independent.

In Japan, the oldest and in many ways the most unusual case, a modern society developed from a centralized feudal state of somewhat unique characteristics. In China, modernization began only after the breakdown of the longest continuous imperial system in the history of mankind. In India and most of southeast Asia (with the exception of Thailand), the first steps toward modernization were taken within the framework of colonial systems. In black Africa, modernization was more or less directly imposed on tribal structures and traditions by colonial administrations.[1]

As we shall see, these different starting points have greatly influenced the form of modernization in each case and the kinds of problems that have accompanied it. But whatever the differences, the breakthrough to modernity in all of these societies can be seen as a continuation of processes of change that have been developing in them for a long time.

BASIC CHARACTERISTICS OF MODERN SOCIETIES

Two distinct yet complementary characteristics of modern social and cultural orders are of special importance: (1) the nature of the revolutionary event or process that causes the breakdown of traditionality and (2) the increase in social differentiation (for which we have precise structural indicators) that accompanies this breakdown.

The gradual emergence or the sudden creation of a modern polity in a traditional society has always had a revolutionary background. The Glorious Revolution in England (1688), the eighteenth-century American and French revolutions, the various nationalist revolutions of nineteenth-century Europe and Latin America, and the anticolonial revolutions of contemporary Asia and Africa, however much they differ, all represent a type of political and social change that is unknown in the traditional imperial systems. Indeed—with the possible exception of the small classical Greek and Renaissance Italian city-states—the scope, rate, and intensity of these changes were virtually unknown in all traditional societies. Or to use the terminology we have developed, revolutionary change, unlike the change that occurred in premodern societies, has been more or less consciously orientated toward changing the basic contours of the societal center—that is, the changes in these contours were not just an aftereffect of other changes. Modernity, from its very beginning, has been so bound up with revolutionary concepts and

---

[1]For the process of modernization in these societies see S. N. Eisenstadt, *Modernization: Protest and Change* (Englewood Cliffs, N.J.: Prentice-Hall, Inc., 1966).

imagery that even the most conservative tendencies in modern settings have, from *their* very beginning, been expressed in revolutionary terms.[2]

Modernization and the transformation of centers

By "changing the basic contours of the societal center" we mean a far-reaching, complete transformation of the centers' (or center's) *contents,* both social and cultural, with correspondingly drastic changes in the patterns of participation in and access to the centers and in the relationships between the centers and the periphery. As for their contents, the major transformation that is concomitant with modernity is the growing secularization of social and political values, together with the assumption that central values can be formulated anew. But, above all, modern social orders are characterized by an ever greater impingement of the periphery on the center in at least four ways: by (1) the periphery's initiative in opening access to the center, (2) the center's permeation of the periphery, (3) the concomitant tendency to obliterate the symbolic differences between the center and the periphery, and (4) making membership in the collectivity a title to access to the center. Impingement on the center can best be seen in the political field.

Whatever the details in each case, the process by which peripheral groups are drawn into the central institutional spheres of a society can be summarized in a brief and familiar phrase: the demand for equality. In modern or modernizing societies, this demand is no longer merely an abstract ideal but is demonstrated by widespread pressure from all groups in society for fuller participation in all spheres of social life. This pressure has been closely related to the tendency (another concomitant of modernization) to establish a civil order in which all citizens, irrespective of kinship, status, and territorial affiliation, participate in the same set of central institutions. One of the consequences of all this, which is of special importance vis-à-vis stratification, is the sociologically demonstrable fact that different social groups and strata become more and more aware of each other's standing in terms of power, prestige, and wealth, and begin to compare their

[2] Ibid. See also S. N. Eisenstadt's introduction to the section "Modern Polity and the Political Sociology of the Modern State" in S. N. Eisenstadt, ed., *Political Sociology* (New York: Basic Books, Inc., Publishers, 1971).

own and other groups' standing in terms of similar values and standards.[3]

Social mobilization and differentiation

Certain major structural characteristics are closely related to but not necessarily identical with these broad political-cultural features of modernity. For our present purposes, these include Karl Deutsch's sociodemographic characteristics of *social mobilization,* which he defines as "the process in which major clusters of old social, economic and psychological commitments are eroded or broken and people become available for new patterns of socialization and behavior."[4] Thus it is clear that social mobilization is an important aspect of what we have been calling modernization. Indeed, Deutsch has stated that some of the main indices of social mobilization are exposure to the quality of modern life by machinery, new buildings, consumer goods, the mass media, etc., together with changes of residence, urbanization, a decrease in agricultural occupations, an increase in literacy and per capita income, etc.

Closely related to these indices are the following more general structural characteristics.

1. Development of a high degree of social differentiation and occupational specialization;

2. Development of specialized and diversified types of social organization that are not embedded in a fixed, ascriptive framework (such as kinship or territorial affiliation);

3. Development, in all major institutional spheres, of (*a*) specialized roles, (*b*) "free-floating" resources (such as money and generalized political support, which are not embedded in an ascriptive social framework), and (*c*) special and wider regulative and allocative mechanisms and organizations (such as market mechanisms in economic life, voting and party activities in politics, and bureaucratic organizations and mechanisms in most institutional spheres).[5]

---

[3]See, for example, W. G. Runciman, *Relative Deprivation and Social Justice* (London: Routledge & Kegan Paul Ltd., 1966), esp. chs. 2–6, 10, 11.

[4]K. Deutsch, "Social Mobilization and Political Development," *American Political Science Review*, 55, no. 3 (1961): 494.

[5]For more about these characteristics and for additional references see S. N. Eisenstadt, *Modernization: Protest and Change*, op. cit., esp. ch. 1.

Perhaps the most important aspect of this differentiation and specialization of roles is the *separation* between an individual's various roles. His economic role is separated from his political role, and both are separate from his cultural role; and this also applies to his family and kinship roles.

The first and perhaps most dramatic stage of this separation occurred among family, kinship, territorial, and economic roles at the time of the Industrial Revolution. Marx and Engels fully described the phenomenon in their studies of the Industrial Revolution and the emergence of the capitalist system, and modern historical research has only confirmed the truth of their account. As a result of the role differentiation and separation at this stage, different organizational units developed within each institutional sphere and tended to organize themselves around the specific goals of each sphere. Unlike their counterparts in traditional societies, they were not connected to a network based on family, kinship, and territory.[6]

Economic modernization and development

In the economic sphere, these developments have manifested themselves not only in the specialization of economic activities and occupational roles but in the development of market-oriented production units and the widening scope and complexity of the markets themselves. Separate markets arose for labor, goods, and money, in which the exchanged resources were no longer embedded in closed, ascriptive units.

The most important factor in the development of modern economies has been the dual transition from an agricultural to an industrial base and from an emphasis on primary to emphasis on secondary and tertiary occupations. Table 7–1 (p. 126) indicates some of these trends in countries for which data are available.

The decline in agriculture as a gainful pursuit (though not, of course, in agricultural production) was accompanied by the continuous development of new occupational categories and groups. In the first stages of modernization, the occupational structure was relatively uncomplicated. There were various manual occupations, both skilled and unskilled; a few "middle" occupations, such as trade and manufacture; and the traditional

---

[6]J. Kahl, "Some Social Concomitants of Industrialization and Urbanization," *Human Organization*, 18, no. 2 (1959): 53–74; T. Parsons, *Structure and Process in Modern Societies* (Glencoe, Ill.: The Free Press, 1960), chs. 3, 4.

TABLE 7-1 LONG-TERM RATES OF DECLINE IN THE AGRICULTURAL
LABOR FORCE IN VARIOUS COUNTRIES AND PERIODS

Country	Early Date	Percent of Population in Agriculture	Later Date	Percent of Population in Agriculture
U.S.S.R.	1925	85.5	1959	48.4
U.S.A.	1820	71.8	1960	7.1
France	1846	57.0	1954	22.5
U.K.	1801	35.9	1951	5.0
Denmark	1870	54.0	1940	29.0
Ireland	1841	51.0	1951	31.0
Sweden	1840	71.0	1940	27.0
Japan	1872	85.0	1936	45.0
Brazil	1872	78.0	1950	58.0
Mexico	1900	70.0	1950	58.0
Puerto Rico	1899	63.0	1948	39.0

Reprinted from Neil J. Smelser and Seymour Martin Lipset, editors, *Social Structure and Mobility in Economic Development*, p. 202 (Chicago: Aldine Publishing Company, 1966); copyright © 1966 by Neil J. Smelser and Seymour Martin Lipset.

professions, principally law and medicine. Later, with economic development, each of these categories was divided into many subcategories. In addition, the creation of many new occupational groups and categories—professional, scientific, technical, and managerial—changed the overall occupational picture almost beyond recognition. Most striking, perhaps, was the growing importance of the white-collar category, especially its professional segment, as can be seen in table 7-2 (p. 127).

Finally, table 7-3 (p. 128) provides additional data for the changes that occurred in the occupational structure of the United States over almost a century, which bear out the main trends outlined above.

Political and cultural modernization

In the political sphere, four aspects of modernization should be singled out for special attention:
1. The development of a highly differentiated institutional structure, based on a centralized polity with specifically political goals;
2. The extended scope of the central, legal, administrative, and

TABLE 7-2 WHITE-COLLAR AND PROFESSIONAL WORKERS AS PROPORTIONS OF ECONOMICALLY ACTIVE POPULATIONS, IN SELECTED COUNTRIES, AROUND 1950

Country	Date	Economically Active Workers (Thousands)	White-collar Workers	Professional Workers
Burma	1953	1,075	39%	4%
South Africa	1946	889	36	. . . .
Israel	1958	319	35	12
U.S.	1950	60,037	35	8
Canada	1951	5,300	33	7
New Zealand	1951	740	32	7
U.K.	1951	22,578	29	6
Sweden	1950	3,120	27	7
Japan	1950	35,574	23	5
Chile	1952	2,188	20	4
Austria	1951	3,361	19	5
Denmark	1950	2,063	16	6
Mexico	1950	8,345	16	2
Costa Rica	1950	272	15	3
Paraguay	1950	437	13	3
Brazil	1950	17,117	12	2
Yugoslavia	1953	7,838	9	3
Pakistan	1951	22,393	8	1
India	1951	101,725	7	2

Ibid., p. 207.

political activities and their permeation of all spheres and regions of society;

3. A continuous spread of power, or the opportunity for power, to ever wider groups in society and ultimately to all adult citizens; and

4. The weakening of traditional elites and traditional forms of legitimation for the rulers.[7]

The culmination of this fourfold process, as it has developed in the most fully modernized systems, has been the participation of the ruled in the selection of their rulers and in the establishment of major political goals, usually by means of elections. In the cultural sphere, a similar weakening of the traditional elites has had the inevitable consequence of increasingly secularizing cultural values (to which reference has already been made). The process has been hastened in most modern countries by the

[7]See G. Lenski, *Power and Privilege* (New York: McGraw-Hill Book Company, 1966), pp. 308–309, 316–319.

TABLE 7-3 SOCIAL-ECONOMIC DISTRIBUTION OF THE U.S. LABOR FORCE (MEN AND WOMEN) 1870, 1910, AND 1950

	Percent of Labor Force		
	1870	1910	1950
Professional persons			
Proprietors, managers,			
officials:	3.0	4.4	8.5
Farmers	24.0	16.5	7.3
Others	6.0	6.5	8.6
Clerks, salespeople, etc.	4.0	10.2	18.9
Skilled workers and foremen	9.0	11.7	13.8
Semi-skilled workers	10.0	14.7	21.7
Unskilled workers:			
Farm laborers	29.0	14.5	4.3
Nonfarm laborers	9.0	14.7	8.3
Servants	6.0	6.8	6.3
Nonreported	. . . .	. . . .	2.3
Total	100.0	100.0	100.0
Number in labor force	12,924,000	37,271,000	56,239,000
Percent of labor-force women	15	21	30
Total population	39,818,000	91,972,000	150,697,000

Adapted from Table 2, "Social-Economic Distribution of the Labor Force," from *The American Class Structure* by Joseph A. Kahl. Copyright 1953, 1954, 1955, and © 1957 by Joseph A. Kahl. Adapted and used by permission of Holt, Rinehart and Winston, Inc.

emergence of a new secular intelligentsia whose influence is based largely on the new professional and entrepreneurial classes.

STRUCTURAL CHANGE IN MODERN SOCIETIES

These basic characteristics of modern social and cultural orders have fostered the development of various structural characteristics at the core of modern systems of social organization in general and stratification in particular. To recapitulate, the most important of them are:

1. The growing number of functionally specific organizations; that is, organizations that are designed for a particular purpose;
2. The growing differentiation between functionally specific and culturally oriented organizations;
3. The growing dissociation between kinship and territorial affiliation; and
4. The growing dissociation between major ascriptive solidarities

(such as status groups and total cultural collectivities) and the traditional kinship, tribal, or territorial groups in which they were formerly embedded.

The most important manifestation of these changes has been the ecological process of urbanization, which gives rise to the agglomeration of continuously expanding parts of the population into centers where the process of social differentiation can be given full rein.

CORE CHARACTERISTICS OF MODERN STRATIFICATION SYSTEMS

What we shall call the core structural characteristics of modern stratification systems are the direct result of the processes and tendencies just described. Of course there are many ways of enumerating and summarizing these characteristics, but the following approach is that of the contemporary British sociologist T. H. Marshall:

(*a*) The abolition of hereditary, legally upheld differences in status;

(*b*) The development whereby social status differences came to be upheld by social rather than legal sanctions;

(*c*) The shift of emphasis through time towards achieved aspects of wealth and occupation.

. . . .

(i) Limitation of inequalities of wealth through State action and taxation;

(ii) The compression of income differences—with residues retained at both ends of the scale; and

(iii) The increased realization, in various fields, of the principle of equality of opportunity.

Some countries had been more affected by these factors than others; those countries had been most affected which had witnessed the rise and development of the middle-class. This, so it seemed, was the first solvent of a rigid stratification system.[8]

Another, closely related characteristic of modern stratifications suggests that these societies are characterized by—more than

[8]In *Transactions of the Third World Congress of Sociology* (London: International Sociological Association, 1956), 8:53.

anything else—the development of a very flexible, and even unstable, status system.

Whatever name or names one may give these tendencies, they seem to denote the same thing: the breakdown of the traditional (whether closed or rigidly segregated) relationships between property, power, and status. Modernization has meant that one's rank in the social sphere is no longer necessarily equivalent to his rank in other spheres. One's place in the political or social spheres is no longer assured, as it was in many premodern societies, by one's economic or occupational standing. Although there have always been strong tendencies in all modern societies toward some form of coalescence between different dimensions of status, this tendency has usually been undermined by continuous processes of social change, especially social mobility. This mobility pertains not only to the movement of individuals and families between relatively fixed positions in the social structure, it also involves the creation of new structural positions—new types of business enterprise, for example, or modern labor organizations and political parties. These new structural developments, in turn, gave rise to new criteria for the evaluation of roles and positions.

The weakening of legal and normative ascription

These developments have also been closely connected, in modern societies, with a weakening of the normative prescription of the linkages among the major components of stratification[9] and the abolition of most legal limitations—first, on access to political participation (or citizenship); second, on the legal or normative-customary prescriptions of belonging to different strata; and third, on the provisions of the various sumptuary laws. The abolition of these legal limitations was the unchanging focal point of political struggle during the spread of modernity from its beginnings in Europe and the United States to India's struggle over the abolition of the lower castes' disabilities.[10] The weakening affected the regulation of access to positions and goals, the control of re-

---

[9]T. H. Marshall, "Citizenship and Social Class," *Citizenship and Social Class* (London: Cambridge University Press, 1950).

[10]Ibid.; R. Bendix, *Nation Building and Citizenship* (New York: John Wiley & Sons, Inc., 1964), pp. 74–104; S. M. Lipset, *The First New Nation* (New York: Basic Books, Inc., Publishers, 1963), esp. pp. 74–98; M. N. Srinivas, *Caste in Modern India* (New York: Asia Publishing House, 1962), ch. 1.

sources, and the interrelationship of these components of social organization and stratification.

Perhaps the most far-reaching change (which most of the literature has taken for granted and therefore has not fully analyzed) has been the opening up—in principle—of all kinds of desiderata and goals to all members of a collectivity. This has led to the weakening or abolition of the ritualistic, legal, or semilegal normative designation of certain patterns of desiderata, goals, and consumption as appropriate only to members of various ascriptively defined subcollectivities.[11]

With the development of modernity—again in principle—no exclusive pattern of consumption, no exclusive combination of desiderata or goals—whether economic, cultural, or social—remained legally or normatively tied (in terms of the norms accepted by the center and most groups and strata) exclusively to a subcollectivity that boasted a differential status identity—especially insofar as it was transmitted in an ascriptive, and especially a hereditary or semihereditary way.

In reality, of course, the picture was quite different. Many "older" groups (aristocratic and oligarchic groups, and even various urban and rural strata) clung to the idea that they and their children had an exclusive right of access to some positions and over various types of resources, especially specific desiderata and styles of life. Similarly, many "new" groups attempted to establish such claims for themselves, claims to social exclusiveness and various types of titles that would regulate the access to desiderata and positions for their own benefit.[12]

These attempts of the old and the new groups constituted (as we shall see) a basic part of the crystallization of social strata in modern societies. But whatever their outcome in different societies, these attempts—in contrast to traditional societies—could not have been fully legitimized by the center either in legal or in ritualistic terms. On the contrary, the very structure and the basic assumption of most modern centers have been opposed to such

---

[11]T. H. Marshall, "Citizenship and Social Class," *Class, Citizenship and Social Development* (Garden City, N.Y.: Doubleday & Company, Inc., 1965).

[12]It is revealing that such attempts can be found even in societies that are characterized by an egalitarian ethos, as in Israel and Australia. For the claims and controversies of various professional groups in these societies see S. N. Eisenstadt, *Israeli Society* (London: Weidenfeld and Nicolson Ltd., 1967), esp. pp. 177–178, 187–190; A. F. Davies and S. Encel, "Class and Status," in A. F. Davies and S. Encel, eds., *Australian Society: A Sociological Introduction* (New York: Atherton Press, Inc., 1965), esp. pp. 30–33; and T. H. Marshall, *Class, Citizenship and Social Development*, op. cit., ch. 6.

claims (as we shall see in greater detail), and hence such claims could have only the partial and informal legitimation of their respective groups.

The opening of access to positions

An "ideal" picture also developed vis-à-vis the access of various groups to resources and positions. Most normative-ascriptive limitations on the access to resources and positions—at least the limitations that were based on some type of formal hereditary transmission of the right of access—were weakened, and were ultimately, with very few exceptions (as with monarchical or aristocratic titles), abolished.

Access to economic and political positions, and in principle to participation in different cultural-social orders, even if gradually and intermittently, became open to all who could qualify on the basis of the prerequisite attributes. In principle, these attributes were more and more often defined in universalistic terms and dissociated from membership in a subcollectivity that was based on familial ties.

Moreover, differential control of any of these resources or positions did not automatically become a title to a specific differential standing in another institutional sphere, although it could serve, of course, as an important base of resources that could be used for obtaining such access.[13]

Hierarchies of wealth, power, and prestige in modern societies

The various changes in the basic characteristics of stratification in modern societies, which were analyzed above, have given rise to a complex situation with regard to the development of the basic stratification hierarchies: wealth, power, and prestige.

On the one hand, a strong tendency of modern stratification systems has been toward the dissociation of the three major bases

[13]The importance of differential control of economic resources in this context will be discussed later in this chapter, but at this point we can adduce specific evidence: for example, the importance of controlling a combination of political and economic resources or skills as the means of gaining access to top political positions in the Soviet Union, or controlling the resources of prestige (as defined in previous chapters) in attaining access to political positions in the United States. For the U.S.S.R. see G. Fisher, *The Soviet System and Modern Society* (New York: Atherton Press, Inc., 1968), chs. 3, 4, 6. For the United States see H. Keller, *Beyond the Ruling Class* (New York: Random House, Inc., 1963), ch. 9.

or dimensions of stratification: wealth, power, and prestige. Increased autonomy in each of these spheres, and the development of new mechanisms that link them in a nontraditional way, have frequently been noted by sociologists. In particular, the increased autonomy of the economic sphere (Max Weber's "class" in his "class, status, and power"[see pp. 81–83]) has been studied in the following aspects:

1. In the development of a trend, at first very gradual and intermittent, toward a situation in which control over economic resources became an increasingly important criterion for the evaluation of many status positions, and

2. In the growing importance of *class,* in both the Marxian and the Weberian sense, as a determinant of access to positions and rewards.

This relative independence of the economic class structure was ushered in by the various European commercial revolutions that began in the sixteenth century. The Industrial Revolution only confirmed an existing trend, in which the individual's standing in various noneconomic hierarchies became less relevant to his access to economic resources. Henceforth the individual would depend more and more on the mercy of the various economic markets. Combined with the growing emphasis on economic activity as a central goal of the collectivity, this process signaled a transformation in the social meaning of economic goals and made economic success an important and legitimate criterion of role evaluation. The continuous development of industrialization in Europe and the United States, and its extension throughout the world, has only increased the autonomy of the economic sphere and therefore of *social class* as a principle of stratification.[14]

But the supremacy of the economic dimension in modern systems of stratification has not gone unchallenged. Side by side with the emancipation of the economic sphere, countervailing forces developed. Similar developments were also occurring in the other major institutional spheres, including the political and the various spheres of social and cultural participation. In all these a growing autonomy developed in terms of control over their resources, organization of their "markets," distribution of their rewards, and the formation of their own criteria of role evaluation.

However, the increased autonomy of the various status hier-

[14]R. Dahrendorf, *Class and Class Conflict in Industrial Society* (Stanford: Stanford University Press, 1959), pp. 3–7.

archies should not be interpreted as meaning that—as compared with traditional societies—they have lost their importance. On the contrary, the very diversification and fragmentation of social organization has increased the importance of these hierarchies as symbolic constructs that order the perception of the social order. At the same time, these hierarchies were never fixed or homogeneous in modern societies.

Continuous structural change in modern societies

The development of a high level of social differentiation—of autonomous hierarchies of wealth, power, or status, as well as wider and easier access to goals, resources, and positions—was not, in modern societies, a unique occurrence. One of the basic characteristics of modern social organization in general and its stratification systems in particular is continuous change. Some of these changes—and especially those that affect the relative standing of different groups or categories of people in different institutional spheres and hierarchies of power, wealth, and status, as well as their control of resources of these spheres and their access to the major positions within them—were of special importance in influencing their processes of strata formation.

Within the economic field, the most important changes of this kind were in the structure of the employment situation:
1. In the degree of authority or autonomy within it,
2. In the degree of autonomy in the use of one's resources,
3. In the degree and the time span of economic security or insecurity that any particular job or assignment entails, and
4. In the levels of remuneration and usable wealth or professional attributes that accompany autonomy.[15]

These developments were also connected with changes in the structure of the basic units of economic organization. The most important trends have been:
1. Changes from small-scale units of production (such as family firms, small factories, and small commercial and banking enterprises), operated for relatively restricted markets, to more centralized, bureaucratized, and larger units of production (such as large corporations, trusts, and cartels), operated in new and more encompassing large-scale markets, and
2. New techniques of production, which greatly affected the

---

[15]For these various aspects of class structure see ibid., ch. 2 and pp. 248–267, and G. Lenski, *Power and Privilege*, op. cit., esp. ch. 11.

structure of the economic process and have been continuously developing, giving rise to a greater and more complicated division of labor within each unit on the one hand and to the growth of new types of interunit relationships on the other.[16]

All of these changes, of course, were accompanied by changes in the channels and the criteria for access to the major occupational positions. And thus the major trend in the history of modern societies has been from broad and diffuse status attributes (transmitted primarily through direct participation in a particular occupational strata based on family, wealth, tribal, or caste-territorial positions) to formal educational qualifications.

The greater importance of educational criteria, in turn, has been due to two interconnected but distinct factors: the greater technological and general knowledge that seems to be necessary for many skills and—certainly no less important—the intensified quest for participation in the cultural and social orders and the attempts to relate the expanding economy and/or technologies to the central symbols of such orders.

Moreover, the greater importance of educational attainments, as criteria of status or for access to positions, has given rise to a situation in which, because of the advance of knowledge, previously acquired skills have become obsolescent. This, in turn, may give rise to status struggles—a result of the decline in the position of groups whose knowledge has become less important or valuable than formerly.

As for the control of property and the relationship between the ownership and the control of units of production, the major trend in modern societies has been from societies or sectors thereof within which the owners of the units were also their managers and masters (as in family farms, haciendas, and plantations in agriculture and family businesses and firms in industry) to large corporate organizations that emphasize the dissociation between ownership and the effective control of the units of production.[17] This distinction between ownership and manage-

---

[16]W. E. Moore, *The Impact of Industry* (Englewood Cliffs, N.J.: Prentice-Hall, Inc., 1965), and C. S. Belshaw, *Traditional Exchange and Modern Markets* (Englewood Cliffs, N.J.: Prentice-Hall, Inc., 1965), esp. pp. 108–130.

[17]For the types of relationships between ownership and control in the agricultural sector see A. L. Stinchcombe, "Agricultural Enterprise and Rural Class Relations," in R. Bendix and S. M. Lipset, eds., *Class, Status and Power* (London: Routledge & Kegan Paul Ltd., 1967), pp. 182–190.

For the dissociation between ownership and control in other economic sectors, with special reference to the situation in the United States, see A. A. Berle and G. C. Means, *The Modern Corporation and Private Property* (New York: The Macmillan Company, 1948), esp. bk. 1, and E. S. Mason, ed., *The Corporation in Modern Society* (Cambridge, Mass.: Harvard University Press, 1959).

ment is, of course, especially crucial in communist or socialist regimes, but it is also important in many sectors of the democratic welfare state, where the ownership of many enterprises has been vested in various publicly owned or controlled bodies, be they governments, trade unions, or corporations.

Changes in income distribution

These differences in the relationship between ownership and management are also closely related to, but not identical with, another structural aspect of economic institutions: the distribution of wealth. But in modern societies, where a polarized distribution of income has gradually given way to wider distribution, remarkable inequalities still persist, if we can judge by the disproportionate share of the total wealth that accrues to some groups—disproportionate, that is, compared to their percentage of the total population. The following tables should make both points clear, even though we could not always find tables that cover exactly the same years for different societies.

In Britain, inequities in the distribution of wealth are even more accentuated, as can be seen in table 7–5.

Table 7–6 (p. 138) shows that a more equalitarian distribution is found in Australia.

As table 7–7 (p. 138) indicates, the situation in Sweden, though more mixed, is more equalitarian than in Britain or the United States.

Of the other forces at work in modern societies (of which income distribution figures are only one aspect), perhaps the most important related economic process has been the almost universal tendency toward inflation. The impact of inflation is hardest on groups and classes whose standing is based on a fixed income, whether as returns from investments or as salaries.

Another force—not, strictly speaking, economic—has been the growing importance of education as a criterion for access to occupational positions. Closely related to inflation and education are changes in the structure of the working situation, especially the growing differences between organizations in which various categories of skilled, unskilled, and white-collar workers are segregated from each other and organizations in which they are not.

Finally, changes in income, education, and work situations are closely related to changes in the security of employment.

TABLE 7-4 ESTIMATED DISTRIBUTION OF WEALTH IN THE UNITED STATES, 1953

Assets	Adult Population*	Wealth*
Less than $3,500	50.0%	8.3%
$3,500 to $10,000	18.4	10.2
$10,000 to $20,000	21.2	29.3
$20,000 to $30,000	5.8	13.4
$30,000 to $50,000	2.7	9.5
$50,000 to $100,000	1.0	6.2
$100,000 to $1,000,000	0.9	16.6
$1,000,000 to $10,000,000	0.04	5.2
$10,000,000 and over	0.0006	1.3
Total	100.0%	100.0%

*Percentages are rounded to nearest decimal point.
From *Power and Privilege* by G. E. Lenski, p. 339. Copyright © 1966 by G. E. Lenski. Used with permission of McGraw-Hill Book Company.

TABLE 7-5 ESTIMATED DISTRIBUTION OF WEALTH IN BRITAIN, 1946-1947

Assets	Adult Population*	Wealth*
Less than £100	60.6%	4.2%
£100 to £999	27.8	11.6
£1,000 to £4,999	8.9	21.0
£5,000 to £9,999	1.4	11.4
£10,000 to £24,999	0.9	16.4
£25,000 to £99,999	0.4	19.2
£100,000 and over	0.06	16.3
Total	100.0 %	100.0%

*Percentages rounded to nearest decimal point.
Ibid.

TABLE 7-6 INCOME DISTRIBUTION IN AUSTRALIA, 1960-1961

Income	No. of Taxpayers	Percent of Total Taxpayers*	Actual Income*	Percent of Actual Income*
£105 to £499	772,000	17.7	£ 237	5.0
£500 to £999	1,410,000	32.4	1,052	22.2
£1,000 to £1,999	1,850,000	42.5	2,453	51.6
£2,000 to £4,999	284,000	6.5	740	15.6
£5,000 to £9,999	29,000	0.7	185	3.9
£10,000 to £19,999	4,300	0.1	58	1.2
£20,000 to £49,999	640	. . . .	19	0.4
£50,000 and over	60	. . . .	5	0.1
Total	4,350,000	100.0	£4,750	100.0

*Entries rounded to nearest decimal point or pound.
Reprinted from A. F. Davies and S. Encel, editors, *Australian Society*, p. 235 (New York: Atherton Press, 1965); copyright © 1965 by F. W. Cheshire Pty. Ltd.

TABLE 7-7 DISTRIBUTION OF INCOME* IN SWEDEN, 1950

Income (Kroner)	Persons in Percent of Total	Income in Percent of Total
600 to 2,000	17.1%	4.1%
2,000 to 5,000	35.9	22.0
5,000 to 10,000	36.6	44.4
10,000 to 20,000	8.6	19.6
20,000 and over	1.8	9.9
Total	100.0%	100.0%

*Before taxes.
From: G. R. Nelson, ed., *Freedom and Welfare: Social Patterns in the Northern Countries of Europe* (Copenhagen: The Ministries of Social Affairs of Denmark, Finland, Iceland, Norway, and Sweden, 1953), p. 54. Reprinted with permission of Greenwood Press, Inc.

Some workers in modern societies are wholly subject to the vagaries of the market, while others attain security through unions or governmental unemployment insurance. But between these two extremes are many intermediate categories.

All of these changes have had, and are having, profound effects on the structure of the economic sphere in modern societies.

Political and cultural changes

Similar changes can be discerned in other institutional spheres. In the political sphere, the most important kinds of structural change seem to be in the scope of political participation, in access to the center and to membership in the elite, and in the power structure (that is, in the way power in a society is spread over different institutional spheres). In the cultural sphere, equally important changes have occurred in the exclusiveness of different groups, in the degree of common participation in various social spheres, in access to various goals, and in the opportunities to share in a common value system (such as the "middle-class values" of American society—as compared, say, with the more exclusive values of subgroups in England).

SOCIAL MOBILITY AND EQUALITY OF OPPORTUNITY IN MODERN SOCIETIES

We have seen that modern social systems are characterized by continuous change, differentiation, and expansion. But to what extent did the continuous expansion of the economy, the continuous structural changes, and the ever present ideological stress on egalitarian participation in all sectors of the social order affect the distribution of population within the different social hierarchies? Several types of research may throw light on this question.

Studies of social mobility

Sociologists have devoted much empirical research to comparing social mobility in different modern societies, but the pioneer study is that of Bendix and Lipset, who attempted to synthesize broad samplings of occupational mobility data, es-

lly from several European countries and the United States
...ad Japan after the Second World War.[18] In all of these countries
they found significant and, on the whole, similar rates of intergenerational mobility, especially between manual and nonmanual occupations. The quantitative roots of this phenomenon,
though not its cultural evaluation—according to this study—were
fairly similar in the countries studied and were traced to the
changes in the occupational structure occasioned by the process
of industrialization.

But these findings do not tell us much about the *range* of
mobility—for example, the occupational status to which the son
of a manual worker can hope to rise. This problem has been
studied more fully by Miller, whose general conclusions are as
follows.

> No nation has considerable movement into the upper levels.
> Only a small part of the manual strata are able to obtain such
> positions. Nations with high overall upward movement . . .
> may not have, for the manual strata, high rates of access to the
> top positions. The range is from less than 2% in 5 nations to
> almost 8% in the U.S.A. and 8.6% in Puerto Rico. . . .
>
> The comparison of the movement into Elite I (the highest
> occupational grouping in this class) of manual workers with
> the corresponding movement of the middle classes shows a
> considerable range. . . . For the nations for which we have
> data, the middle classes are overall three-and-a-half times
> more likely to end up in Elite I occupations than are those
> originating in the manual strata. *In terms of this type of
> long-distance mobility, there is no nation in which it is not a
> distinct advantage to be born in the middle classes rather
> than in the manual strata.*[19]

The same problem is explored further in another study, by
Fox and Miller, who analyzed and compared various aspects of
mobility in four countries. Their conclusions on the opportunities
for sons in various occupational groupings to rise to the elite
stratum are excerpted below.

In Great Britain, sons of middle-class fathers enjoy a distinct

---

[18]R. Bendix and S. M. Lipset, *Social Mobility in Industrial Society* (Berkeley and Los Angeles: University of California Press, 1959).

[19]S. M. Miller, "Comparative Social Mobility," *Current Sociology,* 9, no. 1 (1960): 40, 42.

advantage over sons of skilled, semi-skilled and unskilled in securing membership in the elite stratum. The middle-class sons have almost three times the opportunities of the skilled sons (19/7) of entering the elite, six times the opportunities of the semi-skilled (19/3), and nine times the chances of the unskilled (19/2). But the son of an elite father has the best opportunity to become an elite himself—his chances are five times greater than for the son of a middle-class father (100/19) and fifty times [greater] than for the son of an unskilled father (100/2). . . .

The son of a middle-class father in Japan enjoys almost twice the opportunity of a skilled son (39/21) for gaining admission to elite status, and only slightly more than twice the advantage of the semi-skilled and unskilled (respectively, 39/17 and 39/18). Japanese sons of middle-class origins are more than one-third of the way toward achieving elite entry equality with the sons of elite fathers (100/39).

In the Netherlands, sons of middle-class origins have very little advantage over the sons of skilled origins in securing elite status; their chances are almost equal (22/20). But skilled and middle-class sons have considerably better chances of entering the elite than the semi-skilled or un-skilled sons.

Turning now to the U.S., we find that . . . the sons of middle-class fathers have travelled more than a third of the route leading to equality of opportunity with sons of elite fathers (100/37). Middle-class advantage over offspring of the skilled exists but is less than double the chances of the latter (37/22). The son of a skilled father has almost four times the opportunity of a semi-skilled to reach the elite stratum (22/6).[20]

Bases of stratification and social mobility

Thus it is clear that, given a continuous economic and occupational expansion, there is necessarily a great amount of occupational mobility, that is, transition between specific occupations. But most of the data on mobility seem to indicate that, when occupations are sorted into "high," "middle," and "low," the

---

[20]Copyright © *Studies in Comparative International Development* vol. 1, no. 1, 1965, p. 6. Rutgers University, New Brunswick, New Jersey.

chances of being in the high echelon are better for sons whose fathers already belong to it than they are for the sons of fathers who are in either of the two lower echelons. Nevertheless, the data show that there is much intergenerational occupational mobility, especially from the manual to the white-collar stratum.

Miller's international study shows that these rates of mobility fluctuate from a 8.5 percent to 30 percent (in most cases they are above 20 percent).[21] Although such rates are remarkable, it would be only fair to assume that most of this mobility is toward the *lower* ranks of the white-collar occupations, because the chances for a worker's son to reach the upper levels of the white-collar class are relatively limited. There is even some evidence that the mobility chances of a skilled worker's son may be greater than those of an unskilled worker's son.[22]

The studies of mobility also tell us something about downward mobility—although, here again, measurement is difficult. Miller's study indicates that, in the countries studied, rates of mobility from the white-collar category to manual occupations are significant. The most noteworthy move is from the bottom of the white-collar scale to skilled manual occupations. The down-mobiles from the upper layers of the white-collar category tend to move into its middle ranges rather than into the manual range.[23]

Access to occupational positions

The mobility studies also provide insight into the determinants of differential access to major occupational positions in modern societies. For instance, Bendix and Lipset, drawing on a large body of these studies, have demonstrated that

1. Plans to attend college are not conditioned by level of intelligence only but by class as well.

2. The class factor, not the level of intelligence, seems to be of greater importance in determining the college rate of entry.

3. Certain personality traits—all those related to the will to achieve—are more likely to develop through the patterns of

[21]S. M. Miller, "Comparative Social Mobility," pp. 30–32.

[22]T. Fox and S. M. Miller, "Occupational Stratification and Mobility: Intra-Country Variations," p. 4. *Studies in Comparative International Development,* op. cit.

[23]S. M. Miller, "Comparative Social Mobility," pp. 32–33, 44–51.

socialization that are more often found in the high and middle strata than in the lower stratum.

Thus it seems that the various occupational strata differ not only in the economic but also in the motivational resources they are able to provide their children. This, in itself, is a sufficient determinant of differential access to education, especially higher education, which today is a particularly important avenue for occupational mobility.

As if this were not enough, many studies indicate that parents' occupational positions influence the nature of their sons' first job *regardless* of the latter's level of education. Of course, this is not just a matter of control over economic resources. Every class, or occupational position, can also be rated in terms of prestige, and the combination of high prestige and control of significant economic resources is obviously more influential than either factor taken singly.

It is equally clear, however, that the two halves of this combination exert influence in different ways. Economic resources seem to control access to occupational positions insofar as the positions require different levels of investment. The prestige dimension, on the other hand, seems to provide both the motivation to invest economic resources in occupational opportunities and the social connections for receiving preferential treatment in the occupational market. But the precise way in which these factors combine to determine occupational access has not yet been fully studied.

Another area in which more work is needed is the influence of expanding educational opportunities on class privilege. One would expect that greater openness of the educational system would result in greatly increased opportunities for lower-class children to win access to occupational positions of high income and prestige, but most studies indicate that this increase is not as great as might be expected. Of sociologists' various explanations for this, two in particular are worth mentioning, especially since they reinforce each other.

The first explanation is the fact that secondary schools differ in the emphasis they put on norms of success and mobility— orientations that are passed on to the students. Strong orientations toward success and mobility are cultivated and transmitted primarily by the schools of the upper and middle classes, and, consequently, lower-class children, whose home environment does not tend to encourage aspirations of achievement and success, find a poor and ineffective substitute in the schools. Even for the lower-class children who are mobility oriented, school is seldom much help inasmuch as its academic standards tend to be low. Or, at best, these schools prepare their students for institutions of higher education in which they can learn only the professions that carry low income and prestige (for example, teaching as opposed to medicine or law).

In part, however, this occupational choice is made independently of the school situation since lower-class children, it is argued, prefer to enter professions that can be mastered in a short time and entail a minimal economic investment. (This, of course, is not a matter of absolute preference but economic calculation; the poor would make different choices if they were not poor.)

The other line of explanation is based on the fact that the entry rates of lower-class children into institutions of higher education that have a *good reputation* are low compared to the rates for upper- and middle-class children. This can be attributed partly to the former's limited economic resources and partly to the fact that, because of their poor secondary school background, they cannot meet the high academic requirements. These findings are also important because of a parallel finding that the reputation of the university from which one graduates is a valuable asset in his occupational career. Indeed, it is sometimes even more important than academic achievement.[24]

Much work remains to be done in these areas, but thus far all the studies indicate that differential control over resources in these two spheres (the purely economic sphere and the sphere of prestige and motivation) is the principal determinant of occupational access, at least over a single generation. There are, of course, exceptions to this pattern; nevertheless, it is the dominant pattern, not only in the United States but in all other modern societies that have been studied thus far.

Social equality: more or less?

The results of the social mobility studies necessarily raise the question of the degree to which there has been an increase in equality. No final answer can be given this large question until sociologists devise a satisfactory overall measurement of social equality, but, given the abovementioned dominance of the economic dimension in modern societies, differences in personal

[24]See R. Perrucci, "Education, Stratification, and Mobility," in D. A. Hausen and J. E. Gerstl, eds., *On Education: Sociological Perspectives* (New York: John Wiley & Sons, Inc., 1967).

income can be used (for present purposes) as gross indices of the distribution of social power and prestige. A recent examination of these differences in the United States (by Jencks and Riesman) concludes that, despite an absolute rise in the income level of every income category, the gap between major income levels has remained fairly constant since the 1930s. Nor did they find much change in each category's share of the overall income. The figures on which they base these conclusions are reproduced in table 7–8 (p. 146).

From these findings we can derive a tentative answer to our question about social equality. Clearly, there has been little mobility from the low-income categories to the higher ones. Or to state it differently, there does not seem to have been a substantial change in the distribution of opportunities to attain positions of power and prestige over the years. Of course this conclusion, as the authors themselves recognize, must be viewed with reservations: the congruence between income, prestige, and power is never perfect.

However, it is possible to arrive at a similar conclusion on the basis of other findings in Jencks and Riesman; namely, the figures on the percentage of the American population that finished high school and college (table 7–9, p. 146). According to the data collected by the Census Bureau and the U.S. Office of Education, college graduates are still a distinct minority in the population; most of the increase has been in high school graduates. Presumably, then, the highest social positions are still attainable only by a small part of the population.

Thus it seems that, even in a society that is not burdened by a feudal past and has always placed great emphasis on public education, the expansion of educational opportunity attendant upon modernization has only slightly altered the shape of its social hierarchy. Probably the only exceptions to this trend in modern societies—and temporary exceptions at that—have occurred during the first two generations that followed a violent revolution (as in Russia) and/or in societies that experienced an exceptionally rapid period of industrial expansion, when usually for one or two generations there is a very high increase in the mobility into the school system.

Social mobility in the Soviet Union

Analyses of social developments in the U.S.S.R. are of special interest at this point inasmuch as the intensive development of

TABLE 7-8 AMERICAN FAMILY AND INDIVIDUAL INCOME
BY SEGMENTS, 1929-1962

Year	Top 5 Percent	Next 15 Percent	2nd Fifth	3rd Fifth	4th Fifth	Bottom Fifth	Total
1929	30.0%	24.4%	19.3%	13.8%	12.5%		100.0%
1935/36	26.5	25.2	20.9	14.1	9.2	4.1	100.0
1941	24.0	24.8	22.3	15.3	9.5	4.1	100.0
1947	20.9	25.1	22.0	16.0	11.0	5.0	100.0
1957	20.2	25.3	22.4	16.3	11.1	4.7	100.0
1962	19.6	25.9	22.7	16.3	10.9	4.6	100.0

From: C. Jencks and D. Riesman, "On Class in America," *The Public Interest,* no. 10 (Winter 1968), p. 71.

TABLE 7-9 PERCENTAGE OF U.S. POPULATION
FINISHING HIGH SCHOOL AND COLLEGE

Year of Birth	High School		Four Year College	
	Census Bureau	U.S. Office of Education	Census Bureau	U.S. Office of Education
1855-1859	....	....	....	1.1
1860-1864	11.5	2.5	2.3	....
1865-1869	13.1	....	2.6	1.3
1870-1874	14.2	3.5	2.9	....
1875-1879	16.4	....	3.3	1.7
1880-1884	17.1	6.4	3.4	....
1885-1889	18.5	....	3.8	2.0
1890-1894	20.7	8.8	4.1	....
1895-1899	24.6	....	5.0	2.7
1900-1904	28.5	16.8	6.1	....
1905-1909	34.9	....	7.3	5.8
1910-1914	40.6	29.0	7.4	....
1915-1919	43.4	....	8.1	8.1
1920-1924	54.7	50.8	9.5	....
1925-1929	55.8	....	10.9	....
1930-1934	60.5	59.0	11.0	14.1
1935-1939	63.6	61.1	....	18.2
1940-1944	....	65.1	....	20.0

Ibid., p. 76.

the Soviet economy during the 1930s and after the Second World War created new positions at all levels of the occupational scale. We do not have systematic data on the rates of mobility in this period or the social categories that were most benefited, but there is evidence of great mobility in the creation of many new positions, both skilled and administrative. But even in the thirties, on the other hand, and especially at the beginning of the next decade, countervailing forces began to be felt. By the time Hitler attacked Russia (June 1941), it seems that these countervailing forces reduced the Soviet Union's mobility rates, and especially intergenerational movement from the manual stratum to the middle and upper nonmanual strata.[25]

What lay behind these developments? Although historians and sociologists continue to sift the evidence, at least four factors can be singled out:

1. A decline in the rate of economic development;
2. Widening gaps between the income levels of the different social strata (which is important if only because education, especially higher education, ceased to be free but at the same time became a principal avenue of access to positions of responsibility—in contrast to the more permissive earlier policy);
3. Entrance to certain schools became conditional on the fathers' occupational status, a phenomenon that legally ensured intergenerational, occupational continuity; and
4. The family, contrary to the original Soviet ideology, did not lose its role of status placement; indeed, there are well-attested cases of upper-class Soviet families' circumventing the law with impunity in the process of assuring their children a good education.

During the 1960s, certain reforms (mainly in education) were introduced with the intention of counteracting some of the tendencies described above. It is too early to evaluate the success of these measures, but one may reasonably doubt that they will alter the Soviet system of stratification in a significant way.

An interesting footnote to the Soviet experience is the fact that several recent studies of Latin American countries reveal a similar process of restricted mobility. There are also indications

---

[25]See A. Inkeles, "Social Stratification and Mobility in the Soviet Union," in R. Bendix and S. M. Lipset, eds., *Class, Status and Power*, op. cit., pp. 516–526, and R. A. Feldmesser, "Toward the Classless Society?" in *Class, Status and Power*, pp. 527–533.

that this pattern exists in most underdeveloped countries, even during periods of rapid industrial development and expansion.[26]

SUMMARY

In this chapter we began our analysis of the processes of stratification in modern societies. After pointing out some of the basic characteristics of modern societies (such as their revolutionary origins and their high levels of social differentiation and social mobilization), we examined the characteristics of their systems of organization that are most closely related to stratification.

These characteristics are, on the one hand, a continuously expanding social and economic structure; changes in the patterns of relationships between the center and the periphery, and especially a greater impingement of the periphery on the center and greater accessibility to the center; and the concomitant weakening of ascriptive linkages among the basic components of stratification.

At the same time, the very development of these characteristics poses the question of the degree to which modern societies promote greater social equality in the form of a wider distribution of access to the most important institutional (especially occupational) positions. Various studies—especially those on social mobility—show that, on the whole, this form of social inequality tends to persist in modern societies. At the same time, its effects may be partially counteracted by the general expansion of opportunities and greater accessibility to other—that is, political collective and prestige—positions.

The combination of these characteristics provides the starting point and framework for the dynamics of stratification and strata formation in modern societies, to which we will address ourselves in the next chapter.

---

[26]P. C. Lloyd, "Introduction," in P. C. Lloyd, ed., *The New Elites of Tropical Africa* (London: Oxford University Press, 1966), esp. pp. 21–26, and Dale L. Johnson, "Industrialization, Social Mobility, and Class Formation in Chile," *Studies in Comparative International Development*, 3, no. 7 (1967–1968): 127–151.

Social Dynamics of Modern Stratification Systems

The preceding discussion has brought out some of the most salient aspects of modern systems of stratification, and some of their major problems. First, these systems tend toward continual structural and symbolic expansion. And second, from within this expanding sociocultural structure new types of positions continually emerge and weaken the traditional linkages among the components of stratification. Nevertheless, inequalities and status divisions tend to persist within this framework, although they are not unidimensional. Divisions persist among social strata only because they are maintained by other "nontraditional" types of mechanisms.

Thus the process of strata formation tends to be more complicated in modern societies than in traditional societies. There is no quick and easy explanation of the reason why the former is so complicated, and the search for an answer will begin with consideration of the relationship between two basic social-symbolic categories: occupation and status.

OCCUPATION AND STATUS IN MODERN SOCIETIES

It is, of course, difficult to estimate the extent to which self-evaluation in terms of occupation and status is widespread or "natural" in modern societies or is due primarily to the impact of social research and political class ideologies. However, research on modern social stratification attests to the fact that people, when asked, are able to evaluate their standing in the social order according to these categories. Moreover, even though we cannot always study these phenomena without thereby influencing them, comparative research shows that, in general, the salience of these categories increases with modernization.[1]

But what are the bases on which this "class consciousness" tends to develop in modern societies? First of all, the designation *strata* consciousness, in terms of occupation and class, points to an implicit assumption which can be found in many studies of stratification that strata consciousness is rooted in the economic sphere. Thus most studies of class and class structure in modern societies tend to be based on the assumption that social classes comprise different occupational categories that fall within the broad categories of upper, middle, or lower (or working) class.[2]

It is significant that, although the details of occupations have been continuously changing and expanding, the broad designations of class have seemingly remained fixed throughout the development of modern societies. Thus whatever the changes in specific occupational or economic activities, the general attributes and distribution of classes—of control over economic resources—seem to have persisted in most modern societies.

[1]Evidence for all this can be found in numerous studies undertaken in industrial societies, which indicate that occupation and other related dimensions of status are the foci of classes' self-identification. See, for example, A. F. Davies and S. Encel, "Class and Status," in A. F. Davies and S. Encel, eds., *Australian Society: A Sociological Introduction* (New York: Atherton Press, Inc., 1965), esp. pp. 33–37; L. Broom, F. Lancaster Jones, and J. Zanbrzycki, "Social Stratification in Australia," in J. A. Jackson, ed., *Social Stratification* (London: Cambridge University Press, 1968), pp. 212–233; A. Zloczower, "Mobility Patterns and Status Conceptions in an Urban Israeli Setting," (Ph.D. dissertation, Hebrew University of Jerusalem, 1968), pp. 110–111 (in Hebrew); R. Centers, *The Psychology of Social Classes* (Princeton, N.J.: Princeton University Press, 1949); M. Kahan, D. Butler and D. Stokes, "On the Analytical Division of Social Class," *British Journal of Sociology*, 17, no. 2 (1966): 122–132; N. Rogoff, "Social Stratification in France and the United States," in R. Bendix and S. M. Lipset, eds., *Class, Status and Power* (Glencoe, Ill.: The Free Press, 1953), pp. 577–588; and K. Odaka, "The Middle Classes in Japan," in R. Bendix and S. M. Lipset, eds., *Class, Status and Power* (London: Routledge & Kegan Paul Ltd., 1967), pp. 541–551.
For some interesting contrasts, compare the above with the evidence for perception in various African societies, for which see P. C. Lloyd, "Introduction," in P. C. Lloyd, ed., *The New Elites of Tropical Africa* (London: Oxford University Press, 1966), esp. pp. 49–62.

[2]See for example, S. Ossowski, *Class Structure in the Social Consciousness* (London: Routledge & Kegan Paul Ltd., 1963), esp. pp. 38–49; L. Reissman, *Class in American Society* (Glencoe, Ill.: The Free Press, 1959), esp. pp. 144–164; G. Carlsson, *Social Mobility and Class Structure* (Lund, Sweden, 1958), esp. ch. 3; and G. D. H. Cole, *Studies in Class Structure* (London: Routledge & Kegan Paul Ltd., 1955), ch. 4. See also the references cited in no. 3 below.

Although occupations have been grouped into broad class categories in many different ways, many features are common to most modern societies, as well as some very important marginal cases and problems. Thus the upper class, which is sometimes divided into upper-upper and upper-lower, usually includes upper-upper groups of highly qualified professionals, such as physicians, scientists, lawyers, and college professors; high government officials, such as Supreme Court justices, diplomats, and cabinet members; and top business managers or owners, such as bankers and members of boards of directors of large corporations.

The upper-lower stratum of the upper class includes such professionals as teachers, engineers, artists (writers, painters, musicians in symphony orchestras); medium-level government administrators and businessmen, such as accountants; and owners of medium-size businesses and enterprises.[3]

The middle class is usually divided into two subcategories, which include the upper-middle professionals, such as newspapermen, radio announcers, technicians, owners of small businesses, welfare workers, and similar white-collar workers; and the lower-middle stratum of highly skilled manual workers, owners of small businesses, white-collar office workers, and salesmen.

The lower class is also usually subdivided into upper-lower, or semiskilled manual workers, service workers and clerks, and lower-lower, or unskilled workers.

Another of the classification systems consists of drawing a line between such broad categories as manual and nonmanual occupations. A refined and often used system follows the gradations in each grouping; for example, manual occupations are further categorized as skilled, semiskilled, and unskilled, and the nonmanual occupations are subdivided into variants of such groupings as professional and technical; managerial, administrative and proprietary, and sales and clerical.

But whatever the criteria for grouping occupational pursuits

---

[3]This categorization is based on the NORC's scale of occupational prestige (for which see R. Bendix and S. M. Lipset, eds., *Class, Status and Power*, 1953, pp. 411–426) and on suggestions in J. A. Kahl, *The American Class Structure* (New York: Rinehart & Co., 1959), pp. 76–77, and H. J. Crockett, Jr., "The Achievement Motive and Differential Occupational Mobility in the United States," *American Sociological Review*, 27, no. 2 (1962): 196–197. It is perhaps worthwhile to note that most studies construct social classes by the indices of occupational prestige and related dimensions, such as education, place of residence, income, etc. In this connection see G. Lenski, *The Religious Factor* (Garden City, N.Y.: Doubleday & Company, Inc., 1961), p. 73; A. B. Hollingshead and F. C. Redlich, *Social Class and Mental Illness* (New York: John Wiley & Sons, Inc., 1958), pp. 390–397; and R. A. Ellis, W. C. Lane, and V. Olensen, "The Index of Class Position: An Improved Intercommunity Measure of Stratification," *American Sociological Review*, 28, no. 2 (1963): 271–277.

into classes, there are always many types of "doubtful" or "marginal" occupations, of which the most important are those of the so-called "new middle classes" and "new working classes," which often tend to cut across one another. These classes include skilled manual workers whose occupational evaluation and/or income seem to equal those of the "older" middle class, especially such white-collar workers as minor professionals, technicians, clericals, and staff members in government and business who approach some of the older middle class in terms of income but for the most part are salaried employees. Obviously, this complicates the bases on which occupations are evaluated.

Occupational prestige

Such complications will become even more evident when we examine the evaluation of occupations in different modern societies. In its first phase, comparative research showed marked similarities in these evaluations, as in the studies that compared the United States, Germany, Great Britain, New Zealand, Japan, and the U.S.S.R.[4]

Apart from the similarity in ranking major occupational groups, the principal finding was that agreement was highest on the ranking of professional occupations and lowest for service occupations. These groupings are listed below, in descending order, according to the agreement on rankings among the countries.

Professionals, such as doctor, minister, teacher
Industry, such as industrial worker, company director, factory manager, engineer
Politics, such as judge, civil servant
Traditional crafts, such as bricklayer, carpenter
Clerical and commercial, such as accountant, bookkeeper, salesman, small businessman
Agriculture, such as farm owner and operator, farmhand
Services, such as shoe shiner, barber, porter, streetcar conductor

These convergences are attributed to the spread of industrialization and to the alleged needs or prerequisites of the industrial system. As the researchers concluded:

[4]A. Inkeles and P. H. Rossi, "National Comparisons of Occupational Prestige," *American Journal of Sociology*, 61, no. 4 (1956): 329–339.

Our examination of occupational ratings in six modern industrialized countries reveals an extremely high level of agreement, going far beyond chance expectancies, as to the relative prestige of a wide range of specific occupations, despite the variety of socio-cultural settings in which they are found. This strongly suggests that there is a relatively invariable hierarchy of prestige associated with the industrial system, even when it is placed in the context of larger social systems differentiated in important respects.

In addition, the fact that the countries compared also have in common the national state and certain needs or values, such as interest in health, apparently also contributes to the observed regularity of the ratings since both professional and political occupations are foci of agreement. . . .

In the majority of cases, however, the disagreement appears to involve classes of occupation, notably agricultural and service, about which there is only modest agreement. Disagreement probably reflects differences in the length and "maturity" of industrialization in various countries but also clearly results from differentiations in socio-cultural systems which may well be relatively enduring.[5]

However, a closer look at the evidence will show us that this is only a partial view. In particular, three points should be made.

1. Economic standing is only one dimension of status. Whenever such "noneconomic" occupations as judge, professor, etc., have been studied, they have always been rated higher than either their value in the job market or their social class standing would seem to justify.

2. The relationship between an occupation's prestige and its purely economic value is far more complicated than the six-country study might imply. Some hint of this is provided by the NORC study (cited in n. 3 above), which—for example—more or less equates the following occupations in terms of their prestige: banker, government scientist, county judge, head of a department in a state government, minister, architect, chemist, dentist, lawyer, member of a board of directors of a large corporation, nuclear physicist, priest. It is clear, however, that these occupations differ considerably in their economic rewards.

An even more striking example is provided by the similar

prestige scores of the following occupations: building contractor, economist, instructor or teacher in a public school, railroad engineer, farm owner and operator. Even though the overall prestige ranking of this group was much lower than that of the preceding group, the effect of noneconomic factors was present.

3. Recent examination of the research discussed above advances a thesis that, if true, throws an entirely new light on prestige ratings. The authors of this critique discovered that when prestige scores for less industrialized countries were compared with those for the industrialized countries, the overall rankings of major occupational groups remained much the same.

> We can observe an impressive amount of agreement between the occupational prestige hierarchy of the U.S. and those of twenty-three other countries. . . . The gross similarity between occupational-prestige hierarchies, in the U.S. and elsewhere, is not substantially altered by inclusion of less industrialized nations. . . . These findings suggest that it is impossible to argue, at least for newly developing countries, that similarities in levels of industrialization induced similarities in the hierarchical evaluation of occupations, since without any substantial progress toward industrialization, many "new nations" have achieved a structure of occupational evaluations quite similar to that observed in the U.S. . . .
>
> Putting our doubts about the data aside for the moment, the findings do suggest that for newly developing nations there may be an important causal link in the direction opposite to that usually posited; structural similarities may be in part the product of similarities in occupational evaluation. Development hinges in part upon the recruitment and training of persons for the skilled, clerical, managerial, and professional positions necessary to support an industrial economy. Thus, acquisition of a "modern" system of occupational evaluation would seem to be a necessary precondition to rapid industrialization, insofar as such an evaluation of occupations insures that resources and personnel in sufficient numbers and of sufficient quality are allocated to more occupational positions most crucial to the industrial development of a nation. In one important regard, then, adoption of an occupation-prestige hierarchy similar to that of industrial nations may be a prerequisite for development, notwithstand-

ing the fact that increased development may in turn induce further similarities in occupational prestige evaluations.[6]

The authors conclude that the amount of prestige a society confers on different occupations depends not so much on whether it is highly industrialized but on whether it *wants* to be industrialized or "modern." And thus a modern self-image is sometimes more powerful than modernity itself.

Dimensions of prestige

But this is not the end of the matter. The very concept of modernity, as numerous studies show, is open to various and sometimes conflicting interpretations. Among societies that think of themselves as modern, there can be as many sets of criteria for evaluating occupations as there are definitions of modernity.

The variety of these criteria is endless, but they can be sorted into categories—and by no means are all or even most of the categories economic, nor can they be referred to the imperatives of industrialization. In addition to their economic attributes (such as income), occupations in even the most highly industrialized societies may be judged in terms of their charismatic appeal and various social, cultural, or political qualities—either separately or in combination. Nor is this a casual impression; it is a sociological fact, firmly established by research studies (even if they are not always conclusive in other respects).

In particular, a study undertaken in 1958 among residents of Warsaw turned up some remarkable examples of incongruity between the prestige ranking of occupations and the material rewards connected with them.[7] Another finding of this study, which strenghtens our argument, is that skilled industrial jobs were rated higher than white-collar jobs that do not require an academic education and various private entrepreneurial occupations. In fact, skilled industrial jobs were ranked just under white-collar jobs that require an academic education. This last finding, however, also exhibits an ideological impact inasmuch as

[6] "A Comparative Study of Occupational Prestige," by Hodge, Treiman, and Rossi from *Class, Status and Power*, eds. Reinhard Bendix and Seymour M. Lipset. © 1966 by The Free Press.

[7] A. Sarapata and W. Wesolowski, "The Evaluation of Occupations by Warsaw Inhabitants," *American Journal of Sociology*, 66, no. 6 (1961): 581–591.

it reflects the official policy of the Polish Communist government, it does not result from purely economic considerations.[8]

In a less dramatic way, but no less pervasively, the importance of noneconomic factors is also brought out in studies of occupational prestige in western Europe,[9] whose examples of variations in prestige are attributable to such factors as education and social background, and even the occupations of the raters. People sometimes evaluate occupations whose precise meaning they do not know. In one famous study, for example, the occupation "nuclear physicist" was correctly described by only 3 percent of those interviewed. See the NORC study cited in n. 3 above. The importance of noneconomic factors is nevertheless confirmed for all countries; and these factors include rural-urban differences (especially in underdeveloped countries) and differences of a more cultural nature. The latter are prominent, for example, in the comparative study of Inkeles and Rossi, who found significant intercountry discrepancies in the evaluation of service and religious occupations (no doubt because of the different cultural traditions of these countries).[10]

But as these are rather general remarks, it might be worthwhile to introduce more specific illustrations. In a case study of great interest from our point of view (carried out in Finland in the 1950s),[11] the subjects were asked to rate a sample of their fellow residents by social classes and to assess the relative standings of these classes. The subjects or judges who were chosen for this task employed a great variety of criteria, but occupation was not the governing, or even the most prominent criterion. Some judges rated their fellow residents mainly in terms of their personal characteristics, others in terms of political affiliations or class membership (as defined in Marxist terms), and relatively few judges used occupation as the criterion for their class differentiations, even though the persons they were rating were listed by

[8]Somewhat similar trends are evident in research on occupational prestige in the Soviet Union; see P. H. Rossi and A. Inkeles, "Multidimensional Ratings of Occupations," *Sociometry*, 20, no. 3 (1957): 234–251.

[9]Variations in prestige ratings are possible even within the same society if the raters have different occupations and social backgrounds as is evidenced by the findings in J. Hall and C. Jones, "Social Gradings of Occupations," *British Journal of Sociology*, 1 (1950): 31–55, and M. Young and P. Willmott, "Social Grading by Manual Workers," ibid., 7 (1956): 337–345.

[10]See A. Inkeles and P. H. Rossi, "National Comparisons of Occupational Prestige," pp. 334, 338–339.

[11]Sakari Sariola, "Defining Social Class in Two Finnish Communities," *Transactions of the Second World Congress of Sociology*, 2 (1953): 108–118.

occupation. The standards employed in this case, especially the economic-political ones, no doubt reflect the sometimes violent political struggle that has characterized Finnish society since the beginning of this century, which has been focused around the relative predominance of traditional hierarchy versus egalitarianism.

Even more important for our analysis are the research studies that deal with the values and prestige of social strata that, because of their recent origin, cannot be fitted into the traditional picture of society. For instance, there has been controversy whether the so-called new middle class is really middle. It seems that the appropriateness of the traditional labels depends upon which aspect of class behavior one is considering. Thus some studies have made much of the similarity between the prestige ranking of skilled manual and low-level nonmanual jobs.

But the real question is what conclusion are we entitled to draw from this. Does it indicate a blurring of traditional class lines? Or do these two occupational groupings differ in other dimensions of social stratification that may be more important to their status identity than prestige ranking?

The latter possibility is suggested in a study undertaken in Britain by Runciman, who based his approach on the work of Goldthorpe and Lockwood.[12] Among a sample of manual workers, Runciman found that those who rated themselves as middle class attached such meanings to the term that it was impossible to infer that they shared the values of the old middle class. However, contrary indications are given in other studies, especially in one made in France by Crozier, which seems to show that salaried workers of working-class origin tend to develop various middle-class orientations, at least when they are employed by large industrial enterprises.

The multidimensional approach

These data and their various interpretations indicate some of the problems in assigning an occupation to a particular social class. Nevertheless, we can draw five highly provisional conclusions from them.

1. Occupational groupings may be similar in prestige ranking

---

[12]J. H. Goldthorpe and D. Lockwood, "Affluence and the British Class Structure," *Sociological Review*, 11, no. 2 (1963): 133–163; W. G. Runciman, "'Embourgeoisement': Self-rated Class and Party Preference," *Sociological Review*, 12, no. 2 (1964): 137–152.

but different in income and life chances or—vice versa—similar in income but different in prestige and life chances.

2. Even within an occupational grouping, individuals may identify themselves, or be identifiable, as members of a different class, which may be different from the class to which other individuals (including researchers) more or less arbitrarily assign them.

3. The upgrading of an occupational grouping in prestige ranking and income is not necessarily accompanied by acquisition of the class outlook and style of life that is usually associated with that level of income and/or prestige.

4. In general, the designation of an occupation as especially belonging to a particular social class (or other category) may be based on income, self-employed as against salaried status, the control of economic resources, style of life, and many other cultural and personal attributes for which there is no commonly accepted classification.

5. There is not an invariable relationship between a specific occupation and a specific cluster of attributes of the type mentioned in (4).

Many research analysts have long made use of the *multidimensional approach,* as the theoretical position outlined above is usually known. In one of the most sophisticated studies of this kind (in Japan) people were asked to rank themselves on the basis of their prestige (upper, middle, low) and their economic class (capitalist, middle class, working class); and some of the findings are quoted below. These findings are of the utmost importance for our analysis because they emphasize the problem of tracing the connections between the various dimensions of social stratification.

> The exception [to the joint appearance of "lower prestige" and "worker" consciousness] is the white-collar, i.e., the clerical worker, the nucleus of the new middle class. In this group, those of "middle prestige" are almost twice as numerous as those of "lower prestige," but those who see themselves as "workers" are almost three times the number of those who claim to be of the "middle economic" class. In other words this group insists upon a contradiction; it is both "middle prestige" *and* worker. . . .
>
> Those who are conscious of belonging to the working class are of course not limited to white-collar workers. They are also to be found among professionals, including teaching

and technical staffs, such as administrators, assistant managers and middle public officials, and university students. According to the results . . . 33% of the entire professional category and 29% of the entire administrative category have a working-class consciousness, and, among university students, 39% regard themselves as of working-class [background].[13]

A similar tendency can be found in a study done in Israel, as can be seen from the data in table 8–1.

TABLE 8–1 SELF-CLASSIFICATION OF SOCIAL CLASS
ACCORDING TO EMPLOYMENT STATUS,
EDUCATION AND OCCUPATION

	Total (N)	Middle Class*	Working Intelligentsia	Labor Class	Working Class†
Entrepreneurs	154	57.8%	3.9%	18.9%	19.5%
Wage earners who finished high school					
Nonmanual	133	27.8	51.0	16.5	4.5
Manual	40	27.5	20.0	25.0	27.5
Wage earners who did not finish high school					
Nonmanual	86	24.5	17.5	36.0	19.8
Manual	221	19.0	2.3	16.8	62.0

*Includes "upper class" and "bourgeoisie."
†Includes proletariat, toilers, low classes.
Adapted from A. Zlochower, "Mobility Patterns and Status Conceptions in an Urban Israeli Setting" (Ph.D. dissertation, Hebrew University of Jerusalem, 1968), p. 81 (in Hebrew).

Here, too, many of those who would ordinarily fall in the middle occupational and educational categories preferred to classify themselves as working class—partly, no doubt, because of their objective position in the economic sphere, but partly because this term has not entirely lost the highly valued connotations of being synonymous with national pioneering, that it had in the Yishuv era.

For our present purposes, the main thing we learn from these studies—which will be a central point of discussion in the next chapter—is that although a person's occupation to a

[13]K. Odaka, "The Middle Classes in Japan," op. cit., p. 546 (edited for idiomatic English).

considerable extent determines his location in a modern system of stratification, this does not mean that a researcher need look no further than the economic sphere. Instead, as we shall see, occupation should be regarded as the point at which various dimensions of stratification meet and intersect.

STRATA FORMATION AND CENTERS IN MODERN SOCIETIES

The various complexities in the evaluation of occupations indicate some of the important characteristics of strata formation in modern societies which have greatly affected the patterns of strata formation. The weakening of the ascriptive prescriptions of status did not abolish the different strata and classes in modern societies. As we have seen, differences in wealth, power, status, and the chances of access to different positions still exist and people still perceive the social order as divided into classes and assign themselves to these classes and status categories.

Beyond all this, sociological research has abundantly demonstrated that people in different occupational or status categories tend to differ in their patterns of participation in social, political, and cultural activities and organizations; in their patterns of consumption; in their time perspectives; in the ways they perceive their opportunities in the social order; in the major types of desiderata they emphasize and around which they tend to develop their distinct styles of life (whether job security, high levels of consumption and the attainment of immediate rewards, or the investment of resources in a future career); in basic attitudes toward their work, jobs, and careers; in their use of language; and so on.[14]

These different patterns of social life, orientations, and motivations denote some of the most important mechanisms by virtue of which members of different classes have different life chances or differential potentials of access to positions.[15] More-

[14]The following are only some of the studies that can be adduced as evidence on this point: J. A. Kahl, *American Class Structure*, pp. 108–119 and chs. 5, 7; H. H. Hyman, "The Value Systems of Different Classes," in R. Bendix and S. M. Lipset, eds., *Class, Status and Power*, pp. 488–499; R. Blauner, "Work Satisfaction and Industrial Trends in Modern Society," in *Class, Status and Power*, pp. 473–487; L. Reissman, "Class, Leisure, and Social Participation," *American Sociological Review*, 19, no. 1 (1954): 76–84; K. Svalastoga, *Prestige, Class and Mobility* (Copenhagen: Gyldendal, 1959); Goldthorpe and Lockwood, "Affluence and the British Class Structure"; and D. Lockwood, "Sources of Variation in Working Class Images of Society," *Sociological Review*, 14, no. 3 (1966): 249–267.

[15]See ch. 7 above, esp. pp. 140–144.

over, many groups in modern societies exhibit a high level of consciousness of their distinctive life patterns and often place great value on these distinctions.[16] But, as has been implied, different styles of life are no longer normatively prescribed by the center in modern societies. They have therefore become much more informal, and hence exclusive, on the one hand but, on the other hand, much more restricted in terms of their institutional scope and legitimacy.

The numerous attempts of various groups to uphold exclusive styles of life and restrictions on participation in various social spheres, positions, and rewards in terms of differential membership in various collectivities have become, in modern societies, less pervasive and more informal, and lack legitimation in terms of the basic premises of the center. However, this does not necessarily mean that these developments have weakened class or stratum identification in modern societies. It means only that such identification must be maintained by different means and mechanisms than those used by traditional societies. Here, then, is the crucial importance of the different role of centers in the process of strata formation in modern societies.

Centers in traditional and in modern societies

In many traditional societies, the center (or centers) to a large degree defines the basic attributes that make up a person's or group's social identity. These include—above all—prestige, its distribution among members of different subcollectivities, and the specific goals and rewards associated with this distribution. This function of the center is closely related to the fact that, in traditional societies, the degree of participation in the center is largely determined by the degree to which membership in a particular subcollectivity entitles one to access to the center— which, of course, is almost wholly regulated by the center. In fact, subcollectivities' prestige is at least partly legitimized by the center or centers. Hence in most traditional societies a large part of the interstrata struggle is focused on acquiring the right of

[16]Such tendencies exist even in societies that are known for their egalitarian ethos, for example Australia, for which see K. B. Mayer, "Social Stratification in Two Equalitarian Societies: Australia and the United States," in R. Bendix and S. M. Lipset, eds., *Class, Status and Power*, esp. pp. 157–158.

For other examples see J. A. Kahl, *American Class Structure*, ch. 7; D. Lockwood, *The Blackcoated Worker* (London: George Allen & Unwin Ltd., 1958), esp. ch. 4; and P. Willmott and M. Young, *Family and Class in a London Suburb* (London: Routledge & Kegan Paul Ltd., 1960), esp. ch. 10.

access to the center and the right to influence it, especially in the regulation and the conversion of peripheral resources and in prescribing ascriptive access to positions and participation in various styles of life.

In modern societies, this situation has undergone far-reaching changes. True, an important part of the stratification or "class" struggle in modern societies has consisted of subcollectivities' attempts to make good their claim of being worthy of the highest rewards the society can offer and to influence the centers in determining the importance of different attributes, or to prescribe the distribution of these attributes among the subcollectivities. But these modern functions have never been as fully institutionalized as the analogous functions of traditional centers. And there is more than one reason for this.

Insofar as access to the social and cultural orders in general and to the center in particular was opened to all members of the collectivity, the significance of participation in the center underwent a radical change. Access to the center tended to become direct; that is, it was not mediated by participation in the subcollectivities and therefore was not contingent on evaluation by the center. Even the most totalitarian modern centers could not, at least in principle, deny most groups their autonomous access to the different sociocultural orders. Therefore participation in the subcollectivities, and the associated prestige, become much more autonomous and much less dependent on the center. At the same time, however, such participation and prestige cannot exact legitimation by the center, and therefore these activities become much more fluid and unstable.

One indication of this is the fact that a large part of the stratification or class struggle in modern societies is the attempt of the subcollectivities and the institutional elites to represent— without the legitimation of the center—all differentially valued attributes. Thus in modern societies the center (or centers) is no longer the sole arbiter of relationships between the components of stratification. Instead, its principal function has become the redistribution of resources and the inculcation of socially desirable motives through (for example) education. It cannot, of itself, prescribe the terms or the form of stratification.

The structure of titles in modern societies

As a result of the changing relationships between centers and collectivities, the whole pattern of strata formation and the stratification class struggle in modern societies, in comparison with traditional societies, has greatly changed. This change is most evident in the changing nature of titles in modern societies.

No less than people in traditional societies, people in modern societies seek to exploit their social advantages, and the overall means are the same in both cases: the regulation of access to the most desirable positions and goals, together with maintaining themselves in such positions, from which they can monopolize access and the setting of societal goals. In modern societies, however, the tactics for establishing and maintaining titles differ in several important respects from those of traditional societies.

First of all—aside from membership in the total collectivity—few modern institutional positions can be said to have an *absolute* title. Second, even if various groups succeed in creating and controlling partial or de facto titles, it is not the normative sanction of the center that enables them to do so. There *are* titles in modern societies, but only titles of a *new kind* are explicitly, legally, or normatively acknowledged. And what these new titles have in common is a relative *lack* of exclusiveness; they are vested in all members of the collectivity (citizenship and civil rights) or in special categories (rights to welfare benefits and various kinds of compensation for the deprived, sick, aged, or disabled) that cut across subcollectivities based on differential participation in the center. In some modern societies, simply being a member of a group defined as "deprived" is itself a title to redress. Thus the basis for exclusion from or admission to participation in such titles tends to be defined in legal terms, not in terms of membership in a prestigious subcollectivity.

Another important characteristic of modern titles is that they entitle people not to position or status so much as to the *qualifications* for acquiring position or status. For instance, needy students may be entitled to receive financial aid for completing college.

Given the center's altered role in the process of strata formation, it is easy to see why the crux of the struggle for titles in modern societies shifted from the right of access to the center to the control of resources and the use of the center for the redistribution of resources. Since differential participation could no longer prescribe direct access to positions or to the center, most of the titles that were retained from premodern times or acquired in modern times were relatively easily upset and changed. Hence a much greater and more continuous reinvestment of resources was required to maintain them. Indeed, their maintenance was predicated on the continuous expenditure of such resources.

The changing place of the family in modern stratification

The resultant changes in the pattern of strata formation are somewhat paradoxical. As we have seen, a basic characteristic of stratification in modern societies is the progressive weakening of ascriptive elements, and especially ascriptive linkages, among the components of stratification (pp. 129–134). At the same time, however, the importance of the family and other ascriptively based units in modern society has been greatly enhanced, and it is precisely because the normative power of ascription has generally been on the wane that the few remaining ascriptive units have been burdened with social tasks they did not have before, tasks that are crucial for stratification. Thus the family, in addition to its traditional role as the agent of initial socialization, is the major agency for inculcating a positive attitude in its offspring toward appropriate goals, desiderata, and value orientations and for enabling them to obtain appropriate placement in the social order. Thus one of the most important aspects of socialization that is still largely influenced by family orientations is the specification of whom one's children will play with, choose as friends, and eventually marry.[17] This is true even in modern societies' later stages of development, when, because of high levels of consumption on one hand and the spread of educational facilities on the other, the importance of the family as a transmitter of distinct patterns of life has tended to decrease. And so, in spite of the loosening of ascription, many material and motivational resources of the family may be of crucial importance in the status placement and the life chances of its members.

Strata formation and class consciousness

A similar paradox has developed in modern societies with the development of strata or class consciousness. In short, the weakening of ascriptive linkages among the major components of stratification and the ascriptive legitimation of titles have been accompanied by a growing awareness in various strata and groups

---

[17]E. O. Laumann, *Prestige and Association in an Urban Community* (Indianapolis, Ind.: The Bobbs-Merrill Co., Inc., 1966), esp. ch. 5; J. A. Kahl, *American Class Structure*, esp. pp. 129–136; A. B. Hollingshead, "Class and Kinship in a Middle-Western Community," *American Sociological Review*, 14 (1949): 469–475; W. G. Goode, *The Family* (Englewood Cliffs, N.J.: Prentice-Hall, Inc., 1964), chs. 4, 8.

of their relative hierarchical standings in the social order, which in turn has made class or strata consciousness an important, and sometimes basic, component of social order. With the possible exception of the Greek city-states, no traditional society has developed class consciousness to the same extent.

In this connection, it should be noted that many of the revolutionary events that ushered in the breakthrough to modernity—the French Revolution, the revolutions of nineteenth-century Europe, and the Russian Revolution—relied on symbols that were couched entirely in terms of class. But these symbols would not have attained wide currency if they had not been symptomatic of a general trend toward awareness that the social order was divided into strata and that one's standing within it was determined by interstrata relationships and mutual orientations and references.

This awareness, combined with the weakened traditional ascriptive bases of strata formation, is less paradoxical if it is examined more closely. The conditions that encourage the development of countrywide strata consciousness are, after all, none other than the accessibility of the basic social, political, and cultural centers to the major status groups and—in general—the impingement of society's periphery upon its center. And these conditions, as we have seen, are virtually synonymous with modernization.[18]

Development of common reference points

An interesting structural consequence of greater strata awareness was the development—within the social, cultural, and political orders—of common reference points among the major groups and strata. Thus different status groups became reference points for each other, and developed common orientations by which they could compare each other. In a modern society, therefore, a group's perception of its standing in the social order tends to be couched in terms of its position or placement within one or more of the major social orders vis-à-vis one or more of the other status groups. The standard by which such a position is likely to be judged is equal and total participation in the order in question. On

[18]See E. A. Shils, "Centre and Periphery," *The Logic of Personal Knowledge: Essays Presented to Michael Polanyi* (London: Routledge & Kegan Paul Ltd., 1961), pp. 117–131, and S. N. Eisenstadt, *Modernization: Protest and Change* (Englewood Cliffs, N.J.: Prentice-Hall, Inc., 1966), ch. 1.

the personal level, one's differential standing in a major social order—as distinct from his socially valued attributes—has become an important focus of self-perception and identity.[19]

These common reference and comparison points, however, are not fixed. On the contrary, differences between the social, cultural, and political orders are constantly emphasized, and so is their changing and even unstable character. There is good reason for this, of course.

Given the dissociation between the hierarchies of power, wealth, and prestige (pp. 130–134), as well as the continuous structural changes in all of these values, a group's point of reference may vary considerably among different sociocultural orders.[20] The criteria by which a group compares its position with others' may differ greatly from one institutional sphere to another or undergo great change within a particular sphere. Given the inherently continuous structural change of modern society, no group can regard its relationship to another group as clear cut and unalterable. In fact, it is more likely to be ambiguous and transitory.

It is precisely because of this instability that most modern strata continuously attempt to maintain or change their status positions, which brings us to the following topic.

STRATA FORMATION IN TRADITIONAL AND MODERN SOCIETIES

In this section we will consider, together with some of the basic characteristics of strata and class formation in modern societies, the similarities and differences of these characteristics vis-à-vis strata formation in traditional societies. Given the basic characteristics of modern systems of stratification, it is easier to

---

[19]This is either implicitly or explicitly illustrated by studies of status inconsistency; see, for example, G. Lenski, "Status Crystallization: A Non-Vertical Dimension of Social Status," *American Sociological Review*, 19, no. 4 (1954): 405–413, and "Social Participation and Status Crystallization," *American Sociological Review*, 21, (1956): 458–464, and J. Goffman, "Status Consistency and Preference for Change in Power Distribution," *American Sociological Review*, 22, no. 3 (1957): 275–281. For a more critical approach to such studies see B. Anderson and M. Zelditch, "Rank Equilibration and Political Behavior," *Archives européennes de Sociologie*, 15, no. 1 (1964): 112–125.

[20]W. G. Runciman, *Relative Deprivation and Social Justice* (London: Routledge & Kegan Paul Ltd., 1966); R. Dahrendorf, *Class and Class Conflict in Industrial Society* (Stanford, Calif.: Stanford University Press, 1959), esp. pt. 2; J. H. Goldthorpe and D. Lockwood, "Affluence and the British Class Structure," op. cit.

understand the aspects of strata formation that have been important in traditional societies, such as the normative prescription of styles of life and conspicuous consumption, or the ritualistic criteria of evaluation, which in modern societies necessarily lose some of their importance.

In modern societies, therefore, other components of strata formation gain special importance, such as

1. The extent to which strata and classes are defined not only in traditional or ritualistic terms but especially in what may be called secular terms; that is, according to their relative standing and participation in the social order;

2. The type and strength of class or strata consciousness and the perception of the social order that follows from it, and especially the degree to which this order is conceived in terms of divisiveness and conflicts; and

3. Most importantly, the orientations and activities that effect changes in the sociopolitical structure of stratification in general and political activities in particular.

Evaluation criteria in modern societies

Our analysis begins with the broad categories of position evaluation that tend to develop in modern societies, and the first such category (or perception criterion of the differences in the social order) is the primordial-territorial unit—whether based on kinship, tribe or region—that is conceived as part of a secular order. Closely related to this perception is the perception of similar differences between rural-urban, traditional-modern, and developed-underdeveloped sectors.

The next broad category in which the social order can be perceived stands entirely apart from traditional attributes and criteria. The former are couched entirely in what may be called secular-social terms, which are based on the perception of the social order as an autonomous dimension of human existence. Within this broad type, various subtypes are of special importance, and the foremost type involves a functional contribution to the maintenance of the social or cultural order. Such evaluation is usually associated—especially as it pertains to higher groups—with a very strong elitist emphasis (which, in traditional societies, we discerned in the Indian system, but in modern societies is usually dissociated from a religious-metaphysical basis).

The second subtype involves the evaluation of positions in terms of relatively narrow attributes and goals and limited styles of life, which, though in principle open to everybody, are usually represented by relatively restricted groups.

The third category of secular evaluations of positions involves the degree to which the major positions approximate or uphold a variety of universalistic, cultural, personal, or control attributes and to which each major group or category has some degree of autonomous access.

The desire for change and stratification struggles in modern societies

The strong emphasis on orientations to change, as has been indicated above, is an especially important aspect of strata formation in modern societies. And furthermore, as we have noted, the breakthrough to modernity has been associated with the general tendency to change. Because of this tendency, a major need of modern societies is the capacity to absorb continuous demands for change, although they do not manage this with equal success. And because this tendency has been closely related to strata formation and class symbolism in modern societies, it is very significant—from our point of view—that the principal revolutionary ideologies were often couched in terms of class symbolism.

Thus the very concept of class became linked with change. Just as class consciousness and class organization are usually oriented toward effecting changes, a country's class system has often been studied with a view to urging changes. But inasmuch as demands for change vary in kind as well as intensity, what *kinds* of things do people want changed?

One way of approaching this vastly complicated question is by way of the concept of institutional spheres or orders. In the economic sphere, for example, such demands may be oriented to new patterns of remuneration or the distribution of resources, or in the structure or conditions of employment, or in the control of a market and accessibility to various marketable resources. Corresponding changes in the cultural sphere might be in access to various goals, in participation in cultural orders and centers, in legitimizing new goals, or in the basic criteria for evaluating different styles of life. In the political sphere, change may be demanded in specific interests or privileges, in the use of political power and standing for the redistribution of resources, in the rules of access to these resources, in access to political participation in general and to the center in particular.

All of these "targets," and others like them, can be reclassified according to their implications for a restructured system of stratification. Accordingly, four basic effects can be distinguished.

1. The bargaining positions of various groups may be changed in their relationship to groups in different institutional markets. Some of the most interesting illustrations of this kind are found in business and industrial organizations, where there are frequent attempts to effect change in the structures of control. Similarly, trade unions attempt the same kind of change when they engage in collective bargaining, as do professional groups when they create monopolistic positions for themselves through licensing arrangements and the like.

2. The distribution of rewards, as well as the rules of access to highly valued positions, may be altered by changes in the major attributes that have been defined as prerequisites for occupying these positions. Also, several subtypes can be distinguished.

2*a*. There may be attempts to redistribute the major types of rewards that accrue to certain positions without changing their conditions of access. The most obvious illustration is income redistribution by means of progressive taxation and similar fiscal measures.[21]

2*b*. There may be attempts to change the rules for obtaining the qualifying attributes for highly valued positions, especially for access to political participation (citizenship) and educational facilities. Indeed, the history of modern societies offers numerous examples of attempts to attain the right of access to the center. Most constitutional struggles in the modern European and colonial nations have focused on such attempts (which are closely related to other types of class struggle [discussed below]).[22]

2*c*. There may be attempts to change the rules of access to various (especially occupational) positions. The most important

---

[21]For the effects of such policies on income redistribution in several European countries and in the United States see A. T. Peacock, ed., *Income Redistribution and Social Policy* (London: Jonathan Cape Ltd., 1954). For a brief critique of the alleged equalizing tendencies that result from income redistribution see J. H. Goldthorpe, "Social Stratification in Industrial Society," in R. Bendix and S. M. Lipset, eds., *Class, Status and Power*, op. cit., pp. 651–653.

[22]R. Bendix, *Nation Building and Citizenship* (New York: John Wiley & Sons, Inc., 1964), pp. 61–105; S. M. Lipset and S. Rokkan, eds., *Party Systems and Voter Alignments: Cross-National Perspectives* (New York: The Free Press, 1967), pp. 13–50, 497–513; E. A. Shils, "The Intellectuals in the Political Development of the New States," in H. Kautsky, ed., *Political Change in Underdeveloped Countries: Nationalism and Communism* (New York: John Wiley & Sons, Inc., 1962).

illustration of this is the attempt to assure access to highly valued positions not on the basis of "universalistic" criteria, such as education or knowledge, but on the "particularistic" criterion of membership in a special collectivity (more often than not a deprived minority or caste).[23]

3. There may be attempts to change the relationships between the major attributes of social and cultural order or between the major socioeconomic categories and groupings. Here again, several subtypes can be discerned.

3*a.* There may be attempts to reevaluate the life styles and the goals of various groups in terms of the attributes upheld by a society's center or centers. Governments and political parties in countries of colonizing immigrants (Australia and Israel, for example) have often pursued these objects (for example, by upgrading the value of the working class and its contributions to the social order).[24] Another illustration is the frequent attempt of the middle class to maintain an exclusive claim as the bearer of various attributes represented by its style of life, education, and pattern of consumption (despite its diminishing income). Such attempts may manifest themselves in social exclusiveness and in attempts to limit access to certain educational facilities.

3*b.* There may be attempts to change the *relative* importance of various attributes in a society's value system. For instance, certain groups may argue that education and technical know-how are more important than participation in the national culture. They are especially likely to do this if they are bent on enhancing the value of their own expertise vis-à-vis simple membership in the collectivity.[25]

Any type of change or attempted change, as has been pointed out, may overlap one or more of the other types. This is not surprising inasmuch as almost every kind of structural change in

[23]G. Lenski, *Power and Privilege* (New York: McGraw-Hill, Inc., 1966), pp. 395–402; M. N. Srinivas, *Caste in Modern India* (New York: Asia Publishing House, 1962), ch. 1.

[24]For Israel see S. N. Eisenstadt, *Israeli Society* (London: Weidenfeld and Nicolson Ltd., 1967) esp. pp. 13–46, 52–54, 151–156, 165, 183–189. For Australia, especially for the emergence of its dominant and radical working-class ethos, see R. N. Rosencrance, "The Radical Culture of Australia," in L. Hartz, ed., *The Founding of New Societies* (New York: Harcourt Brace Jovanovich, Inc., 1964), pp. 275–318.

[25]Some cases in point are the attempts made by various professional groups in Israel and Australia. For Israel see J. Ben-David, "Professionals and Unions in Israel," *Industrial Relations*, 15, no. 1 (1965): 48–66, and S. N. Eisenstadt, *Israeli Society*, op. cit., pp. 177–178, 187–190. For Australia see A. F. Davies and S. Encel, "Class and Status," in A. F. Davies and S. Encel, eds., *Australian Society*, op. cit., pp. 30–33.

society is related either to a redistribution of resources and rewards or to a reevaluation of qualifying attributes. Indeed, both tendencies can be seen in the attempts to broaden the scope of participation in the center, which brings us to the fourth basic type of structural change.

4. A society's power centers and other major determinants of control over positions and resources may be completely restructured, together with its value system. This phenomenon is generally known as revolution, and its subtypes need not be enumerated.

Creation of new positions

Most of the preceding types of structural change have been described as if they refer only to existing positions, attributes, and resources, but in modern societies there is always the possibility that new positions and new attributes may be created, and with them new systems of stratification. Accordingly, the difference between restructuring a system of stratification in terms of existing positions and attributes and creating wholly new positions and attributes is of crucial importance for the ability of modern societies to absorb change. And this ability, as we shall see, determines their capacity for sustained growth. At this point, however, it is important merely to note that the distinction between social change as the reform of existing status systems and as the creation of new ones can be viewed as cutting across all the distinctions we have made between different types of change.

Social hierarchies, segregation, and association in modern societies

Beyond those aspects of strata formation analyzed above, which are specific to either traditional or modern societies, many others are common to both, even if their manifestations vary. Some of these common aspects are the:
1. Segregation of the life styles of different strata,
2. Steepness of class and strata hierarchies,
3. Ways in which the life styles and value orientations of different classes are crystallized in different types of societies,
4. Place of the family and kinship systems,
5. Types of mobility, and especially the differences between sponsored and contested mobility,

6. Perception of the divisiveness of a social class order, and

7. Equal and/or continuous participation in the major institutional spheres—or in other words the degree to which a real, even though nonnormative, congruence develops among the hierarchies of power, wealth, and prestige, or, conversely, the extent to which incongruencies develop.

Because we do not have sufficient space to analyze all of these aspects of modern strata, we will concentrate on (1) the broad categories of attributes that in different modern societies serve as the basic criteria for evaluation of the social order, (2) the degree and the nature of different status groups' segregation or association (which is closely related to [1]), and (3) the major orientations to change, both in general and vis-à-vis political class-oriented or class-based change. The other aspects of strata formation, which were mentioned above, will not be analyzed systematically or in detail but only touched upon in passing.

CLASS BEHAVIOR AND POSITION

What conditions influence the development of these different aspects or components of strata formation in modern societies? Our analyses of different types of traditional societies, as well as general characteristics of modern societies, indicate two types of conditions from which tentative hypotheses can be developed.

The first of these is continuous structural differentiation, or continuously changing and expanding economic, social, and political structures. The second is the emergence of modern centers and potential participation in them by all members of a society. All of the structural changes in the major social spheres necessarily affect not only the relative positions of various groups but the ways in which they perceive these positions and attempt to change them.

It may seem, because of the preceding, that a group's class or stratification behavior within an institutional sphere is determined solely or mainly by its standing in that sphere—that, for instance, an economically disadvantaged group will concentrate on improving its economic standing. However, such perfect correspondence between class position and class behavior is rarely encountered in practice because of two sets of closely interconnected factors:

1. A group may have a different standing in each institutional sphere or hierarchy. For instance, it may have lost much of its

income through inflation but nevertheless maintain (as best it can) a relatively exclusive social standing.

2. A group's feelings of contentment or deprivation in an institutional sphere are not determined only by its objective situation. Rather it is mostly influenced by evaluation of its standing relative to that of other groups with which it habitually compares itself—or by what sociologists have labeled *relative deprivation*. That is, if a group alters the terms of comparison it might not feel deprived, without otherwise changing the situation. This comparative element in the behavior of social strata is partly determined by the structure and orientation of the centers.

Because much of a group's feeling of contentment or deprivation can be traced to the relationship it sees between itself and the society's center or centers, and this is equally true of both modern and traditional societies, we need not—up to a certain point in our analysis—change our classification of types of centers in dealing with modern societies. Thus we can say that the U.S.S.R., and some of the rightist authoritarian regimes (such as Mussolini's Italy or Franco's Spain), are societies with single, power-oriented centers whereas the United States is a polycentric society. We could also point out, inasmuch as the ways in which these various kinds of centers influence strata formation are much the same in modern and traditional societies, that a modern, power-oriented center attempts—like a traditional power-oriented center—to segregate its different status groups and to encourage a high degree of sponsored mobility.[26] Similarly, modern societies whose centers emphasize participation in an all-embracing secular or scientific tradition bear a strong structural resemblance to traditional societies that emphasize participation in an all-embracing religious tradition. In these types of modern and traditional societies, therefore, the life styles of different status groups tend to overlap and the elite groups develop a high degree of strata consciousness.[27]

Despite all this, there is no doubt that some of the most important aspects of strata formation in modern societies, such as the attitudes of different strata toward changes in the system of stratification, the degree to which groups engage in class-oriented

[26]For the Soviet Union see A. Inkeles, "Social Stratification and Mobility in the Soviet Union," in R. Bendix and S. M. Lipset, eds., *Class, Status and Power*, op. cit., pp. 516–527, and R. A. Feldmesser, "Toward the Classless Society?" in *Class, Status and Power*, pp. 527–534.

[27]A. Touraine, "Anciennes et nouvelles classes sociales," in G. Balandier, R. Bastide, Y. Berque and P. George, *Perspectives de la sociologie contemporaine: Hommage à George Gurevitch* (Paris: Presses universitaires de France, 1968), pp. 117–156.

or class-based political activities, and the segregation of occupational groups, are not explicable in terms of the orientation of centers—or not to the same extent as in traditional societies. Thus, although the U.S.S.R., some of the Latin American countries, and a few of the new nations (Guinea or Burma, for instance) might reasonably be said to have power-oriented centers, few observers would deny that there are great differences in the structure of their centers.[28] Such differences persist even when allowance is made for the different levels of economic development between, say, Russia and the various Latin American oligarchies. Similar differences can be found between the American and Australian middle classes and between the upper classes of England and the Scandinavian countries, although the centers of all these comparable societies have very similar orientations.

Moreover, it would be easy to point out differences in aspects of stratification that would not be present if the role of the centers were the same as in traditional societies. As has been mentioned above, some of these aspects of strata formation are the type and the degree of attempts to effect changes in the system of stratification, the scope and the orientation of political activities, and the segregation of occupational groups.

Plurality of center orientations in modern societies

To understand why the influence of the structure of modern centers is more complex than that of traditional centers in the processes of strata formation, we must consider two factors in addition to those specified on pages 161–163. The first of these is the former's development of an additional, and central, economic orientation. In the United States, parts of Europe, various western type dominions, and Latin America, it is represented by the activities of individuals, families, and private groups that engage

---

[28]For these countries see Z. K. Brzezinski, *Ideology and Power in Soviet Politics* (New York: Frederick A. Praeger, Inc., 1962), ch. 3; M. Fainsod, *How Russia is Ruled* (Cambridge, Mass.: Harvard University Press, 1953); J. J. Johnson, *Political Change in Latin America* (Stanford, Calif.: Stanford University Press, 1958), ch. 8; M. G. Navarro, "Mexico: The Lop-sided Revolution," in G. Veliz, ed., *Obstacles to Change in Latin America* (London: Oxford University Press, 1965); R. E. Scott, *Mexican Government in Transition* (Urbana: University of Illinois Press, 1959), chs. 6–8; J. H. Badgley, "Burma: The Nexus of Socialism and Two Political Traditions," *Asian Survey*, 3, no. 2 (1963): 89–95; and E. Leach, "The Political Future of Burma," in B. de Jorwenel, ed., *Futuribles: Studies in Conjecture* (Geneva: Droz, 1963), vol. 1: 121–153.

in the pursuit of wealth; in various collectivistic societies, whether the communist or "social democratic" countries of the new nations, it is represented by the orientations to development of the holders of the central political power.[29]

Secondly, a greater plurality of orientations or goals can usually be found in modern societies than in the centers of traditional societies. And of special interest here, perhaps, is the plurality of prestige orientations.

First of all, the definition of almost every national community refers both to universalistic elements—religious, rationalistic, or scientific traditions—and to particularistic elements—specifically, primitive territorial or ethnic. Similarly, modern societies may vary greatly in the degree to which they stress the differential prestige of groups vis-à-vis the universalistic principles of citizenship. England and Sweden, for instance, place much greater emphasis on the prestige levels of their various internal groups than the more democratic or egalitarian countries, such as Australia and Israel.[30]

Of special significance for our analysis is the importance (due primarily to the changing relationships of centers and orders) of a collectivity's concept of the maintenance or increase of its welfare, and the importance of this central orientation is unparalleled in traditional societies. Also important are the ways in which this orientation of the total collectivity combines with orientations of the center to produce strata formation. To illustrate this point, it is not enough to indicate that both the United States and Australia emphasize the pursuit of wealth, nor is it enough to add that this emphasis or pursuit is more "collective" in Australia. As Lipset's and Meyer's analyses have shown, there is a great difference between these two societies in the degree to which membership in the collectivity entitles one to differential rewards and access to

---

[29]T. Parsons, *Structure and Process in Modern Societies* (Glencoe, Ill.: The Free Press, 1960), chs. 3, 4; C. Kerr, J. T. Dunlop, F. H. Harbison, and C. A. Myers, *Industrialism and Industrial Man* (Cambridge, Mass.: Harvard University Press, 1960), ch. 3.

[30]For these countries see S. M. Lipset, "Value Patterns, Class and the Democratic Polity: The United States and Great Britain," in R. Bendix and S. M. Lipset, eds., *Class, Status and Power*, pp. 161–171; S. M. Lipset, *The First New Nation* (London: Heinemann Educational Books Ltd., 1964), pp. 235–237; K. Svalastoga and G. Carlsson, "Social Stratification and Social Mobility in Scandinavia," *Sociological Inquiry*, 31, no. 1 (Winter 1961): 23–46; K. B. Meyer, "Social Stratification in Two Equalitarian Societies: Australia and the United States," op. cit.; R. N. Rosencrance, "The Radical Culture of Australia," op. cit.; and S. N. Eisenstadt, *Israeli Society*, op. cit., esp. pp. 143–148, 151–156, 183–189.

positions, and this difference strongly influences several important aspects of the class structures.[31]

Center and strata formation in modern societies

Another important difference between the ways in which traditional and modern centers influence strata formation comes from the basic change in the relationships between centers and periphery that is concomitant with modernization. In all modern societies, this change has come about through a process of continuous struggle. The dual breakdown of the ascriptive bases of legitimation and the ascriptive regulation of stratification by the centers was not a "natural" process, like soil erosion or organic decay; it resulted from a continuous clash between the forces of modernity and those of tradition, each of which has its own distinctive attitude toward the center.

Because of the breakdown of the ascriptive regulation of stratification by the centers in modern societies, several aspects of social structure that were of only secondary importance in traditional societies became crucial in the process of strata formation in modern societies. Particularly the fact that, in modern societies, the focus for the conversion of resources has shifted from the centers to the various status groups, has completely altered these groups' images of themselves, and thus their attitudes to the resources at their disposal.

Three modern orientations will therefore be distinguished at this point, but their examination will be deferred to a later section.
1. Orientation toward the control of resources as a goal in itself, irrespective of the uses to which they may be put (which may be closely related to conspicuous consumption).
2. Orientation toward converting or directing resources toward goals that seem to epitomize the major attributes a group desires to represent or be preeminently identified with.
3. Orientation toward converting resources on behalf of the development of a broad social or cultural order (which is closely related to the way in which the self-identity of various status groups includes reference and commitment to a broad sociocultural order and/or other groups and their respective centers).

[31]S. M. Lipset, *The First New Nation,* op. cit., ch. 7; K. B. Meyer, "Social Stratification in Two Equalitarian Societies: Australia and the United States," op. cit.

Point 3 has important theoretical implications for our discussion, since it implies that, in sharp contrast to the situation in traditional societies, the modern center cannot completely control its diverse orientations; they are, to a remarkable extent, dependent on the various status groups' attitudes toward the center and on their willingness to invest their resources in maintaining or changing it.

Strong and weak centers

Because of the growing autonomy of orientations to the center, another aspect of centers—their strength or weakness—is also of great importance in strata formation in modern societies. A weak center, though able to perform its technical tasks (such as external political and internal administrative activities, ritualistic and theological functions, etc.), has relatively little control over other centers or symbolic orders of social life. It cannot derive strength and legitimation from other centers or social and cultural orders, nor can it fully discharge its charismatic ordering and legitimizing function. Thus it commands only minimal commitment beyond its limited sphere, and sometimes not even within it. Its relationships with other centers and with broad social groups and strata are usually adaptive (as were, for instance, the relationships of many nomad conquerors with the religious organizations of the conquered peoples). And sometimes a weak center is subjugated by centers it is supposed to rule or guide (some of the religious centers of southeast Asia, for example, were almost entirely submerged in the political centers).[32]

In contrast, a strong center enjoys such access to other centers that it can derive its legitimation from them, either by monopolizing and controlling them or by forming alliances with them.

Strong and weak centers, of course, also existed in traditional societies, and even influenced various aspects of strata formation, but—given the basic characteristics of traditional societies—this distinction was of secondary importance. In modern societies, on the other hand, the differences between strong and weak centers have been crucial.

Thus, for our present purposes, we must distinguish the

[32] For a finer distinction between strong and weak centers see S. N. Eisenstadt's introductions to the sections "Modern Polity" and "The Political Sociology of the Modern State" in S. N. Eisenstadt, ed., *Political Sociology* (New York: Basic Books, Inc., Publishers, 1971). For the structure of southeast Asian societies see J. Bastin and H. J. Benda, *A History of Modern Southeast Asia* (Englewood Cliffs, N.J.: Prentice-Hall, Inc., 1968).

different types of relationships between the center and the periphery. In particular, we must note what the various status groups feel about different kinds of centers, and the possibility that far-reaching differences may easily develop between the orientations of the center and those of the various groups.

SUMMARY

In this chapter, having analyzed some of the major characteristics of the social dynamics of modern stratification systems, we have shown that occupation has become the focus for status crystallization. However—as some of the most important studies of occupational prestige have indicated—this evaluation is based not only on economic factors but on factors of politics and prestige as well, among which there is never full agreement.

Against the background of these studies, we have also analyzed the major differences in the processes of stratification and strata formation in modern as distinct from traditional societies. Among these, the most important are the changing role of the center in strata formation and the structural differences in titles.

These differences, in turn, have given rise to special structural characteristics in the strata formation of modern societies, of which the most important are (1) secular criteria for the evaluation and perception of the social order, (2) weakened normative definitions of the linkages among the major components of stratification, (3) greater orientation to change and to open or public political activities as components of strata formation, (4) the new and paradoxical importance of the family as a basis for status orientation and initial placement, and (5) the growth of countrywide class consciousness as a strong component of strata formation.

At the same time, we have noted the characteristics of strata formation that are common to modern and traditional societies: the relatively segregated life styles of different strata; the scope and type of mobility (especially the importance of sponsored as opposed to contested mobility); the steepness of the stratification hierarchies, as well as the countrywide scope of strata consciousness; and the equal and/or continuous participation of these groups in the major institutional spheres.

Finally, we analyzed the conditions that give rise to different constellations of the components of strata formation in modern societies, again emphasizing some of the conditions that are more important in modern than in traditional societies. The most important condition is the continuously changing socioeconomic structure and the concomitant dislocation of various groups. A second condition is that, because of the changing relationships between the center and the periphery, there are changes not only in the orientations of the center but also in the orientations of various groups to the center, as well as in the strength or weakness of the center.

In Chapters 9 and 10 we will analyze the ways in which these conditions influence the aspects of modern strata formation that, because of space limitations, we have singled out for analysis.

9

Status Segregation and Class Association in Modern Societies

**TYPES OF STATUS SEGREGATION
IN MODERN SOCIETIES**

In this chapter we will see how conditions listed in Chapter 8—the levels of social differentiation, the changing group statuses in the major institutional fields, as well as their orientation to the centers, and the structure and orientations of the center—influence the development of the modern aspects of strata formation on which our analysis concentrates. These aspects, in short, are the development of different criteria of evaluation and the concomitant patterns of social segregation in modern societies. The major types of status, or class struggle in general and its political expression in particular, will be analyzed in Chapter 10.

Thus our analysis begins with the bases and characteristics of status segregation and dissociation among the relatively secular occupational or economic categories of modern societies. Dissociation is shown by a group's low incidence of participation in major institutional spheres; by its rudimentary social, organizational, and political frameworks; and by a high degree of closure in terms of intermarriage and social intercourse.

Segregation, however, may be based on different criteria of perception of the social order: on (1) perception of the social order in terms of the dichotomy between modern and traditional sectors, (2) the "ascriptive" upholding of closed life styles, (3) differential control over resources, or (4) "functional" contributions to the social order.

What, then, are the conditions under which each perception criterion of social order develops, and how do these criteria influence their respective patterns of status segregation?

Status segregation and perception of social order in terms of the modern-traditional (urban-rural) dichotomy

The first type of differentiation criteria, which is based on primordial territorial qualities and on the traditional-modern, urban-rural, etc., dichotomy, is most often found in traditional societies or sectors thereof. Thus in many Latin American[1] and African[2] countries, parts of Indian society, and in southeast Asia,[3] occupational categories seem to be secondary to such premodern stratification categories as tribal, caste, or patrimonial family statuses.

In these societies, the declining validity of the traditional categories of status may foster a perception of the social order in which the primordial categories are submerged in the dichotomy between traditional-modern or urban-rural categories, thereby giving rise to occupational associations or dissociations that are based on these dichotomies.

Side by side with this tendency, and especially within the

---

[1]For Mexico see W. Borrah, *Race and Class in Mexico* (Berkeley: University of California Center for Latin American Studies, 1957), p. 341. For Peru see M. S. Larson and A. E. Bergman, *Social Stratification in Peru* (Politics and Modernization Series, no. 5) (Berkeley: University of California Institute of International Studies, 1969), pp. 43, 52–54. For Guatemala see R. L. Peterson, "Guatemala, Honduras, El Salvador and Nicaragua," in B. G. Burnett and K. F. Johnson, eds., *Political Forces in Latin America* (Belmont, Calif.: Wadsworth, 1968), p. 76. For Ecuador see J. B. Gabbert, "Ecuador" in *Political Forces in Latin America*, pp. 284, 287.

[2]See for example, P. C. Lloyd, *The New Elites of Tropical Africa* (London: Oxford University Press, 1966); S. L. van den Berghe, *Africa: Social Problems of Change and Conflict* (San Francisco: Chandler Publishing Co., 1965), secs. 3, 4; and S. N. Eisenstadt, "Social Change and Modernization in African Societies South of the Sahara," *Cahiers des Etudes Africaines*, 15, no. 19 (1965): 453–471.

[3]The best collection of material on stratification in southeast Asia is K. Odaka and S. Ikuta, eds., "Proceedings of the International Symposium on Social Stratification and Social Mobility in East Asian Countries," *East Asia Cultural Studies*, vol. 4, nos. 1–4 (1965).

more developed urban centers, another trend develops, which can also be found among various oligarchic groups (which will be analyzed later). This trend is characterized by the fact that distinctions between institutional positions in general and occupations in particular are based primarily on their control of resources or their habits of conspicuous spending.

Insofar as perception of the differentiation of a social order is based on the modern-traditional dichotomy, various patterns of segregation develop, based on the one hand on the original traditions of the respective sectors and on the other hand, the sectors' adaptability to new tasks and activities.[4]

Status segregation in two types of oligarchic groups

We now move on to several types of modern societies, or sectors thereof, within which various types of secular perceptions of social order prevail, together with an exclusive or narrowly perceived affinity within status and occupational groups. One of these types consists of semicorporate oligarchic status and professional or occupational groups, such as those in Spain, Portugal,[5] the "traditionalistic-oligarchic" Latin American countries,[6] and—to a lesser degree—France (where there has been much stronger emphasis on the political attributes that are common to such groups).[7]

[4]Some of these developments are best seen in Latin America and Africa. For Latin America in general see, for example, J. Graciarena, *Poder y Clases Sociales en el Desarrollo de América Latina* (Buenos Aires: Paidos, 1968); G. Germani, *Política y Sociedad en una Época de Transición*, 2nd ed., Buenos Aires: Paidos, 1968); and D. B. Heath and R. N. Adams, eds., *Contemporary Cultures and Societies in Latin America* (New York: Random House, Inc., 1965), esp. pt. 3, "Social Organization." For Africa see the citations in no. 2 above. For Indonesia see J. L. Peacock, *Rites of Modernization* (Chicago: University of Chicago Press, 1968).

[5]For Spain and Portugal see, for example, J. Costa, *Oligarquía y Caciquismo: Colectivismo Agrario y Otros Escritos* (Madrid: Aliavia Editorial, 1967), pp. 1–45; Gazolla-Perez, "Funcionarios y Estratificacion Social," *Anales de la Moral Social y Economica*, 7, 1–32; and J. Linz, "The Party System of Spain: Past and Future," in S. M. Lipset and S. Rokkan, eds., *Party Systems and Voter Alignments: Cross-National Perspectives* (New York: The Free Press, 1967), pp. 197–282.

[6]See, for instance, F. Bourricaud, "Structure and Function of the Peruvian Oligarchy," *Studies in Comparativ. International Development*, vol. 1 (1965) and vol. 2 (1966) (Washington University Social Science Institute); A. Touraine, "Social Mobility, Class Relations, and Nationalism in Latin America," *Studies in Comparative International Development*, vol. 1 (1965); and M. S. Larson and A. E. Bergman, *Social Stratification in Peru*, op. cit.

[7]For France see M. Dogan, "Political Cleavage and Social Stratification in France and Italy," in S. M. Lipset and S. Rokkan, eds., *Party Systems and Voter Alignments*, op. cit., pp. 129–195; and J. Pitts, "Continuity and Change in Bourgeois France," in S. Hoffman, ed., *In Search of Modern France* (Cambridge, Mass.: Harvard University Press, 1963), pp. 235–305.

Such traditionally professional or guildlike occupational groups envisage themselves as holders and/or bearers of a special differential social standing vis-à-vis some of the most important attributes of the social order, especially in upholding tradition or distinctive life styles that can be ascriptively defined and whose status perception is often limited to local settings. These groups tend to segregate themselves, even from occupationally similar groups, as well as from most spheres of social life and participation therein, and to use most of their resources for maintaining their traditional goals and styles of life. They rarely attempt to convert their resources, and especially the prestige of their collectivity, into media that might enable them to participate in the broader, modern, and nonascriptively defined social or cultural orders.

These groups also tend to develop a strong ritualistic status closure, which is manifested by their normative limitations on "appropriate" occupations, by the traditional education they give their sons, and their stress on family identity as the central focus of strata identity. These groups are also characterized by an *ever widening* dissociation from modern centers, by their feeble efforts to participate in new spheres of social life, and by a general unreadiness to undertake new roles and activities.

The second major type of self-segregating economic or occupationally oligarchic groups is found among nontraditionalist landowners or industrialists in Latin American countries[8] and among some of the fluid urban groups in many urban centers of the new states.[9] The patterns or bases of their segregation are usually conceived in terms of their greater control of resources or conspicuous consumption, and rarely in terms of representing special types of attributes or participation (even if ascriptively based) in a wider societal and/or cultural order.

Because this type of social segregation is usually couched in terms of control over resources rather than in terms of seminormative life styles, these groups place less emphasis on life styles and family continuity than the first type, they are much more open

---

[8]For Chile see B. G. Burnett, "Chile," in B. G. Burnett and K. F. Johnson, eds., *Politics in Latin America*, op. cit., esp. pp. 348–349. For Brazil see J. López, "Etude de quelques changements fondamentaux dans la politique et la société brésiliennes," *Sociologie du Travail*, no. 7 (1965): 238–253.
For more general information see F. H. Cardoso: "The Industrial Elite," in S. M. Lipset and A. Solari, eds., *Elites in Latin America* (New York: Oxford University Press, 1967), pp. 94–116.

[9]See, for instance, H. Miner, ed., *The City in Modern Africa* (New York: Frederick A. Praeger, Inc., 1966), and A. M. Hauser, *Urbanization in Latin America* (Paris: UNESCO, 1961).

to new occupational, economic and educational activities, and they are more ready to approach the modern centers, if only to use them as a basic resource for their own goals.[10]

Status segregation in power-oriented societies

A third type of segregated or enclosed group, which is only superficially similar to the second type, tends to develop in power-oriented countries and totalitarian regimes—and especially in Russia, although the paucity of relevant data necessitates great caution in formulating generalizations. Nevertheless, some of these data, obtained from Polish investigations and various reports on life in Russia,[11] seem to indicate that, here also, occupational groups tend to develop their own forms of social segregation and to emphasize their particular occupational or professional goals.

Insofar as this segregation is based on secular functional criteria, it probably gives rise to a coalescence of similar groups into relatively closed semistrata in which each group stresses its separation from the others, although stressing similar desiderata, and—moreover—uses the same basic types of institutional commodities and means of exchange.[12]

Legitimation of each subgroup's life style is usually controlled by the monopolistic tendencies of the central elite, which continuously attempts to limit and nullify a stratum's tendencies to transcend its parochial style of life and claim legitimation in terms of wider, central values and independently of the elite. Accordingly, the central elite attempts to minimize the tendency to base life styles and differential access to positions on family transmission. Also, of course, these tendencies necessarily affect

[10]See, for instance, M. S. Larson and A. E. Bergman, *Social Stratification in Peru*, op. cit.

[11]For Poland see A. Sarapata, *Studia nad Uwarstwieniem i Richliwoscia Spoleczna w Polsce* (Warsaw: Ksiazka and Wiedza, 1965), chs. 3, 4. For Soviet Russia and general illustrative material see A. Inkeles and R. A. Bauer, *The Soviet Citizen: Daily Life in a Totalitarian Society* (Cambridge, Mass.: Harvard University Press, 1959), pp. 194–202, and H. K. Geiger, "Social Class Differences in Family Life in the U.S.S.R.," in C. S. Heller, ed., *Structural Social Inequality* (New York: The Macmillan Company, 1969), pp. 284–296.

[12]For evidence of this see W. Wesolowski and K. Slomczynski, "Social Stratification in Polish Cities," in J. A. Jackson, ed., *Social Stratification* (London: Cambridge University Press, 1968), pp. 175–211; Z. Baumann, "Economic Growth, Social Structure, Elite Formation: The Case of Poland," in R. Bendix and S. M. Lipset, eds., *Class, Status and Power* (London: Routledge & Kegan Paul Ltd., 1967), esp. p. 537; and H. K. Geiger, "Social Class Differences in Family Life in the U.S.S.R.," in C. S. Heller, ed., *Structural Social Inequality*, op. cit.

the nature of status groups' participation in the various spheres of social life and in their mutual intercourse.

In principle, most groups in such societies are allowed to participate in the various spheres of life, but their success will depend largely on their standing vis-à-vis the central elite. In practice, participation is possible, and relatively common, in ritualistic-political spheres and communal sporting activities, which are controlled by the central elite, but not in the highest spheres of each stratum or in the more central spheres of the elite.[13]

Insofar as these groups accept the orientations of the center, their segregated status seems to be more or less based on functional criteria and evaluations of their contributions to the social or political order. Insofar as they are apathetic to the center, segregation may be based on perception of the social order either in terms of the dichotomy between traditional-modern or rural-urban dimensions or in terms of their control of resources.[14]

The Polish research and other data also indicate that feelings of affinity may develop among different occupations in these societies, but this seems to be based almost entirely on one of the three abovementioned criteria—or to only a slight degree on approximation to the common attributes to which the groups have autonomous access. Probably, therefore, these orientations only minimally counteract the functional criteria of the elite and give rise to only a very limited secular class or stratum identity.[15]

Although the official ideology of these societies emphasizes

[13]See A. K. Brzezinski, *Ideology and Power in Soviet Politics* (New York: Frederick A. Praeger, Inc., 1962), ch. 3; R. A. Feldmesser, "Social Classes and Political Structure" in C. E. Black, ed., *The Transformation of Russian Society* (Cambridge, Mass.: Harvard University Press, 1960), pp. 235–252; C. E. Black, "Soviet Political Life after Stalin," in A. Inkeles and K. Geiger, eds., *Soviet Society: A Book of Readings* (Boston, Mass.: Houghton Mifflin Co., 1961), pp. 182–189; and D. Allchurch, "Leisure-Time Activities," in *Soviet Society: A Book of Readings*, pp. 520–527.

[14]A. Bauman, "Dreams and Ideals of Warsaw Youth," *Polish Perspectives*, 4, no. 10 (October 1961): 28–37; Z. Josefowicz, S. Novak, and A. Pawelczynska, "Students: Their Views on Society and Aspirations," *Polish Perspectives*, nos. 7, 8 (November, December 1958): 31–43; Z. Josefowicz, S. Novak, and A. Pawelczynska, "Students: Myth and Reality," *Polish Perspectives*, nos. 3, 4 (July, August 1958): 21–28; R. Cornell, "Students and Politics in the Communist Countries of Eastern Europe," *Daedalus*, 97, no. 1 (Winter 1968): 166–183; A. Sarapata, *Studia nad Uwarstwieniem i Ruchliwoscia Spoleczna w Polsce*, chs. 3, 5, 6; W. Wesolowski, "Strata and Strata Interest in Socialist Society: Toward a New Theoretical Approach," in C. S. Heller, ed., *Structural Social Inequality*, op. cit., pp. 465–477; H. K. Geiger, "Social Class Differences and Family Life in the U.S.S.R.," op. cit.

[15]A. Sarapata, *Studia nad Uwarstwieniem i Ruchliwoscia Spoleczna w Polsce*, and R. A. Feldmesser, "Social Classes and Political Structure," in C. E. Black, ed., *Transformation of Russian Society*, op. cit.

class or stratum elements, these concepts are usually used in the pejorative sense against external enemies. As for their internal structures these societies stress the classlessness of "socialist" societies, minimize their distinctiveness vis-à-vis one another, and maximize their togetherness or solidarity against the outside, class-structured world.

A similar type of orientations to occupations and occupational differences can also be found in some of the centers of the new nations, for instance Mexico and India, which stress the functionalistic component rather than the strata or class component of stratification. However, the class component often emerges after the initial establishment of the new order, and especially among the higher or middle groups.[16]

PATTERNS OF STATUS AND CLASS ASSOCIATION

Just as there are societies that segregate closely related occupations, there are other societies in which status dissociation among similar occupational positions is relatively small. In the latter societies, of which the most important are England, Scandinavia, the United States, and to some extent France, Germany (especially after World War II), the "white dominions" (especially Australia and New Zealand), Israel (although it often stresses the functional element), and Japan (especially in the post-World World II period), occupations are encompassed in perceptions that are based on more modern and broader class or stratum categories.[17]

[16]For Mexico see P. González-Casanova, "Dynamics of Class Structure," in J. A. Kahl, ed., *Comparative Perspectives on Stratification: Mexico, Great Britain, Japan* (Boston: Little, Brown and Company, 1968), pp. 64–82; M. G. Navarro, "Mexico: The Lop-sided Revolution," in C. Veliz, ed., *Obstacles to Change in Latin America* (London: Oxford University Press, 1965), pp. 222–230; and P. González-Casanova, "L'Evolution du système des classes au Mexique," *Cahiers Internationaux de Sociologie*, vol. 39 (1965).

[17]For these societies see A. F. Davies and S. Encel, "Class and Status," in A. F. Davies and S. Encel, eds., *Australian Society: A Sociological Introduction* (New York: Atherton Press, Inc., 1965), esp. pp. 33–37; L. Broom, F. Lancaster Jones, and J. Zubrzycki, "Social Stratification in Australia," in J. A. Jackson, ed., *Social Stratification*, pp. 212–233; A. Zloczower, "Mobility Patterns and Status Conceptions in an Urban Israeli Setting" (Ph.D. dissertation, Hebrew University of Jerusalem, 1968), pp. 110–111 (in Hebrew); K. Odaka, "The Middle Classes in Japan," in R. Bendix and S. M. Lipset, eds., *Class, Status and Power*, op. cit., pp. 541–551; W. G. Runciman, *Relative Deprivation and Social Justice* (London: Routledge & Kegan Paul Ltd., 1966), ch. 8; K. Svalstoga and G. Carlsson, "Social Stratification and Social Mobility in Scandinavia," *Sociological Inquiry*, 31, no. 1 (Winter 1961): 23–46 (esp. pp. 30–31); J. Linz, "Cleavage and Consensus in West German Politics," in S. M. Lipset and S. Rokkan, eds., *Party Systems and Voter Alignments*, op. cit., pp. 283–321; M. Dogan, "Political Cleavage and Social Stratification in France and Italy," in *Party Systems and Voter Alignments*, pp. 129–195; Alard D. Robinson, "Class Voting in New Zealand," in *Party Systems and Voter Alignments*, pp. 95–114; and K. M. Bolte, *Deutsche Gesellschaft im Wandel* (Opladen: Leske Verlag (C. W.), 1967), ch. 5.

The ways and the criteria by which various occupations are —so to speak—combined vary greatly among these societies, according to their predominant orientations, but all of them perceive the social order in terms of class or strata; that is, in terms of the approximation of different groups to common attributes to which all have some degree of autonomous access. It is this perception of the differentiation of the social order that constitutes the basis for relatively close status relationships between occupational groups, which are couched in terms of class or strata.

Indeed, this is very much in line with what has been found in traditional societies vis-à-vis the development of countrywide strata consciousness, except that in the former it is not only access to the center that creates this consciousness but the fact that the various groups are seen as the potential bearers of common and basic social and cultural attributes. This high degree of association between closely related occupational groups is manifested in a high degree of participation in various institutional spheres and by a wider and not entirely local or narrowly occupational scope of intermarriage.[18]

At the same time, the high degree of broad status association in these societies does not tell us much about the occupational groups in each class or category, or which groups are marginal vis-à-vis each category, or the degree to which these broad status groups are closed, open, overlapping, or the degree to which their relationships are perceived in conflictual terms. These aspects, of course, are greatly influenced by other variables, and especially by the major orientations of the center and the groups, in a manner similar to that of traditional societies.[19]

On the other hand, there are, of course, many differences in the patterns of strata formation in traditional and modern societies. Some of these differences will be analyzed more fully below, especially when we analyze the orientations to change and the patterns of political activity of different strata and classes in modern societies.

STATUS SEGREGATION AND ASSOCIATION, AND ORIENTATIONS TO THE CENTER

Some of the differences in relationships among occupational and class-strata categories, such as the submergence of occupa-

---

[18]E. Laumann, *Prestige and Association in an Urban Community* (Indianapolis, Ind.: The Bobbs-Merrill Co., Inc., 1966), esp. ch. 5, and P. M. Blau and O. D. Duncan, *The American Occupational Structure* (New York: John Wiley & Sons, Inc., 1967), ch. 10.

tional categories in premodern tribal or caste movements or in broad rural-urban or modern-traditional dichotomies, can—at least at first glance—be explained in terms of the levels of modernization, industrialization, and urbanization. However, differences can still be found between countries with similar levels of modernization. For instance, it seems that a broad urban-rural or modern-traditional dichotomy is more important in such societies as Peru and Brazil than in Mexico, Burma, or Ceylon.[20]

It is even more difficult to explain these differences and variations by a high level of structural differentiation and industrialization. We have noted above that there is little dissociation among occupational groups in most advanced, industrial countries (with the exception of Russia), and this fact may indicate such a relationship. But there seem to have been low levels of dissociation in many of these countries even long before they were highly industrialized and probably less so than countries like Argentina or some sectors of India are today.[21]

Status segregation and distance from the center

We must therefore look for other explanations of these differences. Whatever the variety among societies in which there is a sharp status dissociation among occupations and the professional elite on one hand and class or strata on the other, these societies (or sectors thereof) seem to have two closely related though not identical, and sometimes even dissociated, characteristics. One of these characteristics is an attitude of distance to the modern center; the other is the fact that the activities, goals, and life styles of these groups are only tenuously orientated to

[19]For further details see ch. 6 above.

[20]For Brazil see J. M. Young, "Brazil" in B. G. Burnett and K. F. Johnson, eds., *Political Forces in Latin America,* op. cit., pp. 448–450. Systematic information on stratification in Burma is very scarce; but valid indications can perhaps be derived from books that deal with general topics, such as M. Nash, *The Golden Road to Modernity* (New York: John Wiley & Sons, Inc., 1965), and L. W. Pye, *Politics, Personality and Nation Building: Burma's Search for Identity* (New Haven, Conn.: Yale University Press, 1962). For Ceylon see H. D. Evans, *Kutterwandel a Ceylon* (Baden-Baden, 1964), pt. C; B. Ryan, *Caste in Modern Ceylon* (New Brunswick, N.J.: Rutgers University Press, 1953); and B. Ryan, "The Ceylonese Village and the New Value System," *Rural Sociology,* 17, no. 4 (1952): 311–321.

[21]For the social development of England in the early phases of the Industrial Revolution see, for example, H. Perkin, *The Origins of Modern English Society, 1780–1880* (London: Routledge & Kegan Paul Ltd., 1968).

participation in a modern center or centers. These characteristics appear more frequently in some societies than in others, but within this context perhaps the most interesting cases are those characterized by a weak modern center—a center that, in its transition to modernity, has not established itself as the chief source of stratum identity among a society's most active strata. In less technical language, and with the resultant loss of precision, a weak modern center is one to which most people do not feel strong commitment.

An important subtype of the weak modern center is often found in new nations whose elites are interested in rapid modernization, and where this pursuit gives rise to a tendency to perceive the social order as rigorously separated into traditional and modern sectors. But the traditional sector not only persists, it continues to prevail. However powerful and even overwhelming the modern sector may be, most people regard it as strange and remote. Another common subtype is found in societies whose ruling elites tend to look upon the modern center as, at best, a regrettable fact of social life they can do nothing about, but more often as a resource that exists for their own benefit. (The latter instance is best illustrated by various Latin American oligarchies.)[22] In all of these cases, the modern center does not command a high degree of commitment from the elites.

Conversely, the strong modern center is exemplified by communist-totalitarian societies and, to a lesser extent, by societies that are ruled by a powerful political party.[23] Such centers more or less successfully regulate and control the avenues of access to the center and the various social groups' attitudes of commitment toward it. Insofar as they are successful in both endeavors, these centers are strong in both an organizational and a symbolic sense. Although access to the center is limited and regulated by the center, and cannot be achieved by peripheral groups through manipulation of their resources, the center nevertheless commands the allegiance of these groups. Thus, although

[22]For Peru see M. S. Larson and A. E. Bergman, *Social Stratification in Peru*, op. cit., pp. 273–275. For Latin America in general see the special April 1961 issue of *Sociologie du Travail*, devoted to the workers and trade unions of Latin America.

[23]For the U.S.S.R. see Z. K. Brzezinski, *Ideology and Power in Soviet Politics*, op. cit., ch. 3, and M. Fainsod, *How Russia Is Ruled* (Cambridge, Mass.: Harvard University Press, 1953). For the Soviet bloc in general see Z. K. Brzezinski, *The Soviet Bloc* (Cambridge, Mass.: Harvard University Press, 1967). For Mexico see M. G. Navarro, "Mexico: The Lop-sided Revolution," in C. Veliz, ed., *Obstacles to Change in Latin America*, op. cit., and R. E. Scott, *Mexican Government in Transition* (Urbana: University of Illinois Press, 1959), chs. 6–8.

the situation is not unlike that in traditional societies with power-oriented centers, there are, as we shall see, important differences. Nevertheless, the evaluation of groups in terms of their functional contributions to the social order—which are defined by the ruling elite—is the same in both types of societies, as are the consequent tendencies to status segregation among closely related groups.

Status association and closeness to the center

What, then, are the characteristics of societies in which status association among closely related occupational groups is relatively high? The common denominator in such societies is the strong commitment of their constituent groups to the broad social order and to the center, after the former have attained relatively autonomous access to the latter. In other words, these centers were formed by relatively autonomous participants who acted largely according to their own orientations to the center and thereby asserted the legitimacy of their access to the center.

The history of this phenomenon can be seen in Europe, and especially western Europe, where center formation was rooted in the feudal past. As we have seen, the autonomous bases of access to the center have been most notable in western Europe, and the process was reinforced in the Protestant countries after the Counter Reformation.[24]

A similar pattern, but with different institutional contours, developed in the modern colonist societies—the United States, Australia, Canada, Israel—where new centers were formed by the most active groups and strata, which from the very beginning were strongly oriented not only to economic and colonizing activities (as was the case in many Latin American countries in the second part of the nineteenth century) but also to the formation of a new sociopolitical order and center.[25]

The major groups in all of these societies have participated in the formation of the modern center and have opened it to other groups—if only potentially or after protracted struggle. Indeed, continuous struggles in most of these societies for participation in

[24]S. N. Eisenstadt, "The Protestant Ethic Thesis in Analytical and Comparative Frameworks," in S. N. Eisenstadt, ed., *The Protestant Ethic and Modernization: A Comparative View*, (New York: Basic Books, Inc., Publishers, 1968).

[25]S. N. Eisenstadt, *Israeli Society* (London: Weidenfeld & Nicolson Ltd., 1967), and L. Hartz, ed., *The Founding of New Societies* (New York: Harcourt Brace Jovanovich, Inc., 1964).

the formation of the center have generated the concept of differentiated social orders in terms of secular class or status symbols.

Some of the marginal cases, such as Germany and to some extent France, are also instructive for our analysis. In Germany, many of the new urban and industrial groups were denied access to the center, which was largely dominated by a traditional elite. Although this elite was partially committed to the new center, it also considered it a basic resource for the maintenance of its own position. At the same time, however (under Bismarck), the center had to allow for the symbolic participation of all the groups within it.[26] Hence the German social strata developed a double tendency in the perception of social order and status activities.

On the one hand there developed—especially among some of the middle class and most of the working groups—a broad class consciousness that associated closely related occupations, both in their status activities and in their orientation to the center. On the other hand—and especially among the upper and middle groups—a more segregative tendency developed, based on the combination of traditional criteria and control of resources, which the lower and the new classes countered by a rather militant sociopolitical exclusiveness.[27]

In France, where the revolution created a continuous rift between the traditional and the modern (revolutionary) aristocratic-republican and between religious-secular orientations, a modern and relatively open center developed, but it commanded the loyalty of only part of the society and was seen by many, especially the traditional groups, as alien and distant. Hence side by side with broader class and stratum orientations, which were based on association among closely related occupational groups, strong pockets of segregative, especially traditionalistic or oligarchic, tendencies developed among the aristocratic and various traditional groups.[28]

Other case histories

The continuing importance in modern stratification systems of the orientations of centers can be further illustrated by a few

---

[26]See G. Roth, *The Social Democrats in Imperial Germany* (Totawa, N.J.: The Bedminster Press, Inc., 1963).

[27]G. Roth, ibid. and R. Dahrendorf, *Society and Democracy in Germany* (London: Weidenfeld & Nicolson, 1967).

[28]See R. Aron, "La classe comme représentation et comme volonté," *Cahiers internationaux de Sociologie*, 38 (1965): 11–31, and S. Mallet, "La nouvelle classe ouvriere française," ibid., pp. 57–73.

case histories. In the development of the Mexican system, for instance, our analysis can discern four major trends. The first trend is toward perceiving social order as separated into traditional and modern sectors. The second trend, which was especially evident before the revolution of 1910–1917 but seems to have weakened since then, is characterized by the predominance of exclusive or relatively segregated status groups, both traditional and modern. The third trend is toward conceiving the social division of labor according to the "functionality" of each group, defined in terms of the groups' supposed contributions to the revolutionary social order. (This conception, of course, is fostered by the revolutionary elite.) The fourth trend—as yet rather weak—is toward the development of autonomous social strata.[29]

Of course, this short summary inevitably gives the misleading impression of completeness and finality, but in fact there is very little good material on the class situation in Mexico. However, the available material seems to indicate that, for the many rural-traditional groups that remain in a semicolonial status, the modern center is rather distant and strange, though not necessarily lacking in authority. During the period between independence and the outbreak of the revolution, Mexican society was characterized by a weak center and by status groups that had little commitment to centrality. The development of a more functional approach, as part of the elitist orientations remarked on above, can be traced to the transformation of the Mexican center after the 1910–1917 revolution. The center became strong, and soon it was able to inculcate commitment to itself as part of the collective identity of many groups. The development of class consciousness, on the other hand, may derive from the fact that the center has become more open in recent years and has legitimized, at least for some urban groups, the possibility of autonomous access.

A somewhat similar development pattern can be discerned in Turkey after the Kemalist revolution,[30] when the older pattern of stratification, in which there was a sharp distinction between those in power and those outside the power circle, was trans-

---

[29]See, for example, P. G. González-Casanova: "L'evolution du système des classes au Mexique," *Cahiers internationaux de Sociologie,* 39 (1965); J. Johnson, *Political Change in Latin America* (Stanford: Stanford University Press, 1958), pp. 129–136, 138; and M. G. Navarro, "Mexico: The Lop-sided Revolution," in C. Veliz, ed., *Obstacles to Change in Latin America,* op. cit., pp. 222, 228.

[30]See S. Martin, *Historical Determinants of Stratification: Social Class and Class Consciousness in Turkey—Comparative Administration Groups* (Bloomington, Ind.: American Society for Public Administration, 1967).

formed in two directions. The first transformation was toward a strong dichotomy between the rural and traditional on the one hand and the urban and modern on the other. The dichotomous perception of the social order was strongest in the rural areas, which had not been fully incorporated into the new national entity. The other change was the secular evaluation of occupational groups according to their supposed function in the new society; but this was not as revolutionary as it sounds. The highest evaluation was given to the political and bureaucratic elites, which was in line with Turkey's traditional emphasis on power. Then—as in Mexican society, and for the same reasons—autonomous class consciousness began to develop among a few of the more centrally placed social strata.

India is also of interest in this context. Of all the modernizing societies, it is in India that various groups' access to centers has most closely approached autonomy. During its transition to modernity, therefore, a stratification system has developed in which the association between occupations and social strata tends to be relatively close (see p. 187). This is seen most clearly in the great adaptability the caste system has shown in its response to new occupational opportunities. At the same time, and *because* of the predominance of traditional caste organizations, many of these newly created status references are expressed in traditional terms, or in terms of dichotomies between traditional-modern and rural-urban patterns.[31]

Simultaneously, and especially in the middle and lower segments of the more active castes, there may be attempts to make such attributes as valor, sanctity, etc. (which in the traditional system were connected with specific castes) accessible to the members of all groups, and thus potential bases for new stratum-class identities are created.[32]

And because India is a new nation with an initially strong (though apparently deteriorating) political center, it tended to evince different types of elitist-functionalist components in its system of stratification.[33] But insofar as the new center was not able to maintain its initial strength or implant strong center

[31]See M. N. Srinivas, *Social Change in Modern India* (Berkeley and Los Angeles: University of California Press, 1966), esp. chs. 2 and 3, and A. Beteille, *Castes Old and New* (London: Asia Publishing House, 1969).

[32]See L. Rudolph and S. Rudolph, *The Modernity of Tradition* (Chicago: University of Chicago Press, 1968), pp. 36–88.

[33]See A. Bopegamage and P. U. Veeraraghavan, *Status Images in Changing India* (Delhi and Bombay: UNESCO Research Center, 1966), esp. ch. 2, and A. Beteille, *Castes Old and New,* op. cit., esp. chs. 8 and 9.

commitments in the status orientations of many groups (especially the more active ones), these groups tended to develop a resource-consuming attitude to the center and concomitant decentralized status orientations and activities.[34]

Finally, several features of modern Japan also are worth mentioning. The first modern Japanese center, established after the Meiji revolution (1868), can be characterized as a strong center that was oriented to political and economic expansion but was based on traditional symbols of legitimation.[35] The ruling elite of this period displayed a truly Japanese sensitivity to the importance of tradition in social life, but it pursued a policy of undermining the power of the traditional groups. The members of this elite, who stemmed from the secondary aristocracy of the samurai, not only did away with the older aristocracy's and most of the samurai's political and economic power but used traditional (especially imperial) symbols to legitimize these changes. Then, in replacing these traditional groups, the elite created a completely new and much less rigid status system. Except for some religious and urban groups, the groups that took advantage of the new system did not evince a high degree of initial self-transformation, but the ruling elite was successful in using their ambitions and needs in its program of rapid industrialization. Nevertheless, what may be called the neotraditionalism of the elite placed many limitations on the ability of various social and intellectual groups to develop an autonomous stratum consciousness.[36]

Thus because of the combination of a strong, almost power-oriented center and the weakness of the groups' autonomous stratum orientation, Japan's status configuration tended to be segregative, based partly on traditional and partly on functional-secular criteria of service to the state.[37] And hence the system of stratification that developed in Japan, despite the simultaneous urbaniza-

[34]See A. Bopegamage and P. U. Veeraraghavan, *Status Images in Changing India,* report 1 (chs. 2 and 3) and report 2 (chs. 3 and 4), and A. Beteille, *Castes Old and New,* chs. 8 and 9.

[35]See, in general, S. N. Eisenstadt, *Modernization, Protest and Change* (Englewood Cliffs, N.J.: Prentice-Hall, Inc., 1966), pp. 75 ff., and for fuller details, H. Norman, *Japan's Emergence as a Modern State* (New York: Institute of Pacific Relations, American Council, 1940).

[36]See M. Maruyano, *Thought and Behavior in Modern Japanese Politics* (New York: Oxford University Press, 1964), and R. N. Bellah, *Values and Social Change in Modern Japan* (Asian Cultural Studies no. 3) (Tokyo: International Christian University, 1962).

[37]See R. N. Bellah, *Values and Social Change in Modern Japan;* R. P. Dore, ed., *Aspects of Social Change in Modern Japan* (Princeton: Princeton University Press, 1967), esp. chs. 4, 5, 8; and J. C. Pelzel, "Social Stratification in Japanese Urban Economic Life" (Ph.D. dissertation, Harvard University, 1949).

tion and industrialization, was only superficially similar to that of the West. On the whole, the political changes instigated by the Meiji elite formed the pattern for Japan's class structure.

Also, because the political and industrial elites were not great landowners, they did not have much interest in protecting agriculture. The ruling elite, urban from the very beginning, was strongly bureaucratized, both in government and in large business corporations, and independent entrepreneurs of the American "robber baron" type were almost unknown. Entry to this class was based largely on formal education criteria.

A similar pattern of bureaucratization developed in the professions, and especially in the legal professions, whose members were more often than not employed in the state or corporation bureaucracies. The number of independent lawyers who were organized in strong corporate, professional bodies was very small compared with the number in the United States or western Europe.

Thus various corporate units, not local or semiprofessional groups, constituted the major status units of Japanese society. It was only later, beginning in the 1930s but especially after the Second World War, that new types of class and status orientations—based to a much greater degree on attributive criteria and tending to a somewhat higher level of association, based on status and class criteria—began to develop in some sectors of Japanese society.[38]

Structural differentiation, centers, and status orientations

The crucial importance of the structure of and access to centers in the strata formation process can be seen in the fact that many strata characteristics that were analyzed above and were illustrated mostly by reference to the traditional classes (whether the higher aristocratic classes, the older types of professional or urban groups, or even—if only by allusion—the peasantry) persisted in modernizing societies even after industrialization had developed new occupations and groups. Usually, only a radical transformation of the center effected far-reaching changes in these characteristics. For instance, among the new classes or occupational categories that developed in most Latin American countries with urbanization and industrialization—such as the new busi-

---

[38]K. Odaka, "The Middle Classes in Japan," in R. Bendix and S. M. Lipset, eds., *Class, Status and Power*, op. cit., pp. 541–551, and E. F. Vogel, *Japan's New Middle Class* (Berkeley and Los Angeles: University of California Press, 1963), ch. 13.

ness and managerial classes, and even the new working classes—the basic status orientations were similar to those in the more traditional upper groups.

Most of these groups, in other words, developed segregative status patterns that were similar to those of the upper groups. These patterns were based on either a growing and intensive dichotomization of the differences between the traditional and modern sectors (the former, in turn, based on ascriptive exclusivity) or—more frequently—on a resource-conversion attitude to the center and to other groups. Within the new groups, these status attitudes alternated according to historical and structural circumstances.[39] Some of these status tendencies, of course—especially among the new urban middle class and working groups—can be explained by the various peculiarities of industrial development or its segregated sectors, or by the countries' dependence on external markets and capital.[40]

But these are no more than partial explanations, because segregated status orientations tend to develop in a different type of industrial setting—in the export market or "colonial" type of industry found in Argentina, as well as in the more internally oriented and more intensive industries found in parts of Brazil (especially São Paulo).[41] Nor do these types of status orientation necessarily develop when, as in India, structural-economic conditions—somewhat similar to those in Brazil—seem to develop.[42] But perhaps the most important comparison is with Mexico,

[39] For the situation in Brazil see F. H. Cardoso: "Le prolétariat brésilien: Situation et comportement social," *Sociologie du Travail*, no. 4 (1961): 50–65, and J. Johnson, *Political Change in Latin America*, op. cit., pp. 164–168. For Peru see F. Bouricaud, *Pouvoir et société dans le Pérou contemporain* (Paris: Armand Colin, 1967), chs. 2 and 3. For Chile see O. Sunkel, "Change and Frustration in Chile," in C. Veliz, ed., *Obstacles to Change in Latin America*, op. cit., pp. 129, 131, and J. Johnson, *Political Change in Latin America*, op. cit., pp. 66–93. For Mexico see M. G. Navarro, "Mexico: The Lop-sided Revolution," in C. Veliz, ed., *Obstacles to Change in Latin America*, pp. 207–218, 224.

[40] For Brazil see F. H. Cardoso, "Le proletariat brésilien: Situation et comportement social," in *Sociologie du Travail*, op. cit. For Mexico see K. F. Johnson, "Mexico," in B. G. Burnett and K. F. Johnson, eds., *Political Forces in Latin America*, op. cit., pp. 34–36. For Chile see O. Sunkel, "Change and Frustration in Chile," in C. Veliz, ed., *Obstacles to Change in Latin America*, op. cit., pp. 132–133, 136.

[41] For Brazil see F. H. Cardoso, *The Structure and Evolution of Industry in São Paulo: 1930–1960* (Spokane, Wash.: Washington University Social Science Institute, 1965), vol. 1.

[42] See, for instance, M. D. Morris, *The Emergence of an Industrial Labor Force in India* (Berkeley and Los Angeles: University of California Press, 1965). See also J. Kuznets, *Economic Growth and Structure* (New York: W. W. Norton & Company, Inc., 1965), pp. 176–194, which stresses the importance of noneconomic factors in explaining the differences between the undeveloped countries and the first developmental stages of the developed countries.

where industrial conditions similar to those, for instance, in Brazil, seem to exist, and these types of status orientation seem to have developed in only an embryonic way (especially, as we have seen, after the Mexican revolution).

Although the new groups in these societies seem to have developed broad status orientations similar to those of the older groups, their political expression tended to be radically different. The greater orientation to the center and the more numerous claims to participation in it necessarily gave rise to new types of political orientation and expression, which we shall analyze in greater detail later. Indeed, the same kind of continuity can also be discerned in power-oriented societies, such as Russia, whose urbanization and industrialization display some of the same status orientations among most (or almost all) of its group workers and managers. In most of these groups we can also discern evidence of social segregation and rudimentary but common or widespread status orientations that spring from the basic premises of modernity.[43]

A similar continuity in basic orientations is also found in most of the countries that initially had a high degree of status association among closely related occupational categories. Especially with the development of new and basic political orientations (such as followed from collective political participation, social and welfare policies, perception of status or class, and the encompassment of different occupations within broad class or status categories), these countries acquired a functional tinge, but this orientation is much different from the situation that prevails in power-oriented societies.[44] In the former instance, "functionality" is not defined only in terms of contributions to the tasks set by the political center but, beyond this, according to a group's standing in an order or center in whose formation and definition of basic attributes it has participated.

Of the highly industrialized nations, the major exceptions to

---

[43]For evidence of this see H. K. Geiger, "Social Class Differences and Family Life in the U.S.S.R.," op. cit.

[44]The emphasis on the functional element may be explained by the growing importance of occupational specialization and education in industrialized societies, as well as by the fact that part of the stratification struggles in these societies is focused on these elements.
For some reasons why similar levels of industrialization are not accompanied by similar stratification patterns in societies that are power-oriented and those that are not, see J. H. Goldthorpe, "Social Stratification in Industrial Societies," in R. Bendix and S. M. Lipset, eds., *Class, Status and Power*, op. cit., pp. 648–659, and R. Aron, "Social Class, Political Class, Ruling Class," in *Class, Status and Power*, pp. 201–210.

this tendency of status association, which nevertheless prove the importance of the center formation process, are Germany and—to a much smaller degree—France (to which we have already alluded). In Germany, some of the basic tendencies of status formation seem to have taken the direction of class-stratum association. But in Germany—as in France—this development was only partially realized after the Second World War, when a somewhat new type of center was established, because of the persistence of "older" attitudes toward the center and social order.[45]

Thus, in all these societies, it was primarily changes in the orientations of the center and of broadly based groups to the center that changed some of the basic criteria of differentiation within the social order, as well as the scope of association or the differentials between relatively close occupational groups. But such changes could also have occurred—to some degree—irrespective of such purely structural variables as the levels of economic development and the relative placements of groups within an institutional order. Nevertheless, as we will see later, these variables had great influence on the other crucial aspects of strata formation in modern societies.

STATUS ASSOCIATIONS AND DISSOCIATIONS, AND THE STRUCTURE OF ELITES, PROFESSIONS, AND INTELLECTUAL GROUPS

Thus far, because we have dealt mainly with the effects of different types of centers on whole systems of stratification, this discussion has been framed in terms of broad social strata. Accordingly, we will conclude this chapter by analyzing the influence on association and dissociation of relatively close occupational groups and the influence of different types of dissociation on other aspects of modern social organization, namely, the internal and external relationships of elites, professions, and the so-called intelligentsia. (Inasmuch as every broad occupational group is made up of smaller groups, the way in which the latter "get on" together constitutes the *internal* relationships of the overall group. The way in which these larger groups get on with the rest of society comprises their *external* relationships.)

---

[45]See K. M. Bolte, *Deutsche Gesellschaft im Wandel,* op. cit.; M. Schelsky, *An der Suche nach der Wirklichkeit* (Düsseldorf and Cologne: 1965), pp. 331–391; and R. Dahrendorf, *Society and Democracy in Germany,* op. cit.

Elites and society

With regard to the internal relationships of elites, we will be concerned only with the degree of association or dissociation between the various elite groups and with their relationships to broad status groups. In some societies, the elite groups most closely associated with one another tend to be so by virtue of their social origin, style of life, etc. In others, they tend to develop as separate, almost self-enclosed status groups, and are therefore spoken of as dissociated. On the whole, it seems that in modern societies that are characterized by a relatively great distance between the center and the periphery, most of the elite groups tend to dissociate themselves from each other. The same tendency can also be seen in the external relationships of elites in such societies: dissociation between the elite and the society's major status groups.

Both internally and externally, however, this dissociation is exhibited in a variety of subtypes, depending on the major orientation of a society's stratification system. In societies whose systems are based on traditional, ascriptive criteria, the various elite groups usually have a strong familial basis.[46]

In societies whose systems emphasize differential control of resources, elite groups are somewhat less dissociated from one another than they are from the rest of society. Although their style of life is still exclusive, they are no longer so particular about the origin of their members.[47]

In societies whose systems are based on power, and especially in their middle echelons, there tends to be a high degree of dissociation among the elite groups and (in most respects) between them and the rest of society. The reason for this is that, in such a society, a particular group (usually the central political elite) always tries to dominate the others.[48]

[46]Much information on this subject is available, but see especially K. F. Johnson, "Mexico," in B. G. Burnett and K. F. Johnson, eds., *Political Forces in Latin America,* op. cit., pp. 34, 42; B. G. Burnett, "Chile," in *Political Forces in Latin America,* p. 349; F. G. Gil, *The Political System of Chile* (Boston: Houghton Mifflin Company, 1966), pp. 23–24; F. Bouricaud, *Pouvoir et société dans le Pérou contemporain,* op. cit., ch. 1; and J. López, "Etude de quelques changements dans la politique et la société brésiliennes," *Sociologie du Travail,* no. 7 (1965): 238–240.

[47]This situation, as already mentioned, is characteristic of some urban centers of the new states and various sectors of Latin American societies. See, for example, H. H. Smythe and M. M. Smythe, *The New Nigerian Elite* (Stanford, Calif.: Stanford University Press, 1960), esp. chs. 6, 7, 9; F. G. Gil, *The Political System of Chile,* op. cit., pp. 23–24; J. M. Young, "Brazil," in B. G. Burnett and K. F. Johnson, eds., *Political Forces in Latin America,* op. cit., pp. 461–467; and M. S. Larson and A. E. Bergman, *Social Stratification in Peru,* op. cit., pp. 273–274.

Under these conditions, most elites—especially the secondary groups—have little in common except their social origins. Moreover, unlike elite groups in other kinds of societies, they are prevented by the central ruling elite from exercising ultimate control over access to the positions nominally at their disposal. In particular, attempts to transmit these positions on a hereditary basis are rigorously suppressed by the central elite as threats to its own position.[49]

In contrast, elite groups in societies that are characterized by a relative closeness between center and periphery do not usually dissociate themselves from each other, and they tend to be closely interwoven in broader status groups.[50]

Professional groups

The situation is similar for the internal and external relationships of professional groups, which are greatly influenced in both respects by the type of stratification system of which they happen to be part. In this context, two aspects of professional organization are of special interest: the degree to which (1) each profession internally organizes itself as an exclusive body, with strict apprenticeship requirements and a tendency toward making its positions hereditary, and (2) the professions, as a whole, display commitment to a wider social order, real or ideal, as opposed to a commitment that extends no further than fulfilling their respective professional functions.[51]

In modern societies in which there is a relatively large distance between center and periphery, professions tend to be organized along exclusive lines. In more traditional societies, and in the traditional sectors of modern societies, an exclusive professional organization is coupled with very strong emphasis on

[48] See J. H. Goldthorpe, "Social Stratification in Industrial Societies," in R. Bendix and S. M. Lipset, eds., *Class, Status and Power,* op. cit. esp. pp. 655–658; and R. A. Feldmesser, "Toward the Classless Society?" in *Class, Status and Power,* op. cit., pp. 527–533.

[49] See R. A. Feldmesser, "Toward the Classless Society?" in *Class, Status and Power,* op. cit.

[50] R. Dahrendorf, *Class and Class Conflict in Industrial Society* (Stanford, Calif.: Stanford University Press, 1959), ch. 8, and R. Aron, "Social Class, Political Class, Ruling Class," in *Class, Status and Power,* op. cit.

[51] For general analyses of professions see T. H. Marshall, *Class Citizenship and Social Development,* op. cit., ch. 6, and J. Ben-David, "Professions in the Class System of Present-Day Societies," *Current Sociology,* 12, no. 3 (1963–1964) (which contains a good bibliography).

familial transmission of professional positions.[52] In most societies that emphasize differential control of resources, there is little professional commitment to any kind of wider social order.[53] In societies that have power-oriented centers, familial and ascriptive ties are generally deemphasized, and professional organizations are closely supervised by the central elite. Naturally, this supervision discourages commitment to a wider social order.

Conversely, societies in which broad status groups develop, encompassing many occupations, tend to have professions that are less exclusive and, at the same time, more interested in their "public responsibility." But they also develop differences, according to their major orientations. In prestige-oriented societies, such as England and Holland, the self-image of professions centers mainly on their styles of life and orientations to broader responsibilities.[54] In societies based on wealth, there is more emphasis on professional functions as such, but there is also a basic acceptance of public responsibility. Finally, it must be remembered that all of these generalizations are very tentative, and that a full investigation would disclose many more subtypes than those we have enumerated.[55]

Intellectual groups

The intelligentsia is another group that takes its form from the dominant values by which a society is stratified. This is most clearly seen in the relationships between the intelligentsia and the center, which can be analyzed under three headings: (1) the degree to which the intelligentsia perceives itself as participating in the creation or maintenance of a sociocultural order that is shared by other groups and strata; (2) the degree to which the intelligentsia's sociocultural order is upheld by the society's

---

[52]For Spain and Portugal see, for instance, J. Costa, *Oligarquía y Caciquismo: Colectivismo Agrario y Otros Escritos*, op. cit., pp. 1–45, and José Gazolla-Pérez, "Funcionarios y Estratificación Social," *Anales de la Moral Social y Económica*, 7: 1–32.

[53]See, for instance, F. Bouricaud, "Structure and Function of the Peruvian Oligarchy," *Studies in Comparative International Development*, vol. 2, and J. C. Agulla, *Eclipse de una Aristocracia* (Buenos Aires: Ediciones Libera, 1968).

[54]See W. J. Reader, *Professional Man* (New York: Basic Books, Inc., Publishers, 1966) and R. Lewis and A. Mande, *Professional People* (London: Phoenix Home Ltd., 1952).

[55]For the United States see K. S. Lyon, ed., *The Professions in America* (Boston: Beacon Press, 1965).

center or centers; and (3) the degree of autonomy the intelligentsia enjoys in forming such an order.

In societies with weak centers and elite groups that attempt to monopolize the center and/or use its resources exclusively for their own benefit, two types of intelligentsia tend to develop. The first is composed almost exclusively of members of the traditional professions, or at any rate those who share their values; it upholds a relatively exclusive style of life, not unlike that of other elite groups; and it tends to uphold a cultural order whose relationship to the center is external rather than internal. In other words, this type of intelligentsia tends to consider its pursuits as "purely intellectual" and having little reference to the social center. Having little motivational commitment to this center, it nevertheless usually enters into some sort of de facto alliance with it. This type of intelligentsia is probably best represented by the typical Latin American society during the early post-independence years.[56]

The second type of intelligentsia is characterized by its attempts to create mostly in a revolutionary way, a wholly new cultural order. Members of this intelligentsia have at most only a weak commitment to the existing social order, especially when its requirements conflict with their own interests, whether rational or cultural.

Both types of intelligentsia enjoy a high degree of autonomy in relation to the center and the major social strata. However, because this autonomy is based on segregation, mutual points of interest are few, and only a drastic transformation of the center can reconcile an intelligentsia in this kind of society. Of course, these intelligentsias are not always wholly averse to participating in such a transformation.[57]

The structure and orientation of intelligentsias in societies with strong, power-oriented centers are of a somewhat different order. Historically (in Soviet Russia, for instance), many of them developed from intelligentsias of the second type (above), but once these erstwhile rebels found themselves in power they

---

[56]F. Bonilla, "Cultural Elites," in S. M. Lipset and A. Solari, eds., *Elites in Latin America*, op. cit., pp. 242–249. For more details see J. L. Romero, *A History of Argentinian Political Thought* (Stanford, Calif.: Stanford University Press, 1965), part II; R. A. Humphrey and J. Lynch, eds., *The Origins of the Latin American Revolutions* (New York: Alfred A. Knopf, Inc., 1965); G. Germani, *Política y Sociedad en una Época de Transición* (Buenos Aires, 1968), pp. 195–217; and J. Garciarena, *Poder y Clases Sociales en el Desarrollo de América Latina* (Buenos Aires, 1968), chs. 2, 5.

[57]F. Bonilla, "Cultural Elites," in *Elites in Latin America*, op. cit., pp. 242–249; S. Bagu, *Estructura Social de la Colonia* (Buenos Aires: El Ateneo, 1952), ch. 3; L. M. Vega, *Roads to Power in Latin America* (London: Pall Mall Press Ltd., 1964), ch. 1.

tended to develop attitudes much like those of the professional elites. Eventually, however, rebellious subgroups tend to emerge even in this kind of intelligentsia, which is partly the result of the continuous forces of change and differentiation that are concomitant with modernity.[58]

Finally (at least for the purposes of this discussion), a still different type of intelligentsia tends to develop in societies in which there is a close association between the major occupational categories and the rest of the social order. Its two outstanding characteristics are a general lack of exclusiveness in relation to other status groups and a good deal of intellectual independence. However, this independence is not a form of alienation from social order as such; this intelligentsia looks to a better kind of social order. Its major prototypes in the history of western societies are the various Protestant groups and, later, the more diversified intellectual and professional groups.[59]

Thus, coincident with the growing differentiation and professionalization of intellectual life, a closer proximity developed between the intelligentsia and professional groups. On the other hand, an "oppositionary," protest-oriented substream also developed, oriented toward the creation of a new social order.[60] However, the details of these developments are beyond the scope of our analysis.

Thus various aspects of the relationships between center and periphery—especially those that derive from actual and symbolic distance from the center, the distinction between strong and weak centers, and the major strata's basic status orientations to the center—are the most important determinants of the principles by which the differentiation within the social order is perceived and the degree to which different but relatively close occupational categories are dissociated or associated in common status frameworks. And thus we have seen that, in modern societies, distance from the center tends to connote a high degree of dissociation between relatively close occupational groups.

---

[58]R. Pipes, "The Historical Evolution of the Russian Intelligentsia," in R. Pipes, ed., *The Russian Intelligentsia*, (New York: Columbia University Press, 1961), pp. 47–62; D. Burg, "Observations on Soviet University Students," in *The Russian Intelligentsia*, pp. 80–100.

[59]See S. N. Eisenstadt, ed., *The Protestant Ethic and Modernization: A Comparative View*, op. cit.; U. Lüthy, "The Intellectuals: France," *Encounter*, 5 (August 1955): 5–15; G. Many, "The Intellectuals: Germany," *Encounter* (June 1955): 42–49; E. A. Shils, "The Intellectuals: Great Britain," *Encounter* (April 1955): 5–16.

[60]See E. A. Shils, "The Intellectuals," in *International Encyclopedia of the Social Sciences* (New York: The Macmillan Company, 1968).

To sum up: a high degree of association between closely related occupational categories or groups seems—according to our analysis—to be a function of the groups' proximity to the center, their participation within it, and the measure of their autonomous access to it.

SUMMARY

This chapter picked up the thread of the last one, in which some of the characteristics of modern strata formation and the conditions that give rise to them—in contrast to traditional societies—were pointed out. However, the analytical focus in this chapter has been on the development of modern secular evaluative criteria for perception of the social order and the former's influence on the patterns of status segregation and dissociation, as well as status (class) association, that tend to develop within modern societies.

We have distinguished several types of status segregation: those based on a dichotomous perception of the social order in terms of traditional-modern, two broad types of oligarchic groups, and the types that develop among groups in power-oriented societies; and we have analyzed the differences among them.

In contrast to these patterns of segregation are the patterns of class-status association that developed in the societies of western Europe, the United States, Canada, Australia, Israel, and Japan.

We have seen that the major determinant of status segregation, as opposed to status association, does not lie in sociodemographic factors but in the relationships between status groups and the center. We have also seen that the different types of status segregation are closely related to their distance from the center whereas the development of status and class association is closely related to participation in the process of center formation.

In addition to using illustrative material from western societies, we have illustrated the importance of all these determinants by analyzing several Asian and Latin American countries, such as Mexico, India, and Japan. The importance of these determinants was also illustrated by demonstrations that patterns of status segregation tend to develop among new socioeconomic groups (such as the middle and the working classes) so long as their basic relationships to the center—as well as the orientations of the center—do not change.

We also illustrated the influence of these patterns of status segregation and/or association on the structure of elites, professions, and intelligentsias.

However, the distinction between status segregation and status (and class) association does not imply a constantly harmonious relationship between the different classes or a harmonious perception of the nature of a social order. On the contrary, the very symbolism of class is often conceived as divisive and conflictual. Indeed, the most articulate expression of division and conflict is the political expression of class symbolism, which will be analyzed in Chapter 10.

10

Class and Politics in Modern Societies

We have seen, in our general discussion of the processes of strata formation in modern societies, that usually the former are openly and legitimately connected with political orientations and activities. In fact, these orientations and activities are some of the major ways in which the ever present desire for change expresses itself in modern societies. Although their forms are often consciously based on class interests and expressed in terms of class symbolism, this does not mean that all political activity in modern societies is necessarily of this kind. It *does* mean, however, that class or stratum elements enter into modern political activities in a great variety of ways and conversely, that many types of political activities and organizations are part of the strata formation process in modern societies.

Thus, in explicating the nature of this political element in modern strata formation, we shall specify (1) the major class or status components in modern political activities and (2) the conditions under which different types and combinations of these components tend to develop.

POLITICAL ORGANIZATION AND CLASS INTEREST

In this context, the following questions about modern political organizations appear to have special relevance.

1. What are the major types of political activity and organization in modern societies?
2. To what extent are the goals of these organizations oriented toward effecting any of the stratification changes described above (pp. 168–171)?
3. To what extent are the goals of these organizations couched in the vocabulary or symbolism of social class?
4. To what extent are such organizations, in recruitment and membership, homogeneous vis-à-vis social class?
5. To what extent are variations in class or status important foci of political cleavage, or contribute to the intensity of such cleavage?

There is general agreement among social scientists on question 1: of all the types of organization through which political demands are articulated, the most important are special-interest groups, social movements, and political parties. Of course, the first two types are sometimes seen as components of the third type—or, in other words, political parties may be the most effective articulation of the goals and aspirations of various special-interest groups and social movements. Thus, although there can be considerable overlapping of the three types, each type can have an autonomous existence and distinctive orientations.

The special-interest or pressure group is usually oriented toward securing specific and limited objectives, whether economic, religious, cultural, or political. It concerns itself with the wider political machinery of a party or state only insofar as this machinery can be used to promote its interests. This singleness of purpose seems to be found in all special-interest groups, and is probably their most distinctive characteristic.

Social movements, on the other hand, are easily distinguishable as either revolutionary or reformist movements. Revolutionary movements attempt to infuse their values or goals in a particular institutional structure or to transform such a structure on the basis of these aims and values. These movements are usually oriented toward the future, which they depict as inevitably different from the present. They also tend to be highly militant and to demand total obedience and loyalty from their members. Their beliefs are very often apocalyptic, even messianic, and revolutionary groups distinguish more sharply than most other groups between friends and foes.[1] As against this, reformist movements emphasize such symbols to a smaller degree and focus on concrete objects attainable in the framework of the system and, on the whole, are more tolerant, and do not command total allegiance.

Special-interest groups and social movements existed, with certain differences, in premodern societies, but political parties were exceedingly rare. Indeed, one of the most important differences between modern and traditional societies is that in the former, special-interest groups and social movements may become part of the framework of common and continuous activity that we call political parties. The integration of different demands that political parties (or other partylike organizations) provide is achieved through the development of party organs and leadership, the subsumption of special interests under general aims that are likely to appeal to a wider public, and translation of the diffuse aims of social movements into realistic political goals and programs.[2]

Political and class consciousness

Because it is beyond the province of the present discussion to analyze political organizations in all their aspects, we shall limit ourselves to the factors that seem to throw most light on the processes of strata formation in modern societies. Among these, the most important are (1) the circumstances under which special-interest groups, social movements, and political parties—especially insofar as they contain class components—become associated with one another; (2) the ways by which a particular political organization comes to predominate over the others; and (3) the degree to which the development of different class components is related to the basic status orientation of the major strata.

In a sense, however, these factors are only initial steps toward a higher level of analysis—namely, analysis of the specific and

[1]The distinctions between different types of political organizations are more fully elaborated in S. N. Eisenstadt, *Modernization, Protest and Change* (Englewood Cliffs, N.J.: Prentice-Hall, Inc., 1966), pp. 11–15.

[2]For modern political parties see, for instance, S. Neumann, ed., *Modern Political Parties* (Chicago: University of Chicago Press, 1956), and J. La Polambara and M. Weiner, eds., *Political Parties and Political Development* (Princeton, N.J.: Princeton University Press, 1966).

direct relationships of political organizations to various aspects of class or strata formation in modern societies. Accordingly, we must ascertain

1. The degree to which the goals of political organizations incorporate the stratification goals that were outlined above, beginning on page 169;

2. The degree to which basic political ideology is couched in terms of class, together with the connotations or meaning of class symbolism;[3]

3. The degree to which different types of political organization develop in modern societies on the basis of class or strata. That is, the homogeneity (or heterogeneity) of class- or stratum-based support for political activities and organizations, or the degree to which groupings other than those of class or status—be they regional, religious, functional economic, or ethnic—serve as the bases of political organization, activity, and ideology.[4]

4. The degree to which political cleavages and conflicts develop around class foci (in contrast to other foci, be they regional, ethnic, religious, or discrete functional issues), together with their intensity and their impact on the social order and political community.[5]

In the following discussion, therefore, we shall analyze the development of different constellations or types of class and strata components in modern political organizations in relation to some of the basic conditions or variables, such as the fundamental status orientations of major strata, their orientations to basic attributes and resources and to the center, their distance from the center, and the ongoing processes of change and dislocation.

[3]See Stanislaw Ossowski, "Different Conceptions of Social Class," in R. Bendix and S. M. Lipset, eds., *Class, Status and Power,* (2nd ed.; New York: The Free Press, 1966), pp. 86–96; and S. M. Lipset, "Social Class," in *International Encyclopedia of the Social Sciences* (New York: The Macmillan Company, 1968).

[4]The best data on this problem are collected in S. M. Lipset and S. Rokkan, eds., *Party Systems and Voter Alignments: Cross-National Perspectives* (New York: The Free Press, 1967).

[5]See, in *Party Systems and Voter Alignments,* op. cit., M. Dogan, "Political Cleavage and Social Stratification in France and Italy," pp. 129–196; J. J. Linz, "Cleavage and Consensus in West German Politics: The Early Fifties," pp. 283–322; and E. Allardt and P. Pesonen, "Cleavages in Finnish Politics," pp. 325–366. See also the articles in E. Allardt and Y. Lettunen, eds., *Cleavages, Ideologies and Party Systems* (Helsinki: Westermark Society, 1964), vol. 10. Interesting material about a different type of political orientation and cleavage can be found in C. Ionescu and E. Gellner, eds., *Populism* (London: Weidenfeld and Nicolson Ltd., 1969).

Development of special-interest groups

Let us begin by analyzing the conditions under which relatively narrow and discrete special-interest groups, whose aims are attributable to a common class or status, develop in modern societies. These aims are likely to include better market positions for the groups' members, greater social rewards, and greater control of the uses to which their resources can be put. Although the evidence warrants no more than an informed guess, it seems that the most important influences on the development of special-interest groups—whether occupational, professional, local, or religious—are largely the same as those that foster association among elite groups (pp. 200–201).

Thus special-interest groups that are oriented toward attaining their own, rather narrowly defined goals and benefits tend to develop in situations where (1) dissociation among relatively close occupational and elite groups is pronounced, (2) status organization has a narrow local or professional basis, and (3) most of the elite groups are distant, or at least dissociated, from the modern center. Although this analysis needs further refinement, it is a sociological fact that similar conditions have been found in contemporary Spain and Portugal and many east European countries (between the two world wars) and that such groups, largely unmediated by political parties, developed in these countries.[6]

A similar pattern of early political organization can be found among groups that regard the center as a usable resource and organize themselves in broader frameworks to maximize direct benefits from the center. This pattern is often found in later stages of political development in Latin American societies.[7]

A similar pattern of political organization also tends to develop in societies with strong power centers, such as most

[6]See, for instance, J. J. Linz, "The Party System of Spain: Past and Future," in S. M. Lipset and S. Rokkan, eds., *Party Systems and Voter Alignments*, op. cit., pp. 197–282. For eastern Europe see H. Seton-Watson, *Eastern Europe between the Wars* (Hamden, Conn.: The Shoe String Press, Inc., 1963), and Andrew C. Janos, "Eastern Europe between the Wars," in S. P. Huntington and C. H. Moore, eds., *Authoritarian Politics in Modern Society* (New York: Basic Books, Inc., Publishers, 1970).

[7]G. A. Dillon Soares, "The Politics of Uneven Development: The Case of Brazil," in *Party Systems and Voter Alignments*, op. cit., pp. 467–498; S. M. Lipset, "Political Cleavages in 'Developed' and 'Emerging' Politics," in S. M. Lipset, ed., *Revolution and Counterrevolution* (New York: Basic Books, Inc., Publishers, 1968), pp. 179–213; G. Germani, *Política y Sociedad en una Época de Transición* (Buenos Aires: Paidos, 1962).

communist societies.[8] The bulk of the political struggle in these societies is waged by segregated special-interest groups, each of which pursues its parochial aims. However, these groups also work within the framework of a unified, all-inclusive "party" that claims to represent the majority of the people. Accordingly, special-interest groups in communist societies must be distinguished from those in the more traditional power-oriented regimes.

In general, the discrete organizational patterns of special-interest groups develop when the broad social strata are held at some remove from the center. This phenomenon is most common in societies whose centers are oriented to the traditional concepts of prestige and power, and is most pronounced if the central elite has such a firm hold on the society that fundamental change is generally accepted as unlikely.

Development of broad political organizations and activities

Discrete political organizations are weakened, and broader based and oriented political activities and organizations are enhanced by the major structural aspects and dimensions of modernization: economic development and differentiation, urbanization and social mobility, the concomitant development of new occupational groups, and the structural dislocation of old and new groups on the one hand and—above all—their impingement on the center on the other. The development of new groups and their economic and social dislocations need not (as we saw above) change their basic stratification orientations, but it may give rise to new and broader political ideologies and organizations. It may also be connected (as we have also seen) with keener perception of differentiations within the social order in terms of developed-underdeveloped and the equating of this dichotomy with class conflicts.

Thus the development of the major structural and symbolic aspects of modernization breaks down discrete patterns of political organization and enables politics to discover a broader basis.[9]

[8] R. Conquest, *Power and Policy in the U.S.S.R.* (London: The Macmillan Company, 1961), and F. C. Barghoorn, *Politics in the U.S.S.R.* (Boston: Little, Brown and Co., 1966).

[9] See T. Parsons, *Structure and Process in Modern Societies* (New York: The Free Press, 1960), pt. 3; T. H. Marshall, *Class, Citizenship and Social Development* (Garden City, N.Y.: Doubleday & Company, Inc., 1964), pp. 65–123; and S. N. Eisenstadt, *Modernization, Protest and Change*, op. cit., ch. 1.

However, the nature of the resultant political organizations necessarily varies from one modern society to the next, and thus we
must consider the causes of this variation.

Class orientation

What, then, are the conditions under which these broad
political organizations emphasize class interests and values?
Although such emphasis can be detected in most modern political
programs, it always exists in conjunction with religious, nationalistic, ethnic, linguistic, or primordial cultural elements, any of
which may either oppose or reinforce the class element. Hence it
is of special importance, from the point of view of our analysis, to
specify some of the conditions under which the class element
comes to dominate the others.

It is customary to equate the development of class movements
with working-class or socialist movements (though they are not
necessarily the same), and the times and places allotted to this
development are usually nineteenth- and twentieth-century Europe, Latin America, and Asia. Although the obvious expressions
of class-oriented political activity are a product of the rise of the
working classes, it should be borne in mind that a vigorous
ideology of class and class struggle (though a bourgeois, not a
socialist ideology) had developed during the French Revolution.[10]
(Indeed, as a result of the revolutions and counterrevolutions of
1848 it became decidedly conservative in its attitude toward the
working classes.)[11] The class element was also part of the programs of the agrarian parties that developed in Scandinavia,
Australia, and some of the Balkan countries between the two
world wars, and similar parties and class issues seem to have
arisen later in Latin America.[12]

[10]See, for instance, S. Ossowski, "Different Conceptions of Social Class," in R. Bendix and
S. M. Lipset, eds., *Class, Status and Power;* D. Thomson, *Europe since Napoleon* (New York:
Alfred A. Knopf, Inc., 1962), pt. 1, and *The Democratic Ideal in England and France* (London:
Cambridge University Press, 1941); and Alexis De Tocqueville, *The Old Regime and the
French Revolution* (Garden City, N.Y.: Doubleday & Company, Inc., Anchor Books, 1955), pt. 2
and ch. 10.

[11]For the revolutions of 1848 and their aftermath see D. Thomson, *Europe since Napoleon,* op.
cit., pt. 3, and J. L. Talmon, *Romanticism and Revolt: Europe 1815–1898* (London: Thames &
Hudson Ltd., 1968).

[12]For the agrarian parties in Scandinavia see D. A. Rustow, "Scandinavia: Working Multiparty
Systems," in S. Neumann, ed., *Modern Political Parties,* op. cit., p. 182, and the articles on
Scandinavia in Allardt and Lettunen, *Cleavages, Ideologies and Party Systems,* op. cit., and in
S. M. Lipset and S. Rokkan, eds., *Party Systems and Voter Alignments,* op. cit.

As has been indicated, class politics takes many forms, but at this stage we shall refrain from analyzing these differences and will, instead, attempt to outline the conditions under which emphasis on class—whether bourgeois, peasant, or working class—becomes an important or even predominant element in the wider forms of political organization.

Most explanations of this development are stated in terms of the emergence of new economic and status groups and the accompanying dislocation of traditional society—of the misery of some groups and the discrepancy between their rising expectations and the inequities of the emerging social and economic structure, with its emphasis on wealth.[13] Such explanations no doubt contain strong elements of truth, but they do not *specify* the conditions under which the politics of class—as distinguished from other types of political orientation—develops in modern societies.

Of special importance, it seems, are the far-reaching changes in the structure of economic institutions that manifest themselves as new economic and occupational dimensions. In addition to general economic expansion, these manifestations include far-reaching changes in the distribution of control over economic resources and in the full range of differential life chances. Equally important is the demand of some of the groups undergoing such changes and dislocations for a particular type of access to the center (which, of course, is also changing). Inasmuch as the groups that demand a highly specific kind of access have evolved broad patterns of goals, identities, and attitudes that differ greatly from those of the center, they want, above all, to change the existing order to conform with their orientations. And because their new dimensions of collective identity are based on social or cultural attributes that are perceived as common to all classes, these groups, in their struggle to change the center, develop programs that are based on, and expressed in terms of, social class.

In contrast, the groups that defend the existing system usually place much less emphasis on class elements and symbols. The notion of class, after all, always implies a divisive element in the perception of a social order, and it is in the interest of conservative groups to emphasize elements that can be seen as shared by all classes. Among these elements are the primordial symbols of

[13]For discussions of some of these themes see J. C. Davis, "Toward a Theory of Revolution," *American Sociological Review,* 27 (1962): 5–19.

collective identity (see p. 43) and such universal values as the desire for social order.[14]

Three illustrations of the development of strong class orientations (under the conditions specified above) are most significant. The first of these is the largely successful attempt of the European and American bourgeoisie to bestow the dimension of centrality on economic, professional, and related cultural activities, which hitherto had been reserved to traditional prestige or power elites.[15] The second illustration is the attempt of portions of the European peasantry (especially in Scandinavia and the Balkans) to uphold both their economic autonomy and their autonomous group prestige against the encroachments of the modern national center.[16] The class symbolism of these peasant groups has stressed the "primitive" and "primordial" qualities with which they sought to imbue the center. Finally, and by far the most successful, there are the attempts of working-class and socialist groups to imbue the center with new economic and social orientations, especially economic equality, social security, and changes in the structure of economic control.[17] These groups have also tried to increase the prestige of participation in the broad collectivity vis-à-vis the more limited prestige and individualistic economic orientations of bourgeois centers.

Other types of political orientation: ethnic, regional, and nationalistic

In contrast to class-oriented political programs, other types of broad political orientation, which are also related to the demand

---

[14]S. M. Lipset, "Class, Politics and Religion in Modern Society: The Dilemma of the Conservatives," in S. M. Lipset, ed., *Revolution and Counterrevolution*, op. cit., pp. 89–129; K. Mannheim, "Conservative Thought," *Essays on Sociology and Social Psychology* (London: Routledge & Kegan Paul Ltd., 1953), pp. 74–165, and S. M. Lipset, "Class, Politics and Religion in Modern Society," in S. M. Lipset, ed., *Revolution and Counterrevolution*, op. cit., pp. 159–179.

[15]Karl Marx, *The Eighteenth Brumaire of Louis Bonaparte*, Daniel de Leon, trans., 3rd ed. (Chicago: C. H. Kerr, 1919), and D. Thomson, *Europe Since Napoleon*, op. cit., pt. 5.

[16]See the chapter on Scandinavia in S. M. Lipset and S. Rokkan, eds., *Party Systems and Voter Alignments*, op. cit.; J. Tomasevich, *Peasants, Politics and Economic Change in Yugoslavia* (Stanford, Calif.: Stanford University Press, 1955); R. Trouton, *Peasant Renaissance in Yugoslavia* (London: Routledge & Kegan Paul Ltd., 1952); and H. L. Roberts, *Rumania: Political Problems of an Agrarian State* (New Haven, Conn.: Yale University Press, 1958).

[17]For the spread of socialism see D. Thomson, *Europe Since Napoleon*, op. cit. pt. 4 and 5. For the welfare state see T. H. Marshall, *Class, Citizenship and Social Development*, op. cit. pt. 3.

for easier access to the center, have also been associated with modernization and social differentiation. Generally, these types arise when the identity of the political collectivity vis-à-vis other collectivities is in question (not just the former's internal orientations), so that the resultant political programs are seldom dominated by considerations of class. On the contrary, the results are more likely to be nationalistic and ethnic movements, which may overlap the class programs of religious, tribal, or ethnic groups. This situation is found, for instance, in Canada, Belgium, and to some degree in Italy and many of the new Asian and African states.[18]

Similarly, there is little likelihood of class-oriented political activity in groups that are undergoing social dislocation and are primarily interested in enlarging their participation in a sociocultural order and its basic orientations.[19] There are numerous examples of bourgeois and working-class groups, developed independent of class orientations, that seek to do no more than increase their share in a center whose basic orientations they accept and enlarge their access to it. Also, professional or workers' groups may compete in a particular market without developing class consciousness, especially if the basic control of economic resources is not at stake.[20]

Strata, centers, and class orientations

In principle, therefore, very few groups or strata (with the possible exception of the aristocracy) are more prone than others

---

[18]S. D. Clark, *The Developing Canadian Community* (Toronto: University of Toronto Press, 1962); F. E. Oppenheim, "Belgium: Party Cleavages and Compromise," in S. Neumann, ed., *Modern Political Parties*, op. cit., pp. 395–421; I. Wallenstein, "The Decline of the Party in Single-Party African States," in J. La Polambara and M. Weiner, eds., *Political Parties and Political Development*, op. cit., pp. 201–217; and S. M. Lipset, "Political Cleavages in 'Developed' and 'Emerging' Polities," and "Class, Politics and Religion in Modern Society," in S. M. Lipset, ed., *Revolution and Counterrevolution*, op. cit.

[19]A good illustration of this can be found in F. Ford, *Robe and Sword* (New York: Harper & Row, Publishers, 1967). For general discussions see D. Thomson, *Europe Since Napoleon*, op. cit., pt. 5, and G. D. H. Cole, *Studies in Class Structure* (London: Routledge & Kegan Paul Ltd., 1955), esp. chs. 1 and 4. See also the citations in no. 20 below.

[20]See A. Pizzorno, "The Individualistic Mobilization of Europe," in S. R. Graubard, ed., *A New Europe?* (Boston, Mass.: Houghton Mifflin Company, 1964), pp. 199–224; R. Dahrendorf, "Recent Changes in the Class Structure of European Societies," ibid., pp. 224–270; S. M. Lipset, "The Changing Class Structure and Contemporary European Politics," ibid., pp. 271–303; and A. Touraine, "Management and the Working Class in Western Europe," ibid., pp. 304–335.

to develop class orientations and symbolism. And therefore we can conclude that it is not so much the economic situation of a group or category as its relative structural position (in terms of the variables specified above) that determines its degree of class consciousness. In western civilization, the bourgeoisie and intellectuals, who were the first to think of themselves as classes in the modern sense (if we exclude the traditional aristocracy), were followed by the working class and the revolutionary elites. It is clear, however, that these attitudes toward class could change as their structural positions changed. Thus even working-class groups and revolutionary elites, having gained access to the center and incorporated some of their orientations, tend either to deemphasize their class orientations or transpose them into symbols of internal conservatism. This has happened both in Soviet Russia and in a number of the Social Democratic regimes, including Great Britain, Sweden, and lately in West Germany.

Just as, in principle, almost every stratum is subject to class politics, the rise of class politics, in every society, seems to depend on the major orientation of its center or centers. In the latter instance, the crucial variable is the structural location of the centers and their incumbent elites vis-à-vis the two structural processes that, between them, virtually define modernization: social mobility and the impingement of new groups on the center. But the severity of problems of modernization, which may be sufficient to instigate the process of class politics, does not depend solely on the actions of the center.

In general, these problems are most acute when the demand for access to the center is combined with an attempt to change its basic orientation, and when the center offers strong resistance. This is most likely to happen when the center is power oriented or when a weak center is oriented toward conserving its resources. It is less likely when the process of structural differentiation and change in the structural control of resources is no longer connected with the struggle for access to centers or attempts to change their orientations but, instead, occurs within established centers in which participation has already been assured. This situation is found most often in the late stages of modernization or industrialization, when, in principle, access to the center has been attained by the broadest strata of the society and the centers have attained a large measure of control over the economic structure.

It is at this stage, then, that problems arise over access to new positions and resources, rather than overall control of the economic sphere. In such situations, two different combinations of status and class politics may develop. Stronger emphasis may be placed on specific points of class interest, so that only lip service is paid to class symbolism, and this is most likely to happen in the older, firmly established socialist parties. The other tendency, which is especially common among students, intellectuals, and various professional groups, is toward political protest that focuses upon problems of group autonomy in institutional settings and the possibility of new forms of cultural expression, and is often related to a total negation of the existing center and any possibility of changing it from within. Because this form of protest tends to dissociate the cultural from the political and social dimensions, class symbolism does not play a major part in it. Also the negation of the existing system is not expressed in class terms, although there may develop a tendency toward some symbolic alliance with faraway (i.e., Chinese, Latin American) class symbols of political struggle.

BASIC TYPES OF CLASS-ORIENTED POLITICAL ORGANIZATIONS AND ORIENTATIONS

In the preceding analysis we talked about class-oriented political organizations in general terms, without much differentiation among them. Although most of them have several elements in common (which are similar to those that can be found in all modern political groups and organizations), we will specify only three of these elements: (1) professional and trade union organizations that are oriented to attaining specific economic interests, such as higher wages, better social security, better bargaining positions, etc.; (2) broad political organization (in parties or movements) that, in turn, attempts to develop broad appeals to public opinion on the basis of class symbolism; and (3) orientation toward change that is couched in terms of class symbolism.

The ways in which these elements have been combined, and the importance of each, have varied greatly in the history of modern political movements. These movements, moreover, have differed (1) in the degree to which the "purer" special-interest groups (such as trade unions) have allied themselves with the broader political groups, (2) in the emphasis they have given each component of political organization, (3) in their specific political aims, and (4) in their perceptions of social orders in general and sociopolitical changes in particular.

Nonpolitical class orientations

The first type of orientations that should be distinguished in terms of these criteria are those of large organizations that have relatively clear-cut class or orientation interests—professional associations, for example, or peasant cooperatives. These groups are characterized by the predominance of specific interests and aims, and they are usually allied with broader political groups and orientations. However, because the nature of this alliance may vary widely among different types of political organizations, two basic subtypes may be distinguished. One of these, which is seen most clearly in the United States but can also be found in other countries, is characterized by congeries of professional and trade union activities that are only loosely related to a political party.

An organization of this kind does not tend to merge into political parties. In fact, its political allegiance often crosses party lines because the different groups in question tend to pursue their respective class interests without much recourse to political organizations. The principal class interests are (1) better marketing and bargaining positions and a larger share of resources, and (2) the favorable (or at least nondiscriminatory) regulation of access to highly valued positions.

The preferred approach in this subtype is to manipulate the institutional markets rather than change the basic policies of the political center. Nor are political and economic demands usually couched in broad class terms and symbols. If, however, class symbolism develops, it is largely confined to the social sphere and emphasizes the possibility of overlapping classes rather than divisions. Nor do many class elements enter into the political symbolism of such groups.[21] (On pp. 226–227 we will analyze the conditions that give rise to this type of nonpolitical class orientation.)

Class and organizational orientations

The other subtype of class-oriented organization is characterized by a close association between professional and trade union interests and political parties. It is typified by the political parties

[21]See R. R. Alford, *Party and Society* (Chicago: Rand McNally & Co., 1963); L. Reissman, *Class in American Society* (New York: The Free Press, 1959); and J. A. Kahl, *The American Class Structure* (New York: Rinehart & Co., 1959).

and movements that arose among the bourgeoisie and intelligentsia in early nineteenth-century Europe and by the socialist and labor movements and parties that developed in most western and central European countries after the 1860s.[22] Although most of these movements were in one way or another associated with professional and political elements, each element retained some autonomy of its own. Indeed, even within the revolutionary socialist parties the trade union elements have retained a significant measure of autonomy vis-à-vis the central party elements.

The most important aims of these movements and parties have been changes in (1) the basic marketing and class situations of their members, (2) the distribution of social rewards, and (3) the rules of access to the center and other highly valued social positions—all of which have been manifested under many forms of political demands. For example, political means have been used to bolster the bargaining position of trade unions and, through various taxation policies, to change the patterns for the distribution of resources. The nationalization of industries and the restructuring of monetary policy, though rather more ambitious aims, also come under the same category, as do many so-called social policies, especially in the field of social welfare. Changes have also been sought in the control structure of industrial enterprises, and this movement has become associated with such slogans as Industrial Democracy and Worker Participation in the management and profit distribution of industry.[23]

These various aims have often been related to demands for changes in the rules of access to the center, as is evident in the struggles for the extension of suffrage, for new orientations to the center, and for the creation of new types of collective goals. At the same time, these aims bore the distinctive stamp of different class movements and therefore differed in their formulation, promulgation, and emphasis on class symbols.

Almost by definition, most of these movements emphasized the divisive nature of social classes and the social order and the importance of restructuring the latter in terms of class symbols. Moreover, the identity of many of these movements during their most intensive political development was expressed in the terms and ideology of class or class warfare. Indeed, the avowed aim of these class-oriented political organizations was the total transformation of the social order in ways very similar to those

[22]See D. Thomson, *Europe Since Napoleon,* op. cit., pt. 3–5.

[23]See the papers by A. Touraine and A. Pizzorno in S. R. Graubard, ed., *A New Europe?* op. cit.

espoused by the revolutionary groups.[24] However, except for such marginal cases as the Social Democrats in imperial Germany and the syndicalist groups in France, these ideologies were rarely— and only very briefly—translated into actual programs.[25]

Class symbols were more readily accepted within social orders that permitted common participation of various strata and the attainment of diverse stratificational goals. Within most of these organizations, therefore, dissociation or dichotomies developed between the more specific stratificational aims of their various components and the more totalistic class ideologies. But even more important, perhaps, was the dichotomy that developed at the policy level over attempts to change only the rules of access to positions and attempts to create new positions. Also, these divisions were usually paralleled by attempts to redistribute resources, on the one hand, and attempts to increase resources in general. It is not surprising, therefore, that many social movements have split and foundered over one or more of these issues.

Revolutionary and extremist class orientations

Another modern subtype of politicized class organizations is usually labeled extremist or revolutionary, and the two most interesting species—from the point of view of our analysis—are the anarcho-syndicalist and the political-revolutionary movements,[26] the best-known example of the latter being the Russian Bolshevik party (and the parties set up elsewhere in imitation of it).[27] In contrast to other types of class-oriented organizations, syndicalist and revolutionary parties are characterized by (1) a single or unique type of organizational unit and (2) a detailed program for overthrowing or completely changing a socioeconomic and political system.

The dominant syndicalist unit is the trade union local, which is also the basic unit for political activity and the class symbol of

[24]See D. Thomson, *Europe Since Napoleon*, op. cit., pt. 5.

[25]Ibid.

[26]For the first types of such revolutionary movements see the articles "Anarchism" and "Syndicalism" in *International Encyclopedia of the Social Sciences* (New York: The Macmillan Company, 1968).

[27]See, for instance, L. Schapiro, *The Communist Party of the Soviet Union* (New York: Random House, Inc., 1959). For the development of the party see A. Ulam, *The Bolsheviks* (New York: The Macmillan Company, 1965).

the revolutionary aspects of the movement. The aims of anarcho-syndicalism, insofar as they go beyond working conditions and power relationships at the local level, are to weaken a society's political centers to the point that they will virtually disappear.

In revolutionary political movements, the political party predominates. Trade union elements are wholly subordinated to the party, which is the sole political center and focus of revolutionary activity. However, the party program usually calls for the establishment of a new political center and a new pattern of economic and political control, and its prime emphasis is on changing the structure of economic enterprise.

Although both types of movements are similar in that they tend to subordinate narrow class interests to the goal of overthrowing a regime, revolutionary movements and parties emphasize the creation of new centers whereas anarcho-syndicalists seek to abolish centers and the systems of central control.

Needless to say, history provides many examples of overlapping and ties among the different types of class-oriented political parties and movements (pp. 219–220). For our analysis, however, the most interesting overlappings are those that developed in modern times in Spain and many Latin American and Asian countries. The resultant situation was frequently a rather uneasy modus vivendi between syndicalist or anarchistic trade unions on the one hand and broadly based political movements or parties on the other. Sometimes these factions merged for brief periods—without, however, renouncing either their political autonomy or goals. Inevitably, this led to constant splits and purges.[28]

The basic aims of most of these movements can be summarized under three headings: (1) changing the rules of access to, and with the help of, the center; (2) broadening the bases of the collectivity whose prestige the center may represent—without infusing new orientations of active commitment to the center, or changing the attitudes of the broader groups' center to a broader sociocultural order, or (least of all) changing the low level of commitment to the center; and (3) changing the pattern for the distribution of resources.[29] However, insofar as these groups

[28]For Spain see J. J. Linz, "The Party System of Spain," in S. M. Lipset and S. Rokkan, eds., *Party Systems and Voter Alignments*, op. cit. For Latin America see V. Alba, *Politics and the Labor Movement in Latin America* (Stanford, Calif.: Stanford University Press, 1968). For Asia see S. Rose, *Socialism in Southern Asia* (London: London University Press, 1958).

[29]See, for instance, V. Alba, *Politics and the Labor Movement in Latin America*, op. cit., and A. Touraine and D. Pecaut, "Working Class Consciousness and Economic Development," *Studies in Comparative International Development*, vol. 3.

approach the center, they tend to oscillate between their desire for immediate and specific rewards and their desire for ever more nebulously conceived changes in the overall system, whereupon intense ideological and political conflicts may develop that often have little to do with restructuring the center or opening new avenues of participation in it.[30]

CLASS SYMBOLISM

What are the conditions that give rise to class-oriented political organizations and the various types of class symbolism?

We have seen that this symbolism, broadly speaking, regards the existing social order as fully capable of accommodating diverse class elements or, alternatively, regards the pursuit of class interests as leading inevitably to the total overthrow of the sociopolitical order. In other words, class symbolism is either reformist or revolutionary. Thus, because class symbolism replicates social attitudes, the most important attitudinal dimensions are those of a class and the center and its elites. Accordingly, a revolutionary or a reformist class ideology develops largely in response to the center's reaction to participative demands from peripheral groups.

Centers and revolutionary class symbolism

Clearly, if not axiomatically, a closed center and a ruling elite that conceive the periphery as a distant and passive entity are likely to encourage the growth of revolutionary class symbolism and ideology. Several types of centers may produce this effect: the traditional, power-oriented type, such as czarist Russia; the power- and culture-oriented type, such as imperial China; and the weak, prestige- and power-oriented type, such as Spain and some of the Latin American countries (which we have mentioned only in passing), whose conception of the scope and activity of the center is very limited.

Other important factors in radicalization are social dislocation among the major strata and elites and various features of modernization. Because modernization proceeds in different

---

[30]See V. Alba, *Politics and the Labor Movement in Latin America*, op. cit., and A. Touraine, "Social Mobility, Class Relationships and Nationalism in Latin America," *Studies in Comparative International Development*, vol. 1.

ways in different societies, the initial and purely administrative modernization of the political center may evince little capacity for symbolic transformation, and this failing may be accompanied by a low rate of economic development. Thus, because of maximum expectation and minimum fulfillment, extremist class politics is almost inevitable. As for social dislocation, syndicalist orientations tend to develop when skilled worker and professional groups are more or less isolated from the rest of society (though they often forge strong ties with similar groups in other countries). Examples of this phenomenon are various workers' unions in Spain and Italy. Similar conditions in rural areas give rise to peasant radicalism, as in Finland, pre-Franco Spain, and some Latin American countries.[31]

Finally, revolutionary parties attract what might be called (for the most part) the secondary aristocratic, intellectual, and professional bureaucratic groups that have become socially dislocated by the processes of economic and administrative modernization.[32]

Centers and reformist class symbolism

Reformist-type class attitudes and symbolism seem to develop under quite different conditions, particularly when elements of a ruling elite, though committed to the center, either foster or do not preclude the participation of peripheral groups in the center. These societies are usually polycentric and culture oriented.

Closely related to this development is the relationship of elites with nonelite groups that (for whatever reason) are undergoing social dislocation. Particularly in western Europe, dislocated but highly self-conscious groups after some struggle, have been able, because of some initial presuppositions of common identity, to attain access to the center and reach some sort of accommodation with the older elites. Therefore certain patterns of social mobility and modernization, based on continuous development

---

[31]J. J. Linz, "The Party System of Spain," in S. M. Lipset and S. Rokkan, eds., *Party Systems and Voter Alignments,* op. cit. For Finland see E. Allardt and P. Pesonen, "Cleavages in Finnish Politics," *Party Systems and Voter Alignments.* For Latin America see V. Alba, *Politics and the Labor Movement in Latin America,* and A. Touraine, "Social Mobility, Class Relationships and Nationalism in Latin America," op. cit.

[32]V. C. Nahirny, "The Russian Intelligentsia: From Men of Ideas to Men of Action," *Comparative Studies in History and Society,* 4 (1962): 403–435; M. Raeff, *Origins of the Russian Intelligentsia* (New York: Harcourt Brace Jovanovich, Inc., 1966); A. Ulam, *The Bolsheviks,* op. cit.

in all sectors of an economy, also favor the emergence of reformist as opposed to revolutionary movements, as does a former political modernization of the center and development of common national and political identity as opposed to merely administrative centralization. And thus, although many groups have been dislocated and class consciousness has been on the rise, the resultant class symbolism has for the most part been expressed in reformist terms and class conflict has generally moved in a reformist direction. This has been the case in most of western Europe.[33]

Insofar as these various tendencies or conditions have been lacking, labor and socialistic movements, with fewer reformist and more revolutionary class orientations have appeared. In Germany, for instance, where the center was relatively inaccessible to the various groups, and especially to new orientations, where the dominant groups were relatively closed, and where the tempo of dislocation was somewhat more intensive and unbalanced, a more revolutionary and monolithic class conception and organization developed among the working-class movements (but not among the bourgeois intelligentsia).[34]

In France and Italy, the combination of relatively weak or divided centers and very uneven sectoral development in the societies at large gave rise to syndicalism. In Spain, a more extreme development of this pattern was associated with the extremist ideology of anarcho-syndicalism.[35] In Finland, the uneven development of different parts of the agrarian sector gave rise to the rather paradoxical emergence of class radicalism in the economically backward peasant regions.[36]

---

[33]See M. Dogan "Political Cleavage and Social Stratification in France and Italy," in S. M. Lipset and S. Rokkan, eds., *Party Systems and Voter Alignments*, op. cit.; W. G. Runciman, *Relative Deprivation and Social Justice* (London: Routledge & Kegan Paul Ltd., 1966), pt. 2; G. D. H. Cole, *Studies in Class Structure*, op. cit.; H. Perkin, *The Origins of Modern English Society* (London: Routledge & Kegan Paul Ltd., 1968); and D. Thomson, *Europe Since Napoleon*, op. cit., p. 5.

[34]A. Mohler, *Die konservative Revolution in Deutschland, 1918–1932* (Stuttgart: F. Vorwerk, 1950); Carl Schorske, *German Social Democracy* (Cambridge, Mass.: Harvard University Press, 1955).
G. Roth, *The Social Democrats in Imperial Germany* (Totawa, N.J.: Bedminster Press, Inc., (1963).

[35]For France and Italy, see M. Dogan, "Political Cleavage and Social Stratification in France and Italy," in S. M. Lipset and S. Rokkan, eds., *Party Systems and Voter Alignments*, op. cit. For Spain see J. J. Linz, "The Party System of Spain," *Party Systems and Voter Alignments*.

[36]See E. Allardt and P. Pesonen, "Cleavage in Finnish Politics," *Party Systems and Voter Alignments*.

Reformist class symbolism and the social bases of class politics

Within the general framework of reformist class orientations and their political expression, several very important connotations of symbolism can be discerned, of which the most important are (1) the extent to which society is conceived as divisive classes or as overlapping and gradually merging classes, (2) the degree to which divisiveness is manifested in social and political fields, (3) the relationship of class symbolism to the stratification aims of various groups, and (4) the type of political organization to which such orientations are related.

It seems that the most important factors in these differences are the major orientations of the center and their relationship to the basic desiderata and identities of the major groups that are experiencing structural dislocation and therefore tend to develop more active orientations to the center. Divisiveness, especially in the political field, seems to be minimal in societies that are characterized by a strong, open center and strong economic orientations, such as the United States.[37] Class consciousness is nevertheless strong, but for the most part it is conceived in social terms rather than in terms of political symbolism (see p. 219). However, this class consciousness is connected with a specific type of stratification aim and its political expression.

As we have seen, the major motivation for stratification changes in the United States has been to improve one's position vis-à-vis markets, either directly or by controlling the relevant ascriptive or access processes. Again, such changes are usually effected by manipulation of the economic and power markets and only secondarily through reevaluation of central policies as they apply to the basic attributes of social and cultural orders. Manipulation, in turn, has usually been the tactic of discrete special-interest groups acting only in loose association with political parties. Changes that stem from central legislation, on the other hand, have usually been effected by political parties. Thus in the United States, as Alford has pointed out, class voting—that is, the homogeneity of class support for political activity—has been less pronounced than in Britain or Australia, and more pronounced than in Canada.[38]

[37]E. E. Schattschneider, "The United States: The Functional Approach to the Party Government," in S. Neumann, ed., *Modern Political Parties*, op. cit., pp. 194–218, and Robert R. Alford, *Party and Society*, op. cit.

[38]See R. R. Alford, "Class Voting in the Anglo-American Political Systems," in S. M. Lipset and S. Rokkan, eds., *Party Systems and Voter Alignments*, op. cit., pp. 67–93.

Several factors explain this difference between the United States and other societies. In the United States, of course, the problem of access to the political center was solved almost simultaneously with the initial development of the national polity and, moreover, at a time when the control of economic resources was widely dispersed. The concentration of economic control occurred *after* the problem of access to the center had been solved, and after the new economic orientations of the center had been established. Thus the strong emphasis on economic orientations, together with continuous economic expansion, created a nonpolitical middle-class ethos that involved multiple interlacing allegiances. At the same time, it created even more marginal and—till lately—apathetic lower groups.[39]

The situation was different in England, the Netherlands, and the Scandinavian countries, where the initial orientations of the center consisted of limited social prestige and/or participation in a tradition, together with the gradual infusion of new economic orientations. The aims of the new and active middle-class groups were primarily oriented to incorporating of their prestige within the center and to increasing the importance of economic orientations in the center. Later, the working classes were able to infuse broad social security orientations in the center.[40] Unlike the situation in the United States, the problems that accompanied changes in the structure of economic control developed concomitantly with the problems of access to the center, and sometimes even before these problems were solved.

These circumstances gave rise to the perception of the sociopolitical order in terms of class order, and also gave much stronger emphasis to the divisive characteristics of class—even if, insofar as the center became accessible, this conception was generally of the reformist type. Thus the basic aims of class movements in politics were of a much different nature than those of societies whose basic aims were "economically" orientated.

Among the latter, the most important goals were self-serving changes in the structure of control over economic resources and the life chances of the various groups in the occupational markets.

---

[39]Ibid.

[40]H. Valen and D. Katz, *Political Parties in Norway: A Community Study* (London: Tavistock Publications Ltd., 1964); D. A. Rustow "Scandinavia: Working Multiparty Systems," in S. Neumann, ed., *Modern Political Parties*, op. cit., pp. 169–193; S. Rokkan, "Geography, Religion and Social Class," in S. M. Lipset and S. Rokkan, eds., *Party Systems and Voter Alignments*, op. cit., pp. 367–444; O. Kirchheimer, "The Transformation of the Western European Party Systems," in J. La Polambara and M. Weiner, eds., *Political Parties and Political Development*, op. cit., pp. 177–201.

These demands have been here, however, usually also closely related to some more concrete demands to changes in market positions and in the distribution of concrete economic rewards. Both goals were attained through changes in the rules of access to positions and reevaluation of the basic attributes of the sociocultural order vis-à-vis the various groups and their relationship to the center.

From the point of view of political organization, these European societies have been characterized by the development of political structure with a high degree of autonomous political association, activity, and organization, but strong political parties have coordinated these various activities.[41] Also, their political organizations are based on heterogeneous class and political allegiance. At the same time, however, as Alford has shown, voting patterns reveal a high level of class orientation, awareness and allegiance.[42]

Similar expressions of class awareness have also been noted in collectivity-oriented societies, such as Australia, Israel, and Sweden, where the centers have adopted strong "social democratic" orientations, emphasizing the prestige of the total collectivity and the welfare of its members.[43] From the very beginning, the centers of these societies have upheld collective prestige, but, because of historical reasons, this orientation has been couched in terms of class symbolism. In Australia, this was due to the development of a strong collectivity that is oriented to the labor movement. In Israel, the center's cultural and ideological orientation also upholds socialist-labor values.[44]

The class symbolism upheld by the political parties of these societies was soon adopted by the "establishments," which tailored it to the social consciousness of the major groups and the political symbolism of the parties, thereby weakening its revolutionary content but at the same time adapting it to more specific and pragmatic objectives.

[41]See the material presented in S. Neumann, ed., *Modern Political Parties*, op. cit.

[42]R. Alford, *Party and Society*, op. cit.

[43]G. M. Carter, "The Commonwealth Overseas: Variations on a British Theme—Australia and New Zealand," in S. Neumann, ed., *Modern Political Parties*, op. cit., pp. 85–105; S. N. Eisenstadt, *Israeli Society* (London: Weidenfeld and Nicolson Ltd., 1967); R. N. Rosencrance, "The Radical Culture of Australia," in L. Hartz, ed., *The Founding of New Societies* (New York: Harcourt Brace Jovanovich, Inc., 1962); K. B. Mayer, "Social Stratification in Two Equalitarian Societies: Australia and the United States," in R. Bendix and S. M. Lipset, eds., *Class, Status and Power*, op. cit., pp. 149–161.

[44]Ibid.

Ascriptive class orientation

The last type of class-oriented political organization that we will deal with is most often found in Latin America. It is the product of an uneasy modus vivendi between populist-type mass parties and smaller, more narrowly defined radical (often syndicalist) groups. Or, in a variant form, it may group broad types of professional and trade union organizations in an uneasy alliance with a populist party whose basic orientations may contain strong class elements or symbolism.[45] In any event, their common denominator—whatever their "explicit" class ideology—is a closed form of stratum or class segregation (even if they are made up of rather broadly based status groups).

Four conditions facilitate this kind of organization:
1. Relatively weak centers, which are oriented toward upholding traditional patterns of prestige and privilege;
2. Widespread political mobilization, combined with a low level of economic development;
3. Urbanization, despite a low level of industrialization; and
4. Structural-economic dislocations that emphasize the segregation of the various sectors.

The basic aims of political movements that develop under these circumstances are changes in the distribution of rewards by the center and in the rules of access to the center. Thus the major emphasis is on introducing a new kind of ascriptive criteria (see pp. 62–64), not on restructuring the center.

SUMMARY

In this chapter we have analyzed some of the most important aspects of modern strata formation: the ways in which it becomes interwoven with political movements. At the same time, we have seen that a major characteristic of modern strata formation is its open and legitimate connection with political orientations and activities.

Following these general indications, we have analyzed (1) the major ways in which modern political activities are related to class symbolism and organized on class bases and (2) the conditions under which the various types of political activities tend to develop.

[45]See, for instance, F. Weffort, "State and Mass in Brazil," *Studies in Comparative International Development*, vol. 2.

A central problem in our analysis has been the conditions under which class symbolism and orientation, as opposed to other types of symbols and orientations, have become foci of protest and political activity in modern societies.

We have seen that the development of class symbolism as a major focus of protest is closely related to attempts by dislocated social strata to improve their standing in various institutional spheres, together with assuring their access to the center and attempting to impart their major orientations to the center. Different combinations of these orientations, together with the reaction of the centers, in turn explain the different types of class symbolism and activities: the revolutionary, the syndicalist, the reformist, and the ascriptive.

Thus the crucial variable in the formation and orientation of class symbolism, and in the importance of class itself as a symbol of protest, is the interrelationship of the basic orientations of the broad strata and those of the center. Insofar as orientation to the center and access to it are important ingredients of the status orientations of large groups, and insofar as the center is sufficiently flexible to accept these orientations, class symbolism may become an important part of these groups' political orientation.

At this point we come to a paradoxical situation with regard to the relationship between the development of class symbolism and the intensity of class cleavages in the body politic. Although Alford's and Lipset's analyses have shown that class symbolism may be a constant component of mature and relatively stable modern social and political systems,[46] this is true only insofar as class symbolism, which tends to be (or become) of the reformist type, is both based on and related to broad status and class associations among closely related occupational groups—as against the more segregated types of status orientation in such groups.

Insofar as political orientations are developed by large groups or elites and are characterized by segregated status orientations, revolutionary types of class symbolism tend to develop. When these groups evince little commitment to the centers (as in Latin America), ascriptive types of class symbolism tend to develop.

In general, the greater the flexibility of the center—whether it is weak or strong—with regard to participation in it, and the greater the demand for such participation, the greater the tenden-

---

[46]A. Touraine, "Management and the Working Class in Western Europe," in S. Graubard, ed., *A New Europe?* op. cit.; A. Touraine, *La société post-industrielle* (Paris: Editions Denvel, 1969), pp. 41–119.

cy of various social movements and parties to develop strong class symbolism, even if their class basis is rather narrow.

On the other hand, insofar as a country's center and symbols are regarded as totally alien by the broad groups and strata, or access to the center has been attained, class symbolism tends to become less important as a focus of protest. Other symbols, such as ethnic, religious, or primordial and antinomian communal symbols (as in the latest type of protest in developed countries), tend to develop and to replace class symbolism. [47]

The close interrelationships between class and politics are perhaps the best illustration of the basic dynamics, as well as the variabilities, of strata formation in modern societies. Indeed, these relationships indicate that status or class has become a basic part not only of social reality but even the conception of this reality— of the self-definition and perception of social groups.

Nevertheless, the relationships between the different types of symbolism and other components of self-perception, as well as the ways in which stratification aims are connected with this symbolism, vary greatly and change continuously, according to a great variety of conditions (some of which we have analyzed).

For reasons of space, we have touched on only some of these conditions and aspects of class symbolism and activity in modern societies. And some of these, as we have noted, require further research and analysis.

Finally, we have observed that class symbolism and activity are not static quantities or factors; they change continuously, both in the highly developed, so-called postindustrial societies and in developing societies.

But at this point we are in danger of going beyond the scope of our analysis, in which our endeavor has been to explore and illuminate these problems in a systematic way.

[47]See S. M. Lipset, "Social Class," in *International Encyclopedia of the Social Sciences*, op. cit., and R. Alford, *Party and Society*, op. cit.

11

General Conclusions

Throughout this book we have presented brief and sometimes preliminary analyses of various major aspects and problems of social stratification, both in a general sense and by reference to specific cases. We have seen that social differentiation and stratification are basic and distinct aspects of social structures, and that social stratification is intimately connected with basic problems of sociological analysis, such as the nature of social order, the bases of social consensus, the place of force or persuasion in the maintenance of social order and institution building, and the very nature of social systems and their goals and needs.

We have also seen that social differentiation and stratification are factors in every society, but only under certain conditions do they develop as distinct and autonomous organizational and symbolic dimensions of social order. Moreover, the expression and characteristics of strata formation are subject to great variance, even among societies in which they have attained full and autonomous development.

Several variables have been found to be most important in determining the particular form of a stratification system:

1. The overall level of technological development, which determines the level of resources that are available for different positions and in the struggle for access to them;

2. The nature of legitimation in a social order (in which the distinction between traditional and nontraditional societies is most important);

3. A society's major value and goal orientations, and especially those of its centers; and

4. The institutional dynamics of different groups and categories of people—or the changes in their placement in institutional systems and in their relationship to the center.

The importance of these variables tends to vary in different societies. In traditional societies, the value orientations of the centers seem to be of greatest importance; in modern societies, the institutional dynamics of various groups and strata and their relationships to the center seem to be of greater importance in shaping their respective systems of stratification.

In no society, however, is the process of stratification and strata formation merely an abstract aspect of social structure that sociologists analyze in order to indicate the distribution of people according to institutional spheres or the control of resources. Stratification goes beyond this to the hierarchical ordering of social categories and groups, which is a basic component of people's self-identity and conception of themselves as members of societies, of the symbolism of social order, and of the way in which members of society tend to see themselves vis-à-vis others.

Nor is the symbolism of hierarchy peripheral or marginal in the galaxy of social and cultural symbols. In all societies and cultures, the problems of hierarchy—the bases and legitimation for arranging or ordering the relative positions of personal and cultural attributes—are some of the basic problems of social and cultural symbolism and the cultural definition of social order.

It is therefore no accident that strata formation is closely interwoven with the basic value orientations of societies in general and the structure of their centers in particular. The crucial role of the centers in the process of strata formation (which has been stressed throughout our analysis) stems primarily from their technical organization. Their importance also derives, in a secondary way, from their charismatic-symbolic dimensions.

Thus it is not by chance that the organizational, and especially the symbolical, aspects of strata formation are closely related to the orientations of the centers and—even more closely—to the bases of their legitimation, be they traditional or modern.

In traditional societies, the social order has usually been conceived as derived from a religious and metaphysical order, and the social hierarchy as derived from a similar or cosmic hierarchy. Accordingly, the social hierarchy's legitimation was represented in corresponding terms.

Hence, though the various forces of stratification were the cause of many social conflicts, struggles, and changes in every society, only rarely were these forces (or conflicts)—insofar as they focused on the central symbols of a society—conceived solely in terms of social class.

As we have seen, only in modern societies (and to some extent in the city-states of antiquity) has a social order been conceived in secular and autonomous terms, and thus class symbolism has become an autonomous dimension of the symbolic perception of social order, as well as a focus of social change and of attempts to transform social order.

But, as we have seen, the contents of this symbolism, its emphasis on conflict or hierarchies, and its importance among other symbols of social life has varied greatly among different societies and in different periods in the development of a modern society. And whatever importance class symbolism has as a focus of social self-consciousness and activity, the problems of inequality, the hierarchical ordering of human beings in their social interaction, and the legitimation of such interaction will always be with us.

These problems will no doubt always be part of social organization—of the ways in which people perceive themselves as social beings and, indeed, the social order itself. They are, of course, basic problems of the human condition—whatever the changes in its external appearance. Nevertheless, the understanding and exposition of these changes is a major function of sociological study and analysis.

Selected Readings

[Books available in paperbound editions are indicated by an asterisk.]

For discussions of the general problems raised in "Social Roles and Social Structure" and "Social Order and the Individual" the student should consult M. J. Levy, Jr., *The Structure of Society* (Princeton University Press, 1952), H. M. Johnson, *Sociology: A Systematic Introduction* (Harcourt Brace Jovanovich, Inc., 1960), and K. Davis, *Human Society* (The Macmillan Company, 1949). The best illustrations of these same problems, as treated in classical sociological analysis, can be found in Emile Durkheim's *The Division of Labor in Society** (hardbound: The Macmillan Company, 1933; softbound: The Free Press, 1964), *From Max Weber: Essays in Sociology** (hardbound: Grosset & Dunlap, Inc., 1946; softbound: Oxford University Press, 1958), edited by H. Gerth and C. W. Mills, and *Charisma and Institution Building: Selections From Max Weber** (University of Chicago Press, 1968), edited by S. N. Eisenstadt.

The particular problem of the charismatic dimension of centers is discussed in E. A. Shils, "Centre and Periphery," *The Logic of Personal Knowledge: Essays Presented to Michael Po-*

lanyi (Routledge & Kegan Paul Ltd, 1961), "Charisma, Order and Status," *American Sociological Review* 30, no. 2 (April 1965), 199–213, and S. N. Eisenstadt's "Charisma and Institution Building" which is the introduction to *Charisma and Institution Building: Selections From Max Weber.**

In Talcott Parsons' *The Social System* (The Free Press, 1951) and S. N. Eisenstadt's *Essays in Comparative Institutions* (John Wiley & Sons, Inc., 1965) are found analyses of the basic aspects of institution building. It is also useful to refer to the readings cited for Chapters 1 and 2 in order to obtain a more complete view of the subject.

The basic work done on the analysis of social stratification has been collected in *Class, Status and Power* (The Free Press, 1966), edited by R. Bendix and S. M. Lipset. Special attention should be given to part 1. For further discussion of the topic, *Social Stratification* (Harcourt Brace Jovanovich, Inc., 1957) by B. Barber, and *Social Stratification** (Prentice-Hall, Inc., 1967) by M. Tumin are recommended. Talcott Parsons' article, "A Revised Analytical Approach to the Theory of Social Stratification" which appears in *Essays in Sociological Theory* (The Free Press, 1954) should also be noted, as well as *Relative Deprivation and Social Justice* (University of California Press, 1966) by W. G. Runciman. *Power and Privilege* (McGraw-Hill Book Company, 1966) by G. Lenski also is applicable to this subject. See also the article by S. M. Lipset, "Social Class" in the *International Encyclopedia of the Social Sciences,* 15 (1968).

A full treatment of the symbolic aspects of stratification can be found in E. A. Shils' "Deference" which appears in *Social Stratification* (Cambridge University Press, 1968), edited by J. A. Jackson.

For the discussion on "Social Stratification and Social Organization," the most relevant sources, in addition to the readings listed already are: S. Ossowski's *Class Structure in the Social Consciousness* (The Free Press, 1963) and L. Fallers' "Equality, Modernity and Democracy in the New States," in *Old Societies and New States* (The Free Press, 1963), edited by C. Geertz. For an illustration of partial stratification with regard to age groups, see *From Generation to Generation** (The Free Press, 1963) by S. N. Eisenstadt. As general background to the study of primitive societies, see L. Krader, *Formation of the State** (Prentice-Hall, Inc., 1968), M. Gluckman, *Politics, Law and Ritual in Tribal Society** (hardbound: Aldine Publishing Company, 1965; softbound: The New American Library, Inc., 1968), and I. Schapera,

*Government and Politics in Tribal Societies** (Schocken Books,
Inc., 1967). A more detailed distinction between stratified and
nonstratified primitive societies is discussed in "Pre-Industrial
Stratification Systems" by M. G. Smith, *Social Structure and
Mobility in Economic Development* (Aldine Publishing Company,
1966), edited by N. J. Smelser and S. M. Lipset.

Analyses of the macrosocietal order have been done by
Talcott Parsons in "An Outline of the Social System" in *Theories
of Society* (The Free Press, 1961) by T. Parsons, E. A. Shils, et al.,
and E. A. Shils in "Society and Societies" *American Sociology*
(Basic Books, 1968), edited by T. Parsons.

The discussion of imperial societies presented in Chapter 6 is
primarily based on *The Political Systems of Empires* (The Free
Press, 1963) by S. N. Eisenstadt. For material on other types of
traditional societies, see *Political Sociology* (Basic Books, Inc.,
1971), edited by S. N. Eisenstadt.

The student who is interested in more detailed material on
the societies analyzed in this chapter should consult the
following:

For Russia:

J. Blum, *Lord and Peasant in Russia From the Ninth to the
Nineteenth Century** (hardbound: Princeton University Press,
1961; softbound: Atheneum Publishers, 1964) and M. Raeff,
*Origins of the Russian Intelligentsia: The Eighteenth Century
Nobility** (Harcourt Brace Jovanovich, Inc., 1966).

For China:

E. Balazs, *Chinese Civilization and Bureaucracy** (Yale University Press, 1964) and J. K. Fairbank, ed., *Chinese Thought and
Institutions* (University of Chicago Press, 1957).

For India:

L. Dumont, *Homo hierarchicus: Essai sur le système des castes*
(Gallimard, 1966); L. Dumont, ed., *Contributions to Indian Soci-
ology* (Mouton, 1966); M. Singer, "The Social Organization of
Indian Civilization," *Diogenes* 45 (Winter 1964) 84–119; M.
Singer, ed., *Traditional India: Structure and Change** (American
Folklore Society, University of Texas Press, 1959); and M. N.
Srinivas, *Caste in Modern India* (Asia Publishing House, 1962).

For Western and Central Europe:

M. Beloff, *The Age of Absolutism** (hardbound: Hutchinson
University Library, 1966; softbound: Harper Torchbooks, 1962); J.
O. Lindsay, ed., *New Cambridge Modern History,* Vol. 7 (Cam-
bridge University Press, 1957); B. Barber and E. G. Barber, eds.,
European Social Class: Stability and Change (The Macmillan

Company, 1965); and Jacob Katz, *Tradition and Crisis* (The Free Press, 1961).

The basic characteristics and problems resulting from modernization can be found in *Modernization: Protest and Change** (Prentice-Hall, 1966) by S. N. Eisenstadt. However, for the classic exposition of problems to be found in modern society, see Karl Mannheim's *Man and Society in an Age of Reconstruction** (Harcourt Brace Jovanovich, 1964). *Class, Status and Power* (The Free Press, 1966) edited by R. Bendix and S. M. Lipset, as well as *Structured Social Inequality* (The Macmillan Company, 1969) edited by C. Heller, are examples of the best compilations of material on stratification in modern society. In Heller's book, special attention should be devoted to parts 3–5 and 7.

For a general survey of the characteristics of the modern system of stratification, consult *Power and Privilege* (McGraw-Hill, Inc., 1966) by G. Lenski; T. H. Marshall's *Class, Citizenship and Social Development* (Doubleday & Company, Inc., 1964); and R. Dahrendorf's *Class and Class Conflict in Industrial Society** (Stanford University Press, 1959). The most complete analyses of the data on social mobility in modern societies are "Occupational Stratification and Mobility: Intra-Country Variations" found in *Studies in Comparative International Development* 1, no. 1 (1965) by T. Fox and S. M. Miller, and Miller's article, "Comparative Social Mobility" in *Current Sociology* 9, no. 1 (1960).

In addition to the above-mentioned material, discussions on the dynamics of modern systems of stratification are found in the following:
H. H. Hyman, "The Value Systems of Different Classes," in *Class, Status and Power* (The Free Press, 1966) edited by R. Bendix and S. M. Lipset, E. O. Laumann, *Prestige and Association in an Urban Community** (The Bobbs-Merrill Co., Inc., 1966); R. Aron, *Eighteen Lessons on Industrial Society* (Weidenfeld and Nicolson, 1960); S. M. Lipset, and R. Bendix, *Social Mobility in Industrial Society** (University of California Press, 1959); J. H. Goldthorpe and D. Lockwood, "Affluence and the British Class Structure," *Sociological Review*, 11, no. 2 (1963) 133–163; and R. H. Turner, "Modes of Social Ascent Through Education: Sponsored and Contest Mobility" in *Class, Status and Power* (The Free Press, 1966), edited by R. Bendix and S. M. Lipset.

Although uneven in quality, the work done on the various aspects of strata formation in modern societies is extensive. For this topic it would be useful to look at the material suggested for Chapters 7 and 8. In addition the interested student would do well to examine the *Transactions of the Third World Congress on Sociology, 1956* (International Sociological Association, 1957) in which there is abundant material.

For actual case studies, see:

For Germany:

G. Roth, *The Social Democrats in Imperial Germany* (The Bedminster Press, Inc., 1963) and R. Dahrendorf, *Society and Democracy in Germany* (Doubleday & Company, Inc., 1967).

For Asia:

Proceedings of the International Symposium on Social Stratification and Social Mobility in East Asian Countries (East Asia Cultural Studies Series, 1960) and A. Bopegamage and P. V. Veeraraghavan, *Status Images in Changing India* (UNESCO Research Center, 1967).

For Puerto Rico:

M. Tumin, *Social Class and Social Change in Puerto Rico* (Princeton University Press, 1961).

For Latin America:

C. Veliz, ed., *The Politics of Conformity in Latin America* (Oxford University Press, 1968); C. Veliz, ed., *Obstacles to Change in Latin America* (Oxford University Press, 1965); A. Touraine, "Social Mobility, Class Relations and Nationalism in Latin America," *Studies in Comparative International Development* 1 (1965); and S. M. Lipset and A. Solari, eds., *Elites in Latin America* (Oxford University Press, 1967).

For the Soviet Union:

A. Inkeles and K. Geiger, eds., *Soviet Society* (Houghton Mifflin Company, 1961). See especially Chapter 5. Also of interest are A. Inkeles, R. A. Bauer, *The Soviet Citizen: Daily Life in a Totalitarian Society* (Harvard University Press, 1959); H. K. Geiger, "Social Class Differences in Family Life in the U.S.S.R.," in C. S. Heller, ed., *Structural Social Inequality* (The Macmillan Company, 1969); and R. A. Feldmesser, "Social Classes and Political Structure," in C. E. Black, ed., *The Transformation of Russian Society* (Harvard University Press, 1960).

For twentieth-century England:

W. G. Runciman, *Relative Deprivation and Social Justice* (Routledge & Kegan Paul Ltd., 1966).

For some of the more recent developments, consult:

J. A. Kahl, *The American Class Structure* (Holt, Rinehart & Winston, Inc., 1959); A. F. Davies and S. Encel, eds., *Australian Society: A Sociological Introduction* Atherton Press, 1965); S. N. Eisenstadt, *Israeli Society* (Basic Books, Inc., 1968), especially

Chapter 8; and S. R. Graubard, ed., *The New Europe?** (hardbound: Houghton Mifflin, 1966; softbound: Beacon Press, 1966), especially the articles by A. Pizzorno, A. Touraine, and S. M. Lipset.

For those interested in the political aspects of social stratification in modern society, *Nation-Building and Citizenship** (hardbound: John Wiley & Sons, 1964; softbound: Doubleday & Company, Inc., Anchor Books, 1965) by R. Bendix, *Class Structure in the Social Consciousness* (Routledge & Kegan Paul, Ltd., 1963) by S. Ossowski, and G. D. H. Cole's *Studies in Class Structure* (Routledge & Kegan Paul Ltd., 1955) are the basic works. However, the most useful comparative material is found in the analyses of *Party Systems and Voter Alignment* (The Free Press, 1967), S. M. Lipset and S. Rokkan, eds.; *Cleavages, Ideologies and Party Systems* 10 (Westermark Society, 1964), E. Allardt and Y. Littunen, eds.; *Party and Society: The Anglo-American Democracies* (Rand McNally & Co., 1963) by R. R. Alford; and S. M. Lipset's *Political Man: The Social Bases of Politics** (Doubleday & Company, Inc., Anchor Books, 1963).

Index

715121